SCENES FOR LATINX ACTORS:
VOICES OF THE NEW AMERICAN THEATRE

Edited by
Micha Espinosa & Cynthia DeCure

Books by the editors

Monologues for Latino/a Actors: A Resource Guide to the Latino/a Playwrights for Actors and Teachers edited by Micha Espinosa

SCENES FOR LATINX ACTORS:
VOICES OF THE NEW AMERICAN THEATRE

Edited by
Micha Espinosa & Cynthia DeCure

Smith and Kraus Publishers   2018

A Smith and Kraus Book
177 Lyme Road, Hanover, NH 03755
editorial 603.643.6431 To Order 1.877.668.8680
www.smithandkraus.com

Scenes for Latinx Actors:
Voices of the New American Theatre
Copyright © 2018 by Micha Espinosa & Cynthia DeCure
All rights reserved.

Manufactured in the United States of America

CAUTION: Professionals and amateurs are hereby warned that the material represented in this book is subject to a royalty. It is fully protected under the copyright laws of the United States of America, and of all countries covered by the International Copyright Union (including the Dominion of Canada and the rest of the British Commonwealth), and of all countries covered by the Pan-American Copyright Convention and the Universal Copyright Convention, and of all countries with which the United States has reciprocal copyright relations. All rights, including professional, amateur, motion picture, recitation, lecturing, public reading, radio broadcasting, television, video or sound taping, all other forms of mechanical or electronic reproductions such as information storage and retrieval systems and photocopying, and the rights of translation into foreign languages, are strictly reserved.

ISBN: 978-1-57525-931-4
Library of Congress Control Number: 2018948632

Typesetting and layout by Elizabeth E. Monteleone
Cover by Olivia Monteleone

For information about custom editions, special sales, education and corporate purchases, please contact Smith and Kraus at editor@smithandkraus.com or 603.643.6431.

For our students.

TABLE OF CONTENTS

ACKNOWLEDGMENTS 11
FOREWORD 13
   Patricia Ybarra

BIENVENIDO A TEATRO NUEVO AMERICANX 19
HOW TO USE THIS BOOK 23

Section 1: Scenes for Males and Females

REFUGEE HOTEL 29
   Carmen Aguirre

AGE OF SEPIA 37
   Rose Cano

antonia 45
   José Casas

COCKS HAVE CLAWS AND WINGS TO FLY 53
   Amparo Garcia-Crow

HABOOB 61
   Marvin González De León

SWEEP 69
   Georgina Escobar

PREMEDITATION 75
   Evelina Fernandez

CHASING MONSTERS 81
   Gabriel Rivas Gómez

THE HEART'S DESIRE 89
   José Cruz González

DETAINED IN THE DESERT 95
   Josefina Lopez

SONIA FLEW *Melinda Lopez*	103
the living'life of the daughter mira *Matthew Paul Olmos*	109
HEART SHAPED NEBULA *Marisela Treviño Orta*	115
COMIDA DE PUTA (F%@KING LOUSY FOOD) *Desi Moreno-Penson*	121
EL CHE *Marcelino Quiñonez*	131
MOTHER LOLITA *Guillermo Reyes*	139
THE SWEETHEART DEAL *Diane Rodriguez*	147
LOS DREAMERS *Mónica Sánchez*	153
FADE *Tanya Saracho*	161
DESTINY OF DESIRE *Karen Zacarias*	167

Section 2: Scenes for Two Females

QUALITY: THE SHOE PLAY *Elaine Avila*	177
FABULOUS MONSTERS *Diana Burbano*	185

La Ruta 191
Isaac Gomez

Maria! Maria, Maria, Maria 203
Lisa Loomer

TO THE BONE 209
Lisa Ramirez

Luchadora! 217
Alvaro Saar Rios

The Hours are Feminine 223
José Rivera

¡CURANDERAS! Serpents Of The Clouds 229
Elaine Romero

No More Maids 237
Anne García Romero

Corazón Eterno (always in my heart) 245
Caridad Svich

Section 3: Scenes for Two Males

Parachute Men 253
Mando Alvarado

Sangre de un Ángel (Blood of Angel) 261
Roxanne Schroeder-Arce

Latins in La La Land 267
Migdalia Cruz

My Father's Keeper 273
Guadalís Del Carmen

THE HAPPIEST SONG PLAYS LAST *Quiara Alegría Hudes*	281
MEMBERS ONLY *Oliver Mayer*	287
KILLING OF A GENTLEMEN DEFENDER *Carlos Murillo*	295
icarus burns *christopher oscar peña*	301
SWIMMING WHILE DROWNING *Emilio Rodriguez*	311
EL PASO BLUE *Octavio Solis*	319

Section 4: Scenes for Three +

MÁS (3M AND 2F) *Milta Ortiz*	329
CLOCK (3F) *Monica Palacios*	337
LA GRINGA (3F AND 1M) *Carmen Rivera*	345
MISS QUINCE (3F) *Cynthia Santos-DeCure*	355
MOMMA'S BOYZ (3M) *Cándido Tirado*	365
THE EDITORS	373

Acknowledgements

We offer deep gratitude for the authors who generously shared their work and gave of their time in service of this collection. We wish we could have included many other writers in this volume; however, we are dedicated to new editions and new formats that will create an opportunity to showcase their work. Please look to the LatinoActor website for updates (http://www.latinoactor.com).

Many thanks to Patricia Ybarra for her insightful forward.[1] We are deeply honored that this leader in the field supports our work. We share a mission to transform the landscape by starting in the classroom, the distinction of being working mothers, and the gift of being really good multi-taskers.

---

[1] Dr. Ybarra is an associate professor and chair of the Department of Theatre Arts and Performance Studies at Brown University. Her groundbreaking text in theatre and performance studies, *Latinx Theater in the Times of Neoliberalism,* traces how Latinx theatre in the United States in the previous quarter century has engaged with the policies, procedures, and outcomes of neoliberal economics in the Americas. Past-president of the American Theatre in Higher Education Association, Dr. Ybarra has been a champion for creating a welcoming and more diverse organization. As chair of Brown, she recently found the support to be able to offer full scholarships to MFA's in directing and performance. Ybarra was quoted in Broadway world (February 26, 2018), "In the theatre world, diversity is often hampered by the inability of low-income artists and artists of color to afford to be creators… By expanding access to our program, we expand access to theatre world more broadly - ultimately redefining in really important ways whose stories are being told and by whom."

Sincere thanks to Smith and Kraus for their patience, support, and belief in our vision. We are grateful to our colleagues at Arizona State University and California State University, Stanislaus who supported us in countless big and little ways. Special thanks to the Voice and Speech Trainers Association Mennen Research Grant, Arizona State University's Institute for Humanities Visiting Fellows Grant, and California State University, Stanislaus' College of Arts, Humanities and Social Sciences Grant for funding the many trips needed to finish this project. A special thank you to Arizona State University's School of Film, Dance, and Theatre Director Tiffany Ann Lopez for offering the perfect advice when needed and Arizona State University's School of Film, Dance, and Theatre students; Elizabeth Hernandez (research assistant), Emmanuel Linares (clerical support), and Ricky Quintana (reader). We are indebted to our mentor Catherine Fitzmaurice whose teachings brought us together and fostered our curiosity and radicalness. Because of her example we are embodied women; resourced, awake, and rooted in our identities and community. Last, but not least, we would like to thank our families. The time and energy necessary to complete this project could not have been expended without their help. Our husbands, Marcelino Quiñonez and John DeCure (our extra pair of eyes); our children Kai, Mia, Colin, Aidan, and Ethan. Also, Ray, J.R., y gracias especiales a nuestras mamas Mary and Maria for your help with the kids so that we could write. Mil gracias a todos!

Foreword

Patricia Ybarra

I write this introduction at a time of a call for change within theatre education at the undergraduate and graduate level. The desire to create truly inclusive programs, which allow actors of color to flourish, is present. Ways to make it happen are being discussed at the national level—in university classrooms, at national conferences, within professional organizations, and at coffee shops and offices around the nation. Sexism and anti-blackness are being confronted, procedures to make us safe within classrooms are being drafted, and a new commitment to hiring faculty of color is a part of almost every strategic plan of major arts programs.

And, yet, in showcases and university seasons around the country, I still see very few of the plays excerpted in this book staged or enacted. This may be because so few students learn about these plays in formal educational settings. A recent survey, authored by two MFA students at my own institution, Mauricio Salgado and Tatyana Marie Carlo, suggests as much. While an increasing number of schools are offering Latinx theatre courses—many acting and directing courses still rely on diversifying their curriculum with a very small number of Latinx dramatic texts. This is sometimes because of the paucity of published Latinx texts; at other times, it is simply a matter of ignorance.

I say this with a spirit of compassion, not judgment. Many a non-specialist feels at sea when faced with the breadth of Latinx theatre and drama. These writers come from many national and local cultures, political stances, class positions and racial and cultural backgrounds. And, these plays enact a number of aesthetics and genres transforming them as they utilize them. In these playwrights' hands American realism, telenovela structures, and science fiction/speculative fiction become something else. Take for example, Karen Zacarias' Destiny of Desire. As Zacarias states, "[a]s Latinx theater artists, many of us have an ambivalent relationship to Telenovelas. Love them or hate them, they are the biggest creative export of the Americas and the most popular form of entertainment in the world. Theater Critics often use the word "telenovela" to describe the work of many Latinx playwrights and actors and it's always used derogatively, dismissively and incorrectly. So I decided to purposely write an unapologetic telenovela for the stage that hopefully takes this populist genre to high art. Telenovelas are a very specific genre, with archetypes and conventions that should be examined, honored, and tested." Georgina Escobar, when writing about *Sweep*, her "Spec-Evo" play that travels back to the Garden of Eden with Adam and Eve, informs her readers of the ways in which the play is like a graphic novel, where the actors "move in and out of certain time specific panels." She instructs actors in the scene in the following way, [a]ccess the characters from the outside in. Let the environment you create for yourselves and the energy of the other person dictate how the characters inner life moves. There is very little 'inner life' to these two characters in this scene—they are reactionary, they are obvious, they are direct. This is the first time 'deceit' is introduced and it should physically affect the characters. Overall, play the style, play the hyper and don't fall into the hypo, play the bigness and think of it as a larger than life piece."

Foreword

Escobar's comments bring me to the critical importance of recognizing the variety of acting styles embedded within Latinx plays. Deciding the appropriate acting "style" for these scenes is complicated for those for whom realism is a default aesthetic. Latinx plays often ask actors to work from without rather than from within, to traverse languages and time and space, and push aside certain notions of psychology so key to contemporary modes of creating character. As I have written elsewhere, many Latinx playwrights eschew certain precepts of American realism, even when they do employ it. This is in part because American Realism's adherence to Anglo U.S. ideas of individualism and individualistic psychology, linear plot development and causal "logical" actions in a clearly delineated time and space do not always serve Latinx storytelling. Some playwrights puncture it with other forms of cosmology and ways of knowing. Take for example Desi Moreno-Penson's *Comida de Puta*, which asks her actors to play present day young people as well as inhabiting Yoruba deities Oya and Elegua, gesturing toward the presence of Afro-Caribbean religion within the canon of Latinx drama and the way it asks actors to inhabit two roles simultaneously. Realities collide. In the scene excerpted from the play, an asthma attack pushes up against a different kind of out of body experience:

> *(Sotero kisses her again. Alcidia responds and their lips stay locked for a long moment until we see that Alcidia's body has begun to shake and she begins to cough uncontrollably. Perhaps at this point, there's even a small light change or some sort of an eerie sound to suggest that something supernatural is taking place. Alcidia begins breathing rapidly, almost hyperventilating and her body slowly slumps down to the ground, as a frightened Sotero continues to hold her fast.)*

SOTERO: Cece…what's wrong? What is it? Are you okay? It's okay. Just keep breathing. Keep breathing.
ALCIDIA: (barely able to get the words out; indicating her jacket) M-my inhaler… get…get my inhaler…!
(Sotero immediately searches the pockets of her jacket for her inhaler, tossing everything out in the process.)
SOTERO: (frantic) I don't see it. I don't see it. It's not in here…! Does Manny have it? Cece…listen to me… does Manny have your inhaler?
(Alcidia is unable to answer him and looks as though she has passed out. Now in a complete panic, Sotero yells across the street to Manny.)
SOTERO: Manny! Yo Manny! Something's wrong with Cece; we gotta get her to the hospital! Bro, come on… forget the fucking pizza and get your ass over here! NOW!

The snap back to realism reveals the co-presence of realities, not a magical realism, but a co-present cosmology. Migdalia Cruz pushes the boundaries of meta-theatricality when she asks her characters in *Latins in La La Land*, which features a mash up of a 1940s Hollywood with the real time murders of their parents by the Menendez brothers, to enact drag personae of Dolores Del Rio and Lupe Velez to construct an alibi for themselves. This "dark comedy" plays with the layering of roles and role-playing in fabulous and disturbing ways.

These different forms of dramatic storytelling, then, ask actors to embody and engage texts in ways not always part of traditional acting training. Many Latinx playwrights feel that actors are not trained to do their work—at a physical, linguistic or psychic level. How can we train people to move between worlds and physical realities, Spanish and English within the rhetoric of sustained "character development?" How can we offer a rich enough repertoire of Latinx dramatic literature to train actors in the many techniques necessary to do this work? How do we encourage professional Latinx actors to audition with the rich material provided by Latinx playwrights? How does one do that with short excerpts of scenes in which play worlds have to be created very quickly?

I believe this book is a beginning. It is for this reason that it is such a great pleasure to introduce such a vital anthology of scenes for Latinx actors, complete with interviews by playwrights from a wide variety of cultural backgrounds who explain how they choose to identify as part of the interview. Each author tells their readers a bit about their dramatic texts; many give suggestions to the actors in terms of writing. These interviews replace the generic (or sometimes absent) contextualization for scenes found in standard scene books. They instruct while illuminating. They do important work.

The content of these scenes varies wildly. Some take on contemporary racist and xenophobic political formations, such as Arizona legislation against ethnic studies or the policing of the U.S. Mexico border. Others gesture to the long history and the effects of dictatorships in the Southern Cone. Others take on daily life in American cities, revealing the characters' struggles to survive. There are stories of queer love and coming of age and middle-aged Lesbian parenthood. There are stories of leaving and coming home. There are plays based on Greek myths, plays that re-write history, plays that point to the racism of Hollywood and the industry. All of them are compelling and emotionally gripping, many are slyly humorous, a few are downright heartbreaking.

The repertoire offered here provides actors with a multitude of stories about Latinx life in the Americas in all of its complexity. Nonetheless each scene provides performers with what they need from this volume for classroom and professional presentations: short, incisive, lucid scenes with compelling relationships and play worlds that make the richness of Latinx life perceivable by a variety of audiences. I look forward to seeing more of these plays on the stage, in auditions and showcases around the country.

BIENVENIDO A TEATRO NUEVO AMERICANX

"We are providing a new beginning for the new American theater. We are the theater of New America—theater, by, for and about the New Americans."
– Luis Valdez

"Perhaps the greatest resource we have as Latino/a theatre makers is the force of our collaboration..."
– Brian Herrera

"We exist, we are here, we are entitled to poetry."
– Migdalia Cruz

The quotes above are taken from The Latina/o Theatre Commons 2013 National Convening: A Narrative Report written by Brian Eugenio Herrera, Jayne Benjulian & Jamie Gahlon. The 2013 national convening was, and is, a catalyst for our work. The Commons brought us in contact with many of the playwrights in this book and strengthened the field in ways we could not have imagined. We **are** New American practitioners, Latinx theatre educators and teaching artists who both serve at state institutions with large Latinx populations. We have the shared experience of being the only Latinx professors in our departments. We have both shared a life as performers, adept at navigating casting calls that use offensive stereotypes, skilled in having our Puerto Rican and Chicana identities commercialized and commodified. As teachers, we have watched as our Latinx students navigate the performance or rejection of their identities, using material chosen for them by faculty with a limited view of the New American theatre. Our commitment to Latinx stories and communities is what brought us together. We each have over thirty years in the field. We view this anthology as just one of the ways we can create pathways to equity of access and representation. We are committed to offering cultural competence to our colleagues and students; and so, we offer these scenes with interviews for the development of the field, the diversification of academic theatre programs, and for the players and the students who, we hope, will find material for performance and practice that reflects their identity, speaks to their community, and allows them to engage with a possible future and their past.

In 2015, Latin@ and Latinx began to find their way into the popular narrative with many arguments for and against their usage. We chose to embrace the term Latinx because it disrupts the traditional gender binary, offers an inclusive attitude toward gender and sexual identities, and embraces intersectionality. The Latinx students of our times are redefining identity. They represent every race, nationality, ethnic-identity, age, religion, citizenship, sexual orientation, and theoretical orientation. They are Latinx, an experience that expands but does not define or limit.

For the actor, performance can be the articulation of developing identity. This book serves as a step towards empowering actors, directors, and professors to find new plays that express the multiplicity of our Latinidad. The act of being seen and heard performing our stories can be a very powerful tool in erasing borders and casting new narratives of what the "New American Theatre" has to offer. The New American theatre embraces a hemispheric view and looks toward the Americas with an eye to 2049, the year, according to the Associated Press, that the U.S. will become the first major post-industrial society in the world in which minorities will be the majority.

Each playwright featured here brings a unique voice and aesthetic. We honor these playwrights, as we view them as our societies' truth tellers, myth makers, and interpreters of the times. This book contains not of a single viewpoint, but a multitude of narratives that more accurately demonstrate the range of talent in the field. With this wide array of scenes, we are intentionally amplifying the many voices that have not been heard. Award-winning playwrights and emerging voices appear side-by-side, shattering stereotypes while taking ownership of our narratives con orgullo de nuestra herencia. This collection is our effort to restructure and broaden the lens through which Latinx plays are seen.

- Micha Espinosa & Cynthia DeCure

How To Use This Book

The book is arranged in alphabetical chapter format, beginning with male/female, female/female, male/male, and then scenes with multiple characters. We present these scenes with a short interview from the playwright(s) who created the work. Every chapter was created in collaboration with the playwright. It is important for the reader to connect the work on the page to the playwright: the forty-five men and women in this collection each represent an aspect of the contemporary theatre in North America. They run the spectrum of *Latinidad*, and understanding their stories and themes will illuminate the text when performed. We asked each playwright the same two questions: "How do you identify" and "Where do we find the play"?

Identity

We felt compelled to begin with an identity question, because identity for Latinx gente is complicated: sometimes we identify with our history, the language, the art, the food, the terminology, and sometimes we don't. Our identities are sometimes firm, hyphenated, multiple, constructed, reclaimed, colonized, vilified, commercialized, internalized, and inevitably evolving with the intersectionality of race, class, gender, sexuality, and politics. Not all the writers in this collection identify as Latinx, but all the scenes were chosen with an eye toward Latinx stories. Then, after reading and speaking the text several times, we crafted questions that possibly a young performer approaching the work would ask. These vary from very specific questions about the scene, to broader questions about the play. We approached the interviews from a beginner's frame of mind. This open, eager, curious attitude is one that we hope will encourage the reader as they explore the text. The written work is only part of the story, and we encourage the reader to explore the entire play, the writer's body of work, and their overall journey.

The Scenes

Each scene features a description of the characters and a brief scene set-up providing minimal context for the situation. The text of some scenes has been edited, or reformatted, with the original writers' permission, so that the scenes can easily be performed by two-to-five people. If characters were omitted, the reader will see a note that the scene has been modified. Stage directions, pauses, and beats indicated in the scenes are from the original text of the plays. At times, paragraph breaks or spacing have been reformatted from the original. Unusual punctuation, spelling/misspelling, and other non-standard elements have not been altered from the original texts.

In our process of amassing this collection, we read plays together aloud, employing our skills as actors, professors and *teatristas* to select scenes that can be used in the classroom, actor's studio and showcases. The scenes can serve to challenge the student actor and director and bring greater inclusivity to the acting studio. The scenes are generally five minutes or less, for use in acting competitions, showcases and such.

Language

Several scenes include words in Spanish, and indigenous language, such as Nahuatl. The actor has the opportunity to exercise their skills as a Spanish speaker, and/or discover or reclaim a new sound.

Accents/Dialects

Many scenes call for accents. This creates an opportunity for the actor to dig deeper into character development, and to take time to carefully research the accent. Endeavor to work respectfully, to be specific about the accent and region—the linguistic identity of the character. Seek out native speakers for sound models. Note all the characteristic phonetic sound changes. Resist stereotypes or "general" interpretations. Play close attention to the *prosody*— the rhythm, tone, and musicality of the accent. Prosody is often the most distinguishing factor of accents of Spanish. Identify the operative words— the pitch and tone change of the accent is often tied to the sense and meaning of what the speaker is trying to convey.

Learn More About The Playwrights

We highly recommend that students and teachers become familiar with the 50 Playwrights Project. Created by Latina/o Studies scholar Dr. Trevor Boffone, the 50 Playwrights Project is an online resource that compiles snapshot interviews with Latina/o playwrights (https://50playwrights.org/about-2/). This resource does not have scene or monologue selections, but the online forum offers valuable insight into the leading playwrights of the New American Theatre.

Getting to know playwright's overall journey can lead to resonance and meaning as one explores the work. Playwrights generously offered their work on the New Play Exchange (https://newplayexchange.org), and through their agents, websites, or publishers if available. As noted, a few of the plays are not available at this time. We remind readers who plan on using this material for audition, classwork, or performance that it is crucial to read the entire play whenever possible to best understand the entire context of the scene.

Scenes for Males and Females

REFUGEE HOTEL

Carmen Aguirre

A play about a group of Chilean refugees who arrived in Vancouver in 1974 and were put up in a modest hotel. An uncompromising look at exile, torture, guilt, and betrayal, The Refugee Hotel is ultimately about love and its power to heal.

- **How do you identify yourself?**

    C. Aguirre: I identify myself as a Chilean-Canadian theatre artist and author. I identify as Latinx and as a person of color. I came to Canada as a refugee and I grew up in exile. That is a core part of my identity.

- **Can you tell us about the character names... and why you chose them?**

    C. Aguirre: Condor Passes and Cakehead both tried to take their own lives at the exact same moment. Condor jumped from his hotel window, while Cakehead stuck her head in an oven. Condor landed in a dumpster of fiberglass and survived unscathed. Cakehead didn't realize that the oven was electric, not gas. She burnt her hair, but that's about all that happened to her. Condor's name is Manuel. Cakehead's name is Cristina. After the double suicide attempts, Fat Jorge, another character in the play, "christened" them with their new names.

- **This is an extremely intimate moment and scene. Do you have any advice on how the actors should approach this moment of deep connection?**

    C. Aguirre: Yes, just approach it with absolute honesty and vulnerability. This is near the end of the play; both these characters have figured out that the only way they will survive exile is to form this partnership. This is not a cerebral realization, but rather a visceral one. Both characters are teenagers. They are completely alone in the North. They have lost everything. This moment is about life or death.

- **Where can we find the full text of the play?**

    C. Aguirre: talonbooks: http://talonbooks.com/books/the-refugee-hotel

CHARACTERS
CAKEHEAD: Age eighteen.
CONDOR PASSES: Age seventeen.

IN THIS SCENE
They are both refugees who arrived in Canada a few days earlier. Condor was tortured almost to death in a concentration camp and Cakehead's parents were murdered. They are both completely alone in exile.

(Cakehead knocks on Condor Passes' door. She is holding a cake she just baked. It has one candle on it. Condor Passes opens the door.)
CAKEHEAD: *(in a whisper so as not to disturb the sleeping hotel)* Happy birthday to you, happy birthday to you-
CONDOR PASSES: Cakehead- What the-
CAKEHEAD: -Shhhh!- Happy birthday dear Condor-
CONDOR PASSES: How did-
CAKEHEAD: Shut up- Happy birthday to you!
CONDOR PASSES: I just don't-
CAKEHEAD: Blow!
CONDOR PASSES: Huh?
CAKEHEAD: Blow! The candle!
CONDOR PASSES: Oh.
(Pause as cakehead and Condor Passes stare at each other awkwardly.)
CAKEHEAD: Holy fucking Jesus. Are you gonna blow the candle or do I have to slap you now?
Condor Passes blows the candle.
CAKEHEAD: Spit all over me now too why dontcha.
CONDOR PASSES: Oh, sorry.
CAKEHEAD: So? Can I come in?

CONDOR PASSES: Uh, yeah, yeah. Of course. It's a bit-

CAKEHEAD: Messy? I can see that.

(Cakehead makes her way to the kitchenette and starts to cut the cake, arranging two slices on plates.)

CONDOR PASSES: What time is it?

CAKEHEAD: Around twelve o' five.

(Another big awkward pause as cakehead approaches Condor Passes with his slice. They arrange themselves on the floor, after looking awkwardly at the bed. They begin to eat.)

CONDOR PASSES: This is very good.

CAKEHEAD: You can make them from packages here.

CONDOR PASSES: Packages?

CAKEHEAD: I went to the supermarket up the street, and I found a whole section of different kinds of packages for cakes. You just add water and eggs and that's all. Are you eating?

CONDOR PASSES: Yeah.

(Big awkward pause as they both eat.)

CAKEHEAD: I wonder where we'll be living.

CONDOR PASSES: I don't know. But I'll be a gardener.

CAKEHEAD: And I'll be a baker. Have you ever gardened before?

CONDOR PASSES: No. I worked the assembly line at the RCA Victor factory. And I worked for the union. Night and day. Have you ever baked?

CAKEHEAD: Just the pottery. I make beautiful pottery, you know.

CONDOR PASSES: What does it look like?

CAKEHEAD: Big bowls shaped like salmon and seashells and the craters on the moon.

CONDOR PASSES: You worked with your hands. And so did I.

CAKEHEAD: And we will still work with our hands. I'll knead dough and you'll dig up the earth.
(Pause as they continue to eat and look at each other awkwardly.)
CAKEHEAD: So. You're eighteen now. A man.
CONDOR PASSES: How did you know?
CAKEHEAD: Looked at your passport.
CONDOR PASSES: You looked at my passport?
CAKEHEAD: I looked at your passport.
CONDOR PASSES: You looked at my passport?
CAKEHEAD: Yes, I told you that already.
CONDOR PASSES: When did-
CAKEHEAD: I came into your room the other day and I saw your passport lying on the bed here and I looked at it-
CONDOR PASSES: Why were you in my room?
CAKEHEAD: I wanted to smell it.
CONDOR PASSES: Oh.
CAKEHEAD: I wanted to smell your room and I saw the passport on the bed and I just couldn't help myself.
CONDOR PASSES: How did it smell?
CAKEHEAD: The passport?
CONDOR PASSES: No. The room.
CAKEHEAD: Good. Good. Like home. Your poncho, your sheets, the armpit of your shirt, it all smells like the house where I was born, with the kelp and the seaweed drying on the sill. You smell like our roots, you smell so good, so good, so good, I could burst from the smell of it all, from the smell of you and your pain and the look in your eyes-
(Condor Passes moves closer to her. He positions himself very close to her. She leans over and smells his hair, his skin, his breath, his clothes. He surrenders to her.)

CAKEHEAD: *(smelling in great big breaths)* Ohh! You smell like that floor. Just waxed. And the mud on the road after a fresh rain.

(Cakehead starts to unbutton Condor Passes' shirt. He allows himself to be taken.)

CAKEHEAD: *(smelling his chest, neck and underarms)* You smell like my past, the good past, the one that existed so long ago-

CONDOR PASSES: I come from Santiago. The smell of diesel and peanuts cooking in caramel, the smell of open sewers and tear gas, suffocating me-

CAKEHEAD: Am I suffocating you?

CONDOR PASSES: No! I can breathe, I can breathe, I can breathe you in, but I can't smell. Nothing. I can smell nothing.

CAKEHEAD: Breathe through your nose. *(offering her mouth)* Smell my breath.

CAKEHEAD: Can you taste?

CONDOR PASSES: No. Nothing.

CAKEHEAD: Can you feel?

CONDOR PASSES: I think so.

CAKEHEAD: You're shaking.

CONDOR PASSES: I've never done this before.

CAKEHEAD: Just keep breathing. Breathe like the seven volcanoes in the deep south of Chile.

CONDOR PASSES: I've never been with a woman before.

CAKEHEAD: Oh.

CONDOR PASSES: I'm afraid.

CAKEHEAD: Don't be.

CONDOR PASSES: Wait. There's something I have to tell you. I can't feel down there. I'm numb there. I wasn't born like that. They did it to me.

CAKEHEAD: Does it hurt?
CONDOR PASSES: Nothing hurts anymore.
CAKEHEAD: Let me love you. Let me worship you. You shine like copper and I could kiss you forever.
CONDOR PASSES: Kiss me forever. Kiss me forever....

AGE OF SEPIA

Rose Cano

Two women, a blonde and brunette, meet again after many years in a small vacation town far away from modern life. Jogged by the unearthing of an old sepia-toned photo, they remember the relationship they once shared with "cousin Hank", a budding photographer, when all three were young and naive about love. Twenty-five years ago they spent a summer together at "Granny's" cabin in the woods. Their love and memories of Granny permeate the reality of their relationship, which was documented with Hank's old camera using black and white film. Scenes flash forward and backward in time, accompanied by projections of photos in black & white and sepia.

- **How do you identify yourself?**

    R. Cano: I am a Peruvian-born Latina playwright, actor, director and producer.

- **You wrote this during a playwright workshop with Marie Irene Fornés. How did she influence you?**

    R. Cano: This play first began during a playwriting workshop with Maria Irene Fornes at Theatre for the New City in 1995. The genesis came from the writing exercise using black & white/sepia-toned photos from an anonymous family album that was found at a flea market. The photo of a blonde and a brunette reminded me of the sepia-toned photo albums of my young parents in Peru in the 50's. I noticed that the absence of full color reduced the obvious racial differences and tended to exoticize the people in the portraits. Everyday folks looked like they were in a Hollywood movie of the 40's and 50's. This notion of color versus black & white is explored literally and figuratively in this play about obsessive relationships and family. Fornés guided our imaginations by playing with the time and place of the photos. This defined the tone of the play. The hyper focus of the workshop and Fornés' simple and clear prompts lead to the sparse essential dialogue.

- **Can you illuminate the title of the piece?**

    R. Cano: The play deals with archetypal roles of women and men of the 50's and the stereotypes of blondes, brunettes and skin color. The beige tone sepia photos exoticized the subjects in the portraits in the same way black and white movies exoticized blondes and brunettes. As the women progress from sepia-toned characters of the 50's to full color complex characters of the

2000's, their ideas of gender roles change. I suggest that the actors fully understand the concepts of exoticism (the quality of being attractive through being colorful or unusual; characteristic of a distant foreign country) and the original processes of creating sepia tone.

- **Where can we find the full text of the play?**

    R. Cano: The play can be found at the New Play Exchange www.newplayexchange.org.

CHARACTERS

BRUNETTE: A young Brunette visting a small rural town for the summer. She is from somewhere other than there and has a certain glamour and daring about her. Middle aged, 25 - 30 years later.

HANK: Blonde's cousin who oversees the property for his "grandmother", the owner. He is clean cut and a hard worker around the property. He is a budding photographer. Hank Sr., his father, is played by the same actor. He is a truck driver.

IN THIS SCENE

After spending a romantic summer in Granny's cabin in the woods, the blonde and brunette must part today. The blonde's cousin Hank, whom has been in love with his cousin forever, is intrigued by the brunette and her "exotic" allure in an unexpected way. Hank is drawn to the two women as he struggles to capture their relationship through the lens of his old camera. While the brunette is packing, Hank enters her cabin to say goodbye.

(A video of many Hula-Hoops going around is projected on the back wall. Blondes and Brunettes hula-ing. Twirling waists and twirling hoops in full color.)
(A small bedroom in a cabin. Sparse furniture. A suitcase and clothes are out. Hank enters.)
BRUNETTE: Hank! What are you doing here? Did you help her pack?
HANK: Nah. She was done already.
BRUNETTE: Where is she?
HANK: I just dropped her and Granny off at the store. They said they had to get something last minute. A present for you
BRUNETTE: Are you packed?
HANK: Why should pack? I'm staying.
BRUNETTE: What? Out here? Don't be silly!
HANK: Why is it silly? Granny is happy here.
BRUNETTE: Granny is ancient. She belongs in these woods.
HANK: That's not very nice about someone who's been so hospitable this summer.
BRUNETTE: What I mean is, Granny has lived. We haven't. We can come back to the woods when we're old and tired out.
HANK: Well I grew up here and I've never tired out of these woods. I don't think I ever will. Who knows? I just might extend my summer vacation. *(pause)* This was the best summer I ever had. Thanks to you both.
BRUNETTE: You don't mean thanks to me. I was simply Granny's guest. You can thank her.
HANK: Yes. I will. I owe her a lot.
(She has difficulty closing her suitcase.)
BRUNETTE: Hank. Could you give me a hand? *(He tries to close it while she sits on it.)* Did you help her close her suitcase at least?

HANK: *(struggling)* Who?
BRUNETTE: Who? You know who?
HANK: *(Still struggling to close the locks he accidentally touches her leg)* Sorry about that.
BRUNETTE: You love her don't you. Hank?
HANK: Who?
BRUNETTE: Who? Oh please, Hank! Your cousin
HANK: I don't know what you mean,
BRUNETTE: I can tell, you know, A mile off. I've noticed it all summer. Since the day I got here.
HANK: *(He stares at the ground.)* I don't know what you mean.
BRUNETTE: You've been following us around like a shadow for a month. To the lake, the store, to the woods even.
HANK: Can help it if have a truck? I was just trying to be friendly.
BRUNETTE: You've sure been friendly. Especially to her.
HANK: To both of you.
BRUNETTE: So what do you like about her Hank? Is it her beautiful hair. All shiny and golden. You can tell me. I'm a girl.
HANK: I don't like this.
BRUNETTE: *(laughs)* Is it the little golden hairs on her arms and back of her neck?
HANK: This isn't right.
BRUNETTE: You've noticed she doesn't shave right? Her legs or armpits. She likes to leave them natural.
HANK: I hadn't noticed.
BRUNETTE: You hadn't? *(Grabs the camera around his neck.)* Then what›s in this stupid camera, huh? This

41

damn peeping-Tom thing that you›ve been clicking and clicking for weeks! I'm sick of posing for you. Why did I ever lend it to you. So where are the pictures?

HANK: I haven't developed any of them yet.

BRUNETTE: Hand them over.

HANK: I told you I haven't developed any yet.

BRUNETTE: Give them to me or I swear I'll open this thing and expose the whole roll.

HANK: Please don't. I don't have any prints yet. I swear.

BRUNETTE: *(pause)* Why not? Aren't you curious?

HANK: Yes. I am.

BRUNETTE: Then why haven't you developed them yet?

HANK: I don't know. Afraid I guess.

BRUNETTE: Afraid of what?

HANK: Afraid that they won't turn out right or something. Sometimes I think I'd rather just not remember this summer.

(He sits on the bed and she sits on her suitcase again so that she is higher up than him.)

BRUNETTE: You saw us. *(pause)* You saw us didn›t you?

HANK: What?

BRUNETTE: You saw us through this lens.

HANK: *(pause)* I closed my eyes. They whole time. swear.

BRUNETTE: You wanted to look though. Why didn't you look? You followed us all that way. Didn't you want to see her?

HANK: I did. But I couldn't. So I just snapped some pictures, without opening my eyes.

BRUNETTE: I heard you. Rustling around like a hamster. *(Hold up camera)* Are they still in here?

HANK: Yes. I think so.

BRUNETTE: Why did you follow us, Hank? We were just

having fun.

HANK: I- I don't know. I wanted ....

BRUNETTE: I don't blame you. She's beautiful. You've probably loved her since she was little.

HANK: I guess. I guess I did. I tried to kiss her once but she scratched my face.

BRUNETTE: Did you see how pretty she looked coming out of the water? Shiny. Golden. A goddess in the woods. I hope you got a picture of that at least.

HANK: I can't look at her anymore. Not from that day on.

BRUNETTE: Did you see me coming out of the water, Hank? Did I look sort of like a goddess?

HANK: I told you I closed my eyes.

BRUNETTE: Well they're open now. *(She slowly begins to unbutton her blouse.)* Do you want to take pictures? This time you don't have to close your eyes.

(Hank puts the camera up to his eye then lowers it.)

HANK: Don't leave today. Stay for another week at least. Stay with me. Please.

BRUNETTE: No! Don't ask me that.

HANK: Please stay.

BRUNETTE: She want's me to stay too. Everyone wants me to stay. Even Granny wants me to stay. I'm not staying. *(She buttons blouse)* This summer has been too long. I need to start something. And you should do something with your life too. You're not going to find it out here.

HANK: I've found what I've been looking for.

BRUNETTE: How can you know if you haven't even looked around?

(She grabs her suitcase and heads to the door. He stands in front of the doorway)

HANK: You can't leave without your pictures, can you?
BRUNETTE: *(pause)* What are you going to do with them if you're too afraid to look at them yourself?
HANK: I could show them to Granny. She'd die.
BRUNETTE: Granny's as strong as an ox. She'll never die.
HANK: I could show them to *her*.
BRUNETTE: Who?
HANK: You know who. My cousin.
BRUNETTE: That would be very mean. *(pause)* I don't want her seeing those.
HANK: Why not?
BRUNETTE: I just don't! So shut up about it!
HANK: I'm sorry. Maybe I should open up the back and expose the whole and forget this whole summer ever happened. *(He starts to open the back of the camera.)*
BRUNETTE: No! Wait! What about all our other pictures? With Granny and everything. Our Hula-Hoop. Our goodbye poses. I'd like to leave Granny with something. Please. Don't.
HANK: Don't worry. *(Advances roll)* There›s still one shot left and I can take the roll to be developed. *(pause)* Do you want me to use it on you?
BRUNETTE: *(pause)* O.K.

(She puts her suitcase flat on her bed and stands on it. Slowly she unbuttons blouse and skirt deliberately passing through beautiful poses, like old Hollywood sirens. She freezes like a Roman statue.)

(The video begins to flicker on her body as she slowly turns to catch the images. The images are of profiles of blonde and Brunette pin-ups, Greek and Roman statues)

antonia

José Casas

The play is a Latina Hip-Hop adaptation of the play, Antigone, written by Sophocles. The story revolves around Antonia as she challenges the King to pay proper respects to her murdered brother, a symbol for old-school Hip-Hop.

josé casas

- **How do you identify yourself?**

  J. Casas: Chicano

- **This a mixture of contemporary and classical, do you have any advice as to how actors should approach the contrasting styles?**

  J. Casas: Actors should focus on the rhythmic similarities of the two distinct styles and see how they work as a "bridge" to communicate the ideas being explored.

- **Both characters are going through an emotional roller coaster. Is it just their youth? Why do they struggle to set boundaries?**

  J. Casas: The two characters struggle because they are trying to restore a world that once was. The world of man and Hip-Hop is a battle of those who exploit the culture and those who want to bring it back to the forefront. For these two characters, their approach to a solution is diametrically opposed and not helped by the fact that the relationship is being challenged by the people around them.

- **Where can we find the full text of the play?**

  J. Casas: For a full text of the play, the playwright serves as contact. His contact email is: jcasas@umich.edu

CHARACTERS

achilles: Compassionate. Trying to make change from within the system. Torn between his father and true love.

antonia: Spirited. Headstrong. An advocate for true meaningful Hip-Hop. Fights for Justice.

antonia

IN THIS SCENE
achilles has discovered that antonia has challenged his father, the king. antonia has broken the law and has been punished with a death sentence. A distraught achilles is attempting to get antonia to give up her challenge and find alternatives, not only to save her life, but their relationship.

suavecito & the power of persuasion
(high school prom lights flood the space. achilles and antonia return.)
(malo's "suavecito." achilles and antonia begin to slow dance to the song. as the song ends eventually fades out and the lights disappear. achilles and antonia continue to dance. after, a few moments, they stop dancing; beat. they stare into each other's eyes; happiness replacing the anger from the previous moment.)

achilles: why didn't you tell me?

antonia: would you have listened?

achilles: i would have helped you.

antonia: *(awkwardly sarcastic)* beloved hijo going against beloved papá. i think not.

achilles: *(walking away from antonia)* i wish our paths had never crossed.

antonia: no digas eso.

achilles: te amo…but, now…i don't want to love you anymore.

(extended beat)
(extended beat)

antonia: this is a task i need to accomplish.

achilles: need or want?

antonia: did you not love fuerza? tierra?

(achilles doesn't reply.)

antonia: *(quietly heartfelt)* two men who would've given up their lives for you if asked.
achilles: *(quietly; stinging with guilt)* you're willing to give up your life? *(beat)* for a funeral?
(antonia doesn't reply. she shakes her head in disgust.)
achilles: say something.
(antonia doesn't reply.)
achilles: father warned me about you. he kept telling me that no man would be able to bear the weight of your convictions. he extolled the virtues of your sister. "she is gorgeous." "she is obedient." "she will worship you like no other woman." that's what he said. but, no, i didn't listen and now…here we are. you and i. engaged to be married. a wedding feast being prepared for ghosts. *(beat)* what about our story, huh?
(antonia doesn't reply)
achilles: i have sacrificed-
antonia: -nothing…you have sacrificed nothing!
achilles: hypocrisy be thy name. *(sarcastic)* who are you to say what is art and what isn't?
(antonia doesn't reply.)
achilles: yo entiendo…no lo crees, pero es verdad.
antonia: do you?
achilles: *(pointing out into the distance)* do you not hear the cries of injustice against my father? it's only a matter of time before the gente-
antonia: -preparing for the throne are we?
achilles: no, señorita…hoping he learns from the errors of his ways. *(beat)* sound familiar?
(antonia doesn't reply.)
achilles: el cambio that you crave for is within your grasp.
(antonia doesn't reply.)
achilles: you're so filled with anguish and doubt that the

blinders you wear have kept you from seeing the progress being made. *(beat; indigent)* the progress i've made…me, the one you regard as the blind one.
(extended beat)
achilles: que? cat got your tongue?
(antonia doesn't reply.)
(the dj begins playing a mix of different songs; the featured artists are childish gambino, kendrick lamar and other current rappers who do not "fit" the stereotype of violent misogynist hip-hop. the volume of the music must be audible, but very understated and low.)
achilles: i may be my father's son, but that's where the similarities end. *(beat; pointing)* i am in that mausoleum of a building every day doing what i can to illuminate and resuscitate los dias de oro. i die inside every time the minstrel show begins. *(torn)* if it means that, at times, i have to make a bargain with the devil then so be it. *(beat; annoyed)* you're not the only hip-hop head in this play, entiendes?
(antonia doesn't reply.)
achilles: there are others luchando la misma pelea…fighting the same fight. tú los sabes. *(beat)* the trick is to be subversive without them knowing you're being subversive because nobody notices baby steps hidden in the sand.
antonia: *(defensive)* one millionth of a millionth of a millionth doesn't make for a revolution…a grain of sand doesn't amount to anything in the scheme of things.
achilles: you wear your emotions on your sleeve like a badge of honor, but all that does is put a target on your back. you decry this imperfect world and all its shortcomings. you preach for conscious thought, but the sad thing is-
antonia: *(cornered)* -your way of-
achilles: -pride is stronger than any weapon of mass destruction created by mankind. *(beat; solemnly)* ask eazy and

biggie about pride. *(beat; resigned and walking away)* you will get your opportunity soon enough.
(antonia crosses to achilles. she attempts to embrace him, but he pulls away.)
antonia: if i don't stand behind my principles, i am not worthy of this life i've been given. *(beat)* i do not take this decision lightly, achilles.

achilles: you could've fooled me.

antonia: i must fight for the cultura.

achilles: but, you do not fight for me; the one who holds you close at night. you refuse to make my name yours. you reject the concept of compromise. you'd rather be dead than be with the ones you love.

antonia: a life of slavery is not worth-

achilles: *(hurt)* -you are not a slave-

antonia:*(combative)* -says the master!!!

(extended beat)
(extended beat)

achilles: *(hurt beyond belief)* i don't know you anymore.

antonia: i…

(extended beat)

achilles: there is nothing i can say…is there?

(antonia doesn't reply.)

achilles:*(sincere and conflicted and quietly)* would it kill you, for once, to color inside the lines?

antonia: my love…

achilles: you say it so easily; that word- love, as if you actually understand its meaning. *(beat)* is there not one ounce in your body feel guilt over the decision you are about to make?

(antonia doesn't reply.)

achilles: *(teary-eyed; defeated)* you said, "yes." *(beat)* to me…

antonia

(with those words, antonia looks at her engagement ring. she lovingly fiddles with it for a few moments.)
antonia: thank you for asking me to the prom.
achilles: antonia?
antonia: yes?
achilles: our children still to be born. a boy and a girl. what would you have named them?
(antonia doesn't reply.)
achilles: for my sake. give me something to hold onto. i beg of you.
(antonia ponders the question. it is apparent that she is thinking about the choices she has made/ will be making.)
antonia: (sad smile) luna for our daughter. (beat) our son would be named achilles in honor of the only man who ever made me smile.
(extended beat)

Cocks Have Claws And Wings To Fly

Amparo Garcia-Crow

Sofia and Pedro are happy, well-adjusted grownups when their mother isn't around. But when the 48-year-old mama shows up pregnant, with her shellshocked fiancé and acid tripping youngest son in tow, family tensions reach the breaking point. A touching, darkly humorous look at life's many mysteries.

- **How do you identify yourself?**

    A. Garcia-Crow: I identify as Mexican-American.

- **How does Sofia's heightened emotional state affect her decision-making through out this scene?**

    A. Garcia-Crow: Scott and Sofia have a very balanced and loving relationship except when her parents coming to town. Sofia gets triggered because there is genuine trauma that she has experienced as the daughter of a mother who married at 14 years of age! In many ways Sophia is the mother in that mother daughter relationship. This is the first time that Sophia has had a genuine breakdown--or regression on this level so it is a genuine and painful crisis. The play is a dark comedy so the challenge is to play at bigger than life because it is one of those bigger than life moments in her life and the 'comedy' happens the more seriously it's played.

- **Scott and Sofia come from families with different cultures and traditions. What are the cultural divides that lead to conflict in this relationship?**

    A. Garcia-Crow: Scott comes from a very privileged background. He is genuinely curious and finds her family very entertaining not in a condescending way. He finds them refreshing, complex and entertaining. His family is Republican – – meaning conservative and Christian and repressed. They do not talk about anything genuinely or honestly. So, whenever he is with her family he is relieved and feels very much at home. Sofia, however, is ashamed and very embarrassed about what is unfolding in her family at the moment.

- **Where can we find the full text of the play?**

A. Garcia-Crow: The South Texas Plays

NoPassport Press - Dreaming the Americas SeriesFirst edition 2009 by NoPassport PressPO Box 1786, South Gate, CA 90280 USA NoPassportPress@aol.com

CHARACTERS

SOFIA: 22 years old, Hispanic. Stocky and feisty. A senior at the University of Texas in Austin, majoring in psychology.

SCOTT: Early twenties, White. Boyfriend of Sofia. A musician. Wiry. A very artsy fellow.

IN THIS SCENE

Scott and Sophia's college apartment. Scott is playing an electric guitar. Sophia's mother has just revealed that she is going to have a baby.

(The apartment is collegiate but artsy. Scott sits on the bed picking on an unplugged electric guitar.)

SOFIA: I came this close to slashing my wrists.

SCOTT: Oh, come on baby, it can't be that bad.

SOFIA: It's so humiliating. She's going to have to get married.

SCOTT: Maybe it's a good thing, don't you think? Someone to take care of her?

SOFIA: Someone she can terrorize you mean? You know what she told Guero? She told him they were already married, that she snuck off to Mexico to get married secretly because she didn't want to hurt him and that they have actually been married for several months.

SCOTT: Why would she do that?

SOFIA: To explain the pregnancy.

SCOTT: It's not like Guero doesn't know the facts of life, I mean he just went through all that nightmare with his girlfriend.

SOFIA: Believe me, if I could understand what goes through my mother's head. All I can figure is that she thinks she has to marry him.

SCOTT: Is it safe for someone her age to have a child?

SOFIA: Her own mother didn't have her till she was 48. How could she be so stupid? All of my life, she's done these adolescent things, I'm the one that's supposed to be doing those stupid things, like Guero. We've got every right, too.

SCOTT: So Guero bought the made up secret elopement story?

SOFIA: Who knows? Even if he hears you there's no guarantee that he's heard you. He's getting worse, every time I see him. And my mother won't get him the help he needs.

SCOTT: Is it acid, or what the hell is he taking?

SOFIA: Who knows, but whatever it is, he takes it like aspirin. I wish they would commit him but Santiago has convinced my mother not to because of what he went through after the war. They tortured the poor guy, electric shocks and every kind of mind drug they could think of. So since, my poor uncle is a basket case...

SCOTT: You said uncle.

SOFIA: Yeah, he was my father's uncle. Grand uncle.

SCOTT: It's hard to keep track of all your family babe, you got cousins that are aunts, sisters that are grandmothers, it's not exactly the neat little Brady Bunch thing I'm used to. So your mother is marrying your uncle, is that legal? Sounds like incest.

SOFIA: (screams!!!) They're not related!!! He's my father's uncle.

SCOTT: Okay, alright already, it's confusing, that's all. You don't have to bite my head off.

(Sofia gives him an "oh that's so funny i forgot to laugh" look.)

Sorry. So when's the wedding?

SOFIA: Who knows? I can't get her to talk about it.

SCOTT: What about Guero?

SOFIA: What about him?

SCOTT: Don't you think he'll figure it out? Especially if they have this wedding?

SOFIA: Who cares if he does, now you sound like my mother.

SCOTT: How old is your mom anyway?

SOFIA: I don't know, forty?

SCOTT: Amazing, and your uncle?

SOFIA: I think he's sixty.

SCOTT: Fucking amazing sperms! They just keep going, don't they? That's a frightening thought.

SOFIA: Yeah, especially when you think how long Santiago's sperms have been on the shelf. I worry for them. They can bring a Mongoloid into the world and actually that's the best case scenario.

SCOTT: Come over here and catch your breath at least.

(Signals for her sit on the bed.)

You get so stressed out when your family is in town. You need to relax.

(Starts to stroke her.) All that talk about sperms...

SOFIA: Gross!

SCOTT: It'll relax you.
SOFIA: *(Starts to hug and kiss her.)* I feel weird.
SCOTT: Why?
SOFIA: You're weird to say what you said.
SCOTT: *(Still stroking her seductively.)* Forget what I said, Sofia. Take a deep breath.
SOFIA: There's no way I can get turned on talking about my mom.
SCOTT: I just miss you, sweetie. Take a deep breath... come back, come back wherever you are.
SOFIA: *(Kisses her gently. She suddenly pulls away.)* You *are* too skinny, Scott.
SCOTT: Ooooh honey, I love it when you talk dirty to me.
SOFIA: *(Kisses her again.)* No, you really are.
SCOTT: And you're chubby, so?
SOFIA: Fuck you Scott! That really hurts my feelings.
SCOTT: And just when I'm all hot and bothered and feeling pretty damn good, you tear into me, "You're too skinny, Scott," that hurts my feelings. You know I'm sensitive about that. How come I'm only skinny when your mother is in town?
SOFIA: You have no idea what I've been through. You start feeling me up like that's supposed to feel good right now...
SCOTT: Excuse me?
SOFIA: The last thing I want to do is "do it" right now.
SCOTT: How long is she going to be here?
SOFIA: I don't know.
SCOTT: Don't think I can take it, babe.
SOFIA: You're gonna leave me aren't you?

SCOTT: Well, I'm thinking about it.
SOFIA: Then don't think about it, do it! Get the fuck out!
SCOTT: Why don't you?
SOFIA: Because I asked you to.
SCOTT: It's my apartment, remember?
SOFIA: *(Sofia grabs the nearest item and throws it against the wall.)* Not if I can help it.
(Sofia proceeds to go for other items, Scott grabs her arms, they struggle till she bites him.)
SCOTT: God damn it, you bitch! What did you do that for?
SOFIA: Oh my God…
SCOTT: Your family is possessed, all of you. Now you're turning into a rabid dog.
SOFIA: I'm sorry…
SCOTT: Get out of here, before I call the police.
SOFIA: *(to herself)* What's happening to me?

HABOOB

Marvin Gonzalez DeLeón

Haboob is a story about finding oneself. For our protagonist Vago, a young Mexican-American whose father and grandfather mysteriously died along the border, it's about going to the source their deaths to discover the truth about himself. *Haboob* is a comedic look at that journey into the unknown, set against the magic and beauty of the Sonoran Desert. Like Mexican-American culture, *Haboob* is a mixture of many things filtered through a prism to create one light. By mixing elements of the American family drama, absurdism, and the magic realism of Juan Rulfo, *Haboob* ultimately becomes its own expression of finding identity in a confusing world.

- **How do you identify yourself?**

    M. González De León: That's always a complicated question for people of a Latinx background. I guess, I identify as American, but not really. I identify as Mexican, but not really. I like calling myself Latino, which signifies a connection to all citizens of the Latin American world. I also feel a connection to the Chicanx movement. I call myself Chicano, especially as an artist, because I do have a political bent to my writing and I support the embrace of our indigenous heritage and roots. But, I also feel like that term belongs to a time and place that doesn't belong to me. However, some days I feel like the artistic work that artists of my generation are doing is in a way carrying the torch of those before us. So, on a good day, I call myself Chicano. On a bad day, I call myself *huevón*.

- **The play is a comedy but also has moments of darkness. Do you have any notes on characterization for the actors?**

    M. González De León: Matilde and Vago's relationship is based on one of my own, but I think it reflects something common in many Millennial relationships— the ability to be in synch with one another, just never at the same time. This stems, I think, from a generational impulse to wish for it all, and when it doesn't come easily, to say "screw it." Matilde and Vago both have a strong desire to be with each other, and in the next moment run for the hills. The problem is they never agree on which it is. So, one is always trying to keep the relationship together, while the other has one foot out the door. Ultimately, it's a matter of miscommunication. They hear what they want to hear. They don't listen to each other, so they misinterpret the signals they each put off. This is especially true for Vago, who by the end of the play does learn to listen to, not only Matilde, but all the women in his life.

- **Can you tell us about the chemistry between Vago and Matilde?**

    M. González De León: Short answer: It's complicated. Long answer: They both have strained relationships with their parents. I'm not suggesting this weird Freudian-thing where they seek out younger versions of their messed-up parents, because Vago is not like Matilde's dad, and Matilde is not like Lupe, Vago's mother. I do think, however, that they came from chaotic households. They are used to that sort of energy, and they seek it out in others (as much as they claim they don't). I think they are kind of turned on by each other's neurosis. They both allude to a desire for a stable sense of domesticity at different points in the play, but it also scares them both—probably because they'd be bored with that life. So, I think the chaos they offer each other is bizarrely comfortable and sexy. That's just the world they know.

- **Where can we find the full text of the play?**

    M. González De León: Currently, a full version of the play is unavailable. However, setting up an account on the New Play Exchange is on my to-do list. So, you can expect to find an updated version of the script there in the near future.

CHARACTERS
VAGO VALENZUELA: 30. Latino. Unemployed magazine editor. Navy blue suit. White shirt. Red tie. Straw fedora.
MATILDE LECLERCQ-DUPUIS: Late 20s. Gringa. Vago's ex-girlfriend. A certified massage therapist. A fashionable, floral skirt. Cowboy boots. Also goes by "Mattie."

IN THIS SCENE
In the prologue, we have just seen Vago's father, Beto, give him a pep talk on his fourth birthday, right before he leaves Vago to journey back to Mexico. Twenty-six years later, Vago's girlfriend, Mattie, has finally shored up the courage to also bid him farewell.

(Lights come up on a bedroom. A scattering of U-Haul boxes.
Matilde, in jammies, sits filling an air mattress, smoking a vape pen.)
(Vago, also in jammies, enters.)
VAGO: Well . . . All packed. *(over the noise of the air mattress pump)* All packed!! *(as the pump sound goes off)* Bunch of fucking crap!
(Vago does his "pre-bedtime" Yoga routine as—)
MATILDE: My James Taylor records aren't crap, or my Rumi books; or our Golden Pecan / furniture—
VAGO: Ugghhh! I've got this pain welling in my Root Chakra, drilling all the way up to my Heart Chakra where it's settled like a pool of dirty rainwater.
(Matilde tokes the vape.)
VAGO: There's, like, a cyst in my chest. I've been having nightmares all week. Are you getting high?

MATILDE: Yeah.
VAGO: I thought you quit.
MATILDE: I did. *(taking a big hit)* Want some?
VAGO: My nightmares, Mattie.
MATILDE: *(blowing-out)* It's cool—it'll help your cyst.
VAGO: Really?
MATILDE: *(stoner-esque)* I'm a licensed massage therapist, Vago—I know these things.
(VAGO takes the vape—puff, puff.)
VAGO: Weed makes me wanna dance.
(VAGO does a rain dance thru—)
MATILDE: *(lacking command)* Vago, can we like . . . I need to talk to—

| VAGO: *(oblivious)* That dance class you / got me taking has, like, changed my life. / I mean, not really, I'm still / Vago Valenzuela—unemployed magazine editor. / But, it's opened some doors for me. Not, / like, career-wise, but in the Jim Morrison-sense of the word— | MATILDE: (practically whispering) . . . Vago . . . . . . (ugh) . . . . . . We need . . . . . . (ugh) . . . . . . Vago . . . . . . I'M LEAVING YOU! |

(Vago stops dancing and takes a pensive hit like a soldier.)
VAGO: I'm uuuuuuhhhhh little baked right now, Mattie. I don't think I—
MATILDE: You heard what / I said, Vago—
VAGO: But, we lose the house in a couple days! We're supposed to move in with your uncle Jim— *(Not meaning to be cruel, but—)*

MATILDE: *(interrupting)* Right—you should, like, probably find other accommodations.

(Beat).

VAGO: That's so fucked-up, Mattie!

MATILDE: You can't stay with my uncle now—that's weird!

VAGO: That's not . . . I get that! It's just!

(Vago starts dancing again.)

| MATILDE: What are you doing? / . . . could you / just . . . . . . stop / that . . . STOP DANCING AND I'LL TELL YOU! | VAGO: . . . Dancing! . . . It's the only thing that brings me peace. . . . Just tell me why! Why— Mattie?! What / did I do?! |

(Vago stops dancing.)

MATILDE: *(calm now)* I've got an opportunity to study Interior Design in Dallas. You know I've always / wanted . . .

VAGO: That's great, Mattie! I'll go to Dallas / with you!

MATILDE: Vago—

VAGO: Or, forget about Dallas! We need a "real" shake-up—let's move to Mexico!

MATILDE: You only care now, because I want something. My father was the same way!

(off his reaction) I know it hurts now, but "the wound is the place where light enters you."

VAGO: *(affronted)* Don't quote Rumi at me!

MATILDE: But, he's so wise.

VAGO: *(having a fit)* Ugh! You know I can't handle rejection! You're tearing me apart, / Mattie! MY LIFE IS OVER!! / I'm thirty-years old! / I can't just start over! No! No, I won't settle down, / Mattie. I'm finished!	MATILDE:. . . Stop being so melodramatic! . . . Your life isn't over! . . . Would you settle down? . . . Jesus Christ.

(Vago crawls toward a U-Haul box and grabs something out of it.)
(Matilde grabs his ankle. They start to sort of wrestle on the air mattress.)
MATILDE: What are you doing?
VAGO: I'm gonna light all our shit on fire!
MATILDE: No, you're not!

VAGO: Yes, I am! / I'm going to throw all your Rumi books, James Taylor records, and Golden Pecan furniture / in the swimming pool and I'm gonna start a big-ass, ceremonial bonfire! / Because I don't want any evidence this sordid relationship ever occurred!!	MATILDE: . . . Stop acting crazy! . . . . . . You're ridiculous! . . . . . . You can't erase the last three years!

(Matilde straddles Vago. She has him pinned down.)
VAGO: *(defeated)* Please. You know weed makes me docile.

MATILDE: What is that?
VAGO: Just something I was gonna throw in the bonfire.
(Matilde tries to grab it.)
VAGO: Stop it!
(They wrestle around some more; then— She finally pulls it from his hands—it's an engagement ring. Matilde pulls it out to examine; she puts it on as—)
MATILDE: Oh, my god—Vago.
VAGO: *(introspectively/sad)* I wanted to elope to Mexico . . . but . . . I suck-ass at timing and—
(Romantic music. Matilde kisses Vago mid-sentence. It's very sweet/sexy.
As Matilde and Vago roll around on their makeshift bed kissing.)

SWEEP

Georgina Escobar

Sweep is a femme spec-evo story that follows two sisters and hit women of the splintered worlds whose initial snafu with Adam & Eve catches up with them lifetimes later. Fighting for a last chance to reset humanity's imperfect patterns, the women of Sweep hunt their targets from biblical times to modern-day in order to accelerate humanity's evolution.

Photo credit: Joe Schaefer

- **How do you identify yourself?**

    G. Escobar: Queer playwright de Ciudad Juarez, shaped in Zacatecas, humbled in SoCal, grown in El Paso, marinated in New Mexico, home in Manhattan.

- **We love the alternative narrative that you offer. Why does Adam bite the apple?**

    G. Escobar: Reimagining the way we shape our narratives is an obsession of mine. It's the infinite 'what if' and the quantum logic of human drama that attracts me. I wanted to start from 'the beginning' and explore the what if's of Adam being responsible for original 'sin.' It seems to me, in the type of household I grew up that women are not easily lured by temptation. I wanted to flip the perspective a bit and explore Eve's crisis in trying to set the path of humanity on the right course.

- **How would you describe the physical space between Adam and Eve?**

    G. Escobar: In Sweep, we move through time like a reader's eyes move through panels in a graphic novel. There are places, and there are gutters, or 'in betweens.' The paradise panel is where Adam and Eve start. It is sparse, it is hot, it is hardly paradise, really. As the play progresses they move in and out of different time-specific panels, and even spend some time arguing in an in-between.

- **What advice would you give to the actors?**

    G. Escobar: Access the characters from the outside in. Let the environment you create for yourselves and the energy of the other person dictate how the characters inner life moves. There is very little 'inner life' to these two characters in this scene—they are reactionary, they are obvious, they are direct. This is the first time 'deceit' is introduced and it should physically affect the characters. Overall, play the style, play the hyper and don't fall into the hypo, play the bigness and think of it as a larger than life piece.

- **Where can we find the full text of the play?**

    G. Escobar: The full text of the play can be found in the New Play Exchange or you can reach out to me, check out my website: www.georginaescobar.com

CHARACTERS
ADAM: The original man. A childish man. A man-child.
EVE: The original woman. Willful, tolerant, and expressive, like a Willow.

IN THIS SCENE
Luna and Siri, the Sweepers, have just been sent back to the Paradise Panel to "take out" Adam and Eve. In this scene, we met the targets for the first time, and it is the first time they have a conversation about the forbidden fruit.

(Eve enters the Paradise panel, followed by Adam. They look pretty fucking normal. It's kinda' disappointing actually: How present-time they look and talk. Maybe they're naked, but it's still "Theatre Naked," and stupid.)
EVE: Give them to me again.
ADAM: Pro: We get to taste it. Con: We end up liking it so much it kills us.

PRO: We're in cahoots with the snake. Con: God gets *really* mad.

EVE: Mkay...

ADAM: Pro: We acquire all the knowledge in the world. Con: We acquire all the knowledge in the world. EVE: Hmmm...

ADAM: I'm torn. SOOOO torn. I can't even.

EVE: Let me think about this! If all the animals like it, what could be wrong with it? It's just a fruit. On the other hand, could eating it revert us back to animal state?

ADAM: I can't even!!! I can't live with this stress, Eve. I feel it in my eyes. Eve? Eve. Eve. Eve—eve, eve, eve-eve-eve-eve...

EVE: Oh. My. God. Adam! I am processing!

ADAM: Who are you thinking about?

EVE: Who? Really?

ADAM: Tell me there's no one else but me.

EVE: There's actually, no one else but you. Stop. What are you...Stop touching my...Stop messing with my hair.

ADAM: I like your long hair.

EVE: Stop.

ADAM: But I like it.

EVE: Stop touching my hair!

ADAM: Well, I like it.

EVE: Well, I hate it. Don't touch it. Back to the forbidden fruit.

ADAM: Ever wonder what is out there?

EVE: All the time.

(Adam goes to the end of the Panel.)

ADAM: Ever wonder why we sweat between our legs?

EVE: No...

ADAM: I want to be the best at knowing things, you know. I want the creatures to come to me and be like "Adam, why am I so hairy?" and I can give them a wise answer.

EVE: Really?

ADAM: I don't remember thinking this much before. It's like it hurts and I like it.

EVE: What's your favorite memory?

ADAM: Meeting the snake. Yours?

EVE: When you weren't the center of your own universe.

ADAM: I just can't stop thinking about it.

EVE: The universe?

ADAM: The snake. It kinda looked like mine, you know. But bigger.

EVE: Like what I'm sorry?

ADAM: *(points to his penis)* But bigger.

EVE: Interesting...

ADAM: And stronger. And awesomer. And green and—I'm a changed man.

EVE: I see.

ADAM: I want to be his friend so bad. I want to be cool. I want to be sly. I want to learn things. (*a little too much like Jesus Christ Super Star)* I want to know, I want to know, I want to know MY. GOD.

EVE: That's exciting, I guess.

ADAM: I want to ask him my questions and get some answers. What's a fire and why does it— what's the word?

EVE: Burn?

ADAM: When's it my turn? Wouldn't I love *(sings)* Love to explore the world around us—

EVE: A lust for knowledge and a potential for epic songwriting. This fruit is more complex than I thought...But what's the catch?

ADAM: He said you would say that.
EVE: Oh now you're besties or something? Stop. Don't. Don't touch my hair!
ADAM: I'm sorry Eve. I think I've made up my mind.
EVE: (*picking herself up*) Made up your mind about what? Oh?! That's new.

PREMEDITATION

Evelina Fernandez

In this 1940's-esque noir, about marriage and infidelity, Esmeralda, an unhappy housewife decides that after decades of putting up with her husband she has finally had enough. It's time to get rid of him. She picks up her cell phone and calls the Mauricio, the highly recommended hit man with a conscience. They meet in a hotel room, but a phone number discovered in the hit man's pocket at home leads their perspective spouses to suspect that an affair is at hand.

- **How do you identify yourself?**

  E. Fernandez: Xicana or Mexican American; pronoun: She/ella.

- **What inspired you to write within the noir genre?**

  E. Fernandez: My constant search of ways to express my identity and that of my community led me to my exploration of American and Mexican film noir (*Cine Negro*). Movies such as "The Postman Always Rings Twice" and "La Otra; as well as actors like Lauren Bacall and Maria Felix inform our diasporic collective memory and inspired the style of "Premeditation." Film Noir was wrought with mystery, danger and emotion, as was my life when I wrote "Premeditation." My husband, a professor at UCLA, and his absentmindedness was driving me to the point of wanting to kill him. I wrote a play instead. We are still happily married.

- **The play vacillates between contemporary and stylized 1940's, what advice do you have for the actors about style and playing this scene?**

  E. Fernandez: It is a heightened noir reality and should be played using 1940's stylization grounded in truthful emotion. In other words, the style should not get in the way of truth of the characters and their emotional journey in the scene.

- **Where can the full play be found?**

  E. Fernandez: The full play can be found in "Gestos" (Spring 2015)

PREMEDITATION

CHARACTER
ESMERALDA: An elegant middle-aged woman.
MAURICIO: A middle-aged man.

IN THIS SCENE
Esmeralda has hired a hit man to kill her husband and when he questions her reason for having him murdered an argument ensues. She decides she's hired the wrong hit man.

(Hotel room.)
(Eemeralda is exhausted.)
ESMERALDA: Forget it. I'll hire someone else for the job.
(She begins to put on her coat.)
MAURICIO: Why?
ESMERALDA: Because you're not right for it. You don't have what it takes.
MAURICIO: What do you mean?
ESMERALDA: Just that.\
MAURICIO: How do you know?
ESMERALDA: I can tell.
MAURICIO: How?
ESMERALDA: I just can.
(He gets up and paces, fuming.)
MAURICIO: You don't even know me, lady!
ESMERALDA: Oh, did I hit a nerve?
MAURICIO: You're saying I don't have what it takes to kill somebody? Is that what you're saying?
ESMERALDA: That's exactly what I'm saying. I hired you to kill my husband, I gave you the money, gave you the plan and you want me to give you a good reason?

MAURICIO: It's my thing, okay? I don't like to kill people behind their backs. I like to go up to them and say stuff like "This is for double crossing Chuy" or "You fucked with the wrong man's wife" or "Manny says to say hello to St. Peter for him." You know, it's my thing. How can I put a gun to a guys head and say "This is for not pick up your calzones?" Come on, it's pathetic. It ain't right!

ESMERALDA: A hit man doesn't ask for a reason. A hit man does his job and takes the money.

MAURICIO: *(Insulted)* Do you think I'm in this for the money?

ESMERALDA: You mean, you're not?

MAURICIO: No! I'm in this for justice, lady!

ESMERALDA: Oh, brother.

MAURICIO: I serve the people, all right? I'm the guy that comes to the aid of Mr. & Mrs. Everyman because the system has failed them or because they can't afford to hire a lawyer, but they can afford to hire a hit man. You know how many criminals get away with murder? You know how many people get away with screwing good, honest people? I'm a public servant, lady!

ESMERALDA: *(To herself)* My God, he's serious...

(He takes off his jacket and sits on the bed.)

MAURICIO: Now, think hard. He must've done something... Said something... Have you ever caught him in a lie?

ESMERALDA: No.

MAURICIO: Has he cheated on you?

ESMERALDA: No.

MAURICIO: Does he say bad things about your mother?

ESMERALDA: He says she's a nag.

MAURICIO: Is she?

ESMERALDA: Yes.

MAURICIO: What then?

(She thinks.)

ESMERALDA: He made promises he didn't keep.

MAURICIO: Like what?

ESMERALDA: He told me I would be his queen.

MAURICIO: (In disbelief) And you believed him?

ESMERALDA: Yes. I was born with my umbilical cord around my neck.

MAURICIO: Huh?

ESMERALDA: Only kings and queens are born with their umbilical cord around their necks.

MAURICIO: Oh, yeah? Does that include drag queens? You mean all the queenotas in L.A. Were born with ombligo cords around their necks?

ESMERALDA: You're not homophobic, are you?

MAURICIO: No way! I love women!

ESMERALDA: What?

(They look at each other, confused.)

MAURICIO: So, he said you'd be his queen and you believed him because you were born with your cord around your neck?

ESMERALDA: Yes.

MAURICIO: Lady, the only thing that cord did was stop the oxygen from going to your brain. That "queen" thing is a line. I've used it myself once or twice. "Mi reina, mi vida...," you know.

ESMERALDA: And were they just lines?

MAURICIO: Yeah.

ESMERALDA: How can men do that?

MAURICIO: Do what?

ESMERALDA: Make promises, swear, vow, profess, pledge; only to later deceive, deny, mislead, fool, delude...

MAURICIO: Hold on, lady. What the hell are you talking about?

ESMERALDA: I'm talking about how you men make promises and then you break them.

MAURICIO: You think we mean to? We don't!

ESMERALDA: You don't?

MAURICIO: You know, when you're young and you're in love... you say things, you make promises. You say the things you think she wants to hear because you want to make her happy. It's that time, you know, when you see that look in her eyes, like you can do no wrong. When you know she'll believe anything you say. We say things. Yeah, we make promises. But, when we make them, we don't think we're gonna break them.

ESMERALDA: But, you break them nonetheless. Whether it's intentional or not it still hurts when you realize that everything you believed isn't true. That they were just words.

(She begins to cry.)

MAURICIO: Oh, no, come on. Please, don't cry. *(He turns away)* I can't stand to see a woman cry. No, come on, please... Look, give me blood, guts, pieces of brain matter, the smell of a decomposed body. But, please don't cry.

I can't take it.

(Esmeralda looks at herself in the mirror, sees her make-up is a mess and runs into the bathroom. Mauricio runs after her.)

CHASING MONSTERS

Gabriel Rivas Gómez

An alcoholic struggles to get his life together before his mother dies of cancer. He wants to do right by her. He wants to make her proud. But his demons go back generations, and he struggles to bear the burden of alcoholism that seems to be in his blood.

- **How do you identify yourself?**

    G.R. Gomez: I'm a Latino playwright and English professor at Glendale Community College. My writing often deals with justice issues and I often feature strong women in my work. My plays have been called everything from surreal to unstageable.

- **Dominic is faced with many temptations throughout the scene, what makes him hold strong this time?**

    G.R. Gomez: Dominic's mother, Vanessa, is dying of cancer and this may be his last chance to get on track before she dies. He has always been thought of as a clown and he wants to be seen differently. He has always struggled with temptation but he is trying (perhaps for the first time) to take the long view here.

- **Can you help illuminate the complexity of the bond between Amy and Dominic?**

    G.R. Gomez: In many ways, Amy is emblematic of Dominic's struggle. She is an enabler who is often drunk with Dominic. In fact the script hints that she might have a drinking problem of her own. But she is also one of the few characters in the play (his sister being the other) who accepts him as he is. She doesn't ask him to be like his brother and loves that he is fun. In fact, she seduces him with this in this scene.

- **Where can we find the full text of the play?**

    G.R. Gomez: This play and some of my other plays can be found on the New Play Exchange.

CHARACTERS
AMY: Late 20's Dominic's girlfriend.
DOMINIC: Late 20's, early 30's.

IN THIS SCENE
Dominic has sworn to his dying mother that he will stop drinking. Previously, he had proposed to Amy, but things didn't go as planned and after a big fight, she kept the ring. Dominic is here to get it back.

(Amy waits in her apartment looking stunning. A knock at the door. She opens it for Dom, who strides in with dirty work clothes. Ironically, sober Dominic looks more drunk than ever. He is clammy. Jittery. Anxious.)

AMY: You look like shit.

DOMINIC: Thanks.

AMY: Sit down.

DOMINIC: I'd rather stand.

AMY: Suit yourself. You want a drink?

DOMINIC: No.

AMY: Can we be civil?

DOMINIC: Will you cut the shit?

AMY: I've missed you.

DOMINIC: The ring?

AMY: It's not here.

DOMINIC: Then I should leave.

(He heads for the door.)

AMY: How are we supposed to work this out if you won't even talk to me?

DOMINIC: Talk.

AMY: I had almost convinced myself you had your mother's blessing. That she WANTED you to marry me. But that would never happen. She has no idea, does she?

(Dom is silent. Amy grabs a pair of beers. She opens them, drinks from one and sets one in front of Dom.)

DOMINIC: How much you want?

AMY: Excuse me?

DOMINIC: I'll pay you for it. That's what you're after, right?

(He checks his wallet.)

DOMINIC: I've got forty bucks.

AMY: I don't want your money. I just wanted to be sure you'd listen. Have a drink.

DOMINIC: I don't want it.

AMY: I haven't been able to sleep.

DOMINIC: Me neither.

(Amy eases Dominic to a seat and rubs his shoulders.)

AMY: I've missed you.

DOMINIC: I know what you're doing.

AMY: I'm just talking to you. Do you miss me, Dominic?

DOMINIC: Sometimes.

(She turns to face him.)

AMY: Maybe things don't have to be over. I mean—

DOMINIC: Maybe they do.

AMY: I never broke up with you.

DOMINIC: You're serious.

(She kisses him.)

AMY: You could use a friend right now. We've always been good at making up.

DOMINIC: It's not the making up that concerns me.

(She straddles him.)

AMY: What if we still have a use for the ring? What if this whole thing is just... part of our story?

DOMINIC: We don't.

AMY: Let's go down to the bar. We'll listen to some music, have a few drinks

DOMINIC: You don't listen.

AMY: One drink won't kill you. We'll take the edge off. See if we can figure things out. You still have some clothes here. I can help you get dressed.

DOMINIC: Not happening.

AMY: Then we can just stay here. This dress really wants to come off anyway. We could even—

(She whispers in his ear.)

AMY: And the ring can be our secret until we're ready to tell people.

(Dom stands and moves Amy aside.)

DOMINIC: I don't want to.

(Amy reaches for his crotch.)

AMY: You could've fooled me.

(Dom backs away.)

DOMINIC: I thought you were special, Amy, because you were the only one who didn't want me to change. You liked me just the way I was.

AMY: And that's a bad thing?

DOMINIC: It's... not a good thing. When I'm with you, nothing changes.

AMY: Now it's MY job to change you?

DOMINIC: It was your job to help.

AMY: That's just like you, to blame your problems on me.

DOMINIC: You called the police.

AMY: It wasn't the police. It was my neighbor. I told him to come over if things got loud.

(Dominic chuckles)

DOMINIC: When my dad proposed to my mom, he couldn't afford shit, so he tied a piece of string around her finger and begged her to marry him. My grandma gave them her own ring so they could do things right.

AMY: Your dad left you.

DOMINIC: And he's a loser, but even HE could tell that my mom was something special. That she was a forever girl.

AMY: I can be a forever girl.

DOMINIC: There's nothing "forever" about you.

AMY: Fuck you.

DOMINIC: You're not special, Amy. You're instant.

AMY: What the fuck is that supposed to mean?

DOMINIC: It means who the hell is so desperate they need to hold threats over my head in order to get back together? When my mom is dying? You're pathetic.

AMY: I called you over to try to make things up to you after what YOU did, and you think you can just shoo me away like a dog?

DOMINIC: Dog's always come back if they get fed.

AMY: You're an asshole. I was actually thinking about giving it back.

DOMINIC: It has its price. You weren't giving anything.

AMY: Maybe your father proposed because he needed someone to change him too.

DOMINIC: You're a bitch.

AMY: You need to leave.

DOMINIC: Did you call the cops again?

AMY: I can.

DOMINIC: Right.

(Dom takes a few singles from his wallet and throws them in the air.)

DOMINIC: Take it.

AMY: I don't want your money!

(Dom moves for the door.)

DOMINIC: Use it to buy a little self-esteem.
AMY: I don't know what I ever saw in you.
(He stops then moves back toward Amy.)
DOMINIC: I do. You saw someone more pathetic than you, and seeing someone like that made you feel better, because you knew you had a leg up on somebody. That's why the first thing you do is offer me a drink?
AMY: You'll never get that ring back.
DOMINIC: You will give me my ring back or I will haunt you.
AMY: Look who's doing the threatening now?
DOMINIC: And you know how I'll do it? I'll completely fucking forget about you. When I find somebody WORTH marrying, you'll be the story I tell about "what's her name" with the nice ass and a few screws loose.
AMY: Fuck you.
DOMINIC: Eventually the joke will get old and I won't even remember the punch line.
AMY: Leave.
DOMINIC: You want to give the ring back, maybe we can talk. Until then, consider yourself forgotten.
(Dom leaves. Amy slams the door behind him. She broods for a moment, then pulls the RING the ring out from under her bra and stares at it.)

The Heart's Desire

José Cruz González

The Heart's Desire is a drama about a Mexican-American WWII veteran who returns home with not only a new, young French wife, but also a new outlook on life. He tries to make the best out of his situation and settle down to farm on a small plot of land, he is reminded that his hometown still carries prejudices from his father's generation.

- **How do you identify yourself?**

    J. González: I identify myself as a Mexican American/Chicano.

- **If the actor does not speak French do you recommend performing in English with a French accent?**

    J. González: I recommend that the actor learn the French phrases as written. My play explores how multiple languages can exist in the same moment.

- **Can you elaborate on the cultural divide between Rachel and John?**

    J. González: Both Rachel and John have been shaped by the horror of war as well as their own countries challenges with the issue of race.

- **What is it that ultimately makes Rachel agree with John?**

    J. González: Rachel loves John but she is learning to trust again.

- **Where can we find the full text of the play?**

    J. González: At this current time, the play isn't published. You can reach out to me and request a perusal draft at jcg57@verizon.net.

The Heart's Desire

CHARACTERS
JOHN GUERRERO: mid-twenties, a Mexican-American World War II veteran.
RACHEL GUERRERO: mid-twenties, a French Jew. Married to John Guerrero.

IN THIS SCENE
This scene begins act two. Prior to this scene, John got into a fight with Chicote outside of a diner in town because they don't serve Mexicans.

RACHEL: Qu'est-ce qu'il est arrivé à ton père? (Tell me what happened to your father?)
JOHN: My father? I told you that's in the past.
RACHEL: Why is your papá buried in Valentina's garden?
JOHN: He died. End of story.
RACHEL: Qu'est-ce qu'il lui est arrivé? (What happened to him?)
JOHN: Look, Rachel, I don't—
RACHEL: Do you love me!?!
JOHN: Yes!
RACHEL: Alors, réponds-moi! *(Then answer me!)*
JOHN: All right! My old man loved to eat chiles. Habañeros, jalapeños, poblanos. One thing led to another and he began selling them. Buddy Taylor's old man took issue. He told my old man growin' crops was his business and if he were smart he'd leave town because if he didn't his men would pay him a visit. My old man told him to go to hell.
RACHEL: Pourquoi ne s'est-il pas arrêté? *(Why didn't he stop?)*
JOHN: He was a veteran of the Mexican Revolution. Afraid of no man. He was so stubborn he planted more chiles

but they set fire to his crop. Nobody knew anything. Nobody saw anything.

RACHEL: Et les flics? *(And the police?)*

JOHN: The sheriff didn't do a thing. My old man sat out in that field with a gun

guarding what remained of his chiles. One hot afternoon Valentina took me to the canal to swim. Mimo stayed playing with his butterflies in the barn loft. That's when Taylor's men visited my father.

RACHEL: Ils sont venus ici? *(They came here?)*

JOHN: We heard gunshots.

(Rachel reacts with shock.)

JOHN: They waited until my old man relaxed. He was playing his guitar when

they surrounded him.

RACHEL: And Mimo?

JOHN: What could he do? He watched in fear as they tied my old man's arms behind his back, bound his legs, and they hung him from our oak tree. Then for fun they shot him because he wouldn't stop moving.

RACHEL: Oh, mon Dieu! *(Oh, my god!)*

JOHN: They took everything away from me.

RACHEL: Je suis desolée. *(I'm so sorry.)*

JOHN: Oh, my god, I miss him. We never touched those chiles.

RACHEL: Je comprends. *(I understand.)* It is the same. Hate is hate. Je le vois

dans leurs yeux. I see it in their eyes, their false smiles, their looks indifferent. I know those looks very well.

JOHN: Hey, that was different.

RACHEL: Aucune difference. No different!

JOHN: You can't compare Mercy with what you went through.

RACHEL: It is the same.

JOHN: No, it isn't the same.

RACHEL: Here. This is only the beginning.

JOHN: This country isn't like that 'cause if it is then all those brave men gave their lives for nothing.

RACHEL: Nous devrions partir. *(We should leave.)*
(Rachel starts packing her suitcase.)

JOHN: And where do we go, Rachel?

RACHEL: Nous pouvons trouver un autre village. *(We can find another town.)* It is not safe here!

JOHN: If we leave it means they've won.

RACHEL: These people sont dangereux.

JOHN: I don't want to hide and I don't want us to live in a barn for the rest of

our lives. You and I have a dream.

RACHEL: Tu risquerais ta famille? *(You would risk your family?)*

JOHN: I know how to protect my family.

RACHEL: Comment vas-tu les arrêter s'ils viennent ici? *(How can you stop them if they come here?)*

JOHN: Then when do we stop running? What if the next town we go to the same

thing happens?

RACHEL: Then we will go somewhere else.

JOHN: Rachel, I learned in battle, you never go back and fight for the same land twice.

RACHEL: It is not about fighting but surviving! When the Nazis came to my country I should have left. The signs were all there, the looks, les commentaires, the hate. Instead I stayed. Stupid me. What do I have to show for it? Numbers tattooed to my skin, nightmares, and everything I ever loved taken from me.

JOHN: What do you want me to do?
RACHEL: On doit partir! *(We must go!)* Leave!
   (She closes her suitcase shut.)
JOHN: Rachel, you got to trust me.
RACHEL: No!
JOHN: We've got everything invested in this crop.
RACHEL: No!
JOHN: A few months are all we need!
RACHEL: No!
   (She slaps him.)
JOHN: Please.
   (She slaps him again.)
JOHN: Please.
   (She goes to slap him but he stops her.)
JOHN: I don't know what else to do. I made you a promise. If ever I needed you to believe in me it's now. I can't do this without you. I can't...
   (beat)
RACHEL: Okay.
JOHN: Okay?
RACHEL: Okay.
   (They kiss passionately falling into bed. Lights fade.)

Detained In The Desert

Josefina Lopez

The play parallels two completely different people: Sandi, a second-generation dark-skinned Latina, and Lou Becker, an inflammatory talk show radio host, whose lives converge in the Sonoran desert in Arizona. An Arizona cop racially profiles Sandi, who refuses to show her identification in protest. Her act of rebellion sets her on an unexpected course toward immigrant detention. Conversely, three siblings who have just suffered the loss of their brother due to a hate crime influenced by Lou's racist talk show, kidnap him in hopes of seeking justice. While Sandi is being transferred to another immigrant detention center, her I.C.E. bus crashes in the desert. She escapes only to end up stranded in the desert. Lou is freed by one of his supposedly remorseful kidnappers. Consequently, Sandi and Lou meet in the desert and help each other survive. Both Sandi and Lou come to understand the severity of the plight of the immigrants through a gruesome discovery.

- **How do you identify yourself?**

    J. Lopez: I identify myself as both Mexican-American and Chicana.

- **Was local Arizona law, specifically SB1070, a catalyst for you to write the play?**

    J. Lopez: I was in Tucson on the day SB 1070 was signed into law and wanted to go join my fellow activists at the protest, but I was on a vacation/family reunion with my husband's family and my husband begged me not to go. So I was left with the desire to protest. Two months later I entered a playwriting contest and wrote my protest play in 4 days. I truly believe I channeled it because I took dictation for the divine.

- **What other aspects of the timeframe should be in the actors' awareness?**

    J. Lopez: They have been driving for hours so they are tired and in somewhat of a trance. They are in a hurry to get to L.A. to have lunch with Sandi's mother so there is a little bit of urgency and tension.

- **Matt and Sandi are still getting to know each other in the scene. Matt reveals he is undocumented. Is he scared about revealing his secret?**

    J. Lopez: He's not scared, he trusts Sandi so he shares it as a way of having intimacy with Sandi.

- **Where can we find the full text of the play?**

    J. Lopez: The play is published by WPR publishing and can be purchased online.

Detained in the Desert

CHARACTERS

SANDI BELEN: 20s, second-generation Latina who does not speak Spanish but is dark-skinned and looks almost Native American. She got an MFA in English and considers herself a liberated Latina.

MATT WILLIAMS: 20s, blond-haired and blue-eyed, Sandi's boyfriend of six months. He is an undocumented Canadian.

IN THIS SCENE
Front seat of a car. It is night. Sandu drives with Matt through the Arizona desert. She spots something outside as they drive by.

(Lights fade in on the front seat of a car. It is night. Sandi drives with Matt. She spots something outside as they drive by.)
SANDI: Did you see that?
MATT: No, what?
SANDI: There was a strange man by the side of the road. I wonder if he was waiting to cross, or if he wanted a ride.
MATT: What man?
SANDI: He was on your side.
MATT: No, I didn't see anything. It's so dark outside, except for all the stars.
SANDI: Yeah, it's kind of scary. This reminds me of a horror film I saw once... I would hate to have a tire blow out and get stuck here. *(Sandi turns on the radio. She dials it. A Ranchera song comes on.)* God, I hate Rancheras. Not another Ranchera station. *(After a few seconds she moves*

the dial and settles on a station broadcasting Take Back America. We hear part of the show we just witnessed, the moment when Lou Becker tells Ernesto that what he does is criminal.) This show is so stupid. *(Sandi turns off the radio.)* People in Arizona are so stupid.

MATT: Where are we?

Sandi studies the map and fully opens it to follow a route.

SANDI: I can't wait to get a job so I can buy a car with GPS. This old clunker is ready to die...I just hope it gets us to California.

MATT *(sarcastic, joking)*: With your Master's degree in English, you should be able to get a high paying job.

Sandi laughs. She continues studying the map.

SANDI: We are...we are...in butt-fuck Arizona... Some stupid route close to the border... Why did you get off the Eight Freeway?

MATT: I didn't know I got off...it just sort of kicked us off and put us on this road.

SANDI: We gotta get back on the Freeway, or it's going to take us longer, and I told my mother we'd be there for lunch.

MATT: Well, let me know when you see an opportunity to get back on the freeway.

SANDI: I'm so glad we're going to California now. If I hadn't gotten a scholarship to the University of Texas, I would have never gone to Texas. Man, I should never have left California. I miss San Diego.

MATT: I'm glad you did, otherwise we would have never met.

SANDI: We would have met. I know we were destined to meet... I can't wait for my mother to meet you.

MATT: Are you sure your mother is not going to mind me staying with you over the summer?

SANDI: I spoke to her. She says it's fine.

MATT: I really appreciate it, but you don't think it's going to be awkward... with your mother in the other room?

SANDI: Whoa. Don't tell me you have sexual hang ups?

MATT: No... I just know that if you came to my parents' house in Vancouver, and we slept in the room next to theirs...well...I just wouldn't feel right...My parents are conservative, and I probably couldn't sleep with you in their house, unless we were married.

SANDI: Your parents are definitely more conservative than mine...than my mother. My mother is pretty hip. She's had several boyfriends since my father and doesn't believe in marriage anymore so don't worry about it.

MATT: That's interesting that my parents are more hung up on these things, when you're Mexican and Catholic.

SANDI: I'm not Catholic, and I'm not... Well, I'm different. I am not a typical Latina like the other girls you might have met in college.

MATT: That's true. None of the other Hispanic girls would go out with me.

SANDI: Yeah, the freshmen ones are all afraid their parents are gonna kill them if they lose their virginity while away in college...especially to a gringo.

MATT: I'm not a "Gringo" - I'm a Canadian—

SANDI (*joking*): Any man as pale as you automatically is a "Gringo."

MATT: Yeah, well, I'm the only "Greengo" who doesn't have a "Green- cardo."

Sandi laughs. Matt doesn't. There's a pause in their conversation as Sandi stares at Matt, quickly figuring out that what he is saying is not a joke.

SANDI: No way.

MATT: I can trust you with that information, right?
SANDI: Of course. Of course. I feel honored that you are confiding in me. Your secret is safe with me.
MATT: Good, because you're the only person I've ever told this to. Not even my mother knows.
SANDI: Wow...I never imagined...hmmm.... Well, I feel special knowing you trust me...
MATT: Of course I trust you... I love you.
SANDI: I love you, too. *(Beat)* How did you get all those scholarships?
MATT: I lied about my status and nobody has asked.
SANDI: What about law school? You mean nobody has figured out you're using a fake social security number?
MATT: Oh, it's a legitimate one...I got it from a dead person.

There's a pause as Sandi slowly turns to Matt not knowing if he is just joking. The information takes a few seconds to sink in.

SANDI: Hey, you aren't some serial killer that is gonna take my car and leave my corpse in the desert?
MATT: Why would you ask that?
SANDI: Oh, using dead people's social security numbers isn't something I take lightly.
MATT: Oh, no, no...I paid some guy in Vancouver, and he got me one and... It's actually easier than it sounds... I didn't go to someone's grave and pick out a name or anything like that...
SANDI: So what's your dead man's name?
MATT: Matthew Williamson.
SANDI *(after a beat)*: So what's your real name?
MATT: I can't tell you.
SANDI: Why not?

MATT: Because then I would have to kill you. (*He tickles her and they laugh. The laughter settles down, and he caresses her cheek.*)

SANDI: So come on; tell me your real name.

MATT: Ah... It's Dylan Thompson...

SANDI: Wow, almost like the English Poet...

MATT: Ah, yeah... Just don't call me by that name, OK?

SANDI: OK.

MATT: So forget what I told you, OK?

SANDI: Sure... So what if somebody found out?

MATT: Ah... If I don't go to jail for using a fake security number, then I guess they'll just deport me back to Canada.

SANDI: That will be the day!

MATT: It could happen. One Canadian friend did not renew his Visa, and he was sent back.

SANDI: I would hate for you to be forced to leave this country... (*Beat*) I would marry you.

MATT: Huh? What did you say?

SANDI: I said...I would marry you if it meant keeping you in this country... I know we've only been dating six months so I don't want to creep you out by making you think I want to get married...like right now...but I truly care about you.

MATT: Wow. That's the most beautiful thing anyone has ever said to me...If I weren't driving, I would kiss you.

SANDI: You should pull over soon at the next gas station. We're almost out of gas.

MATT pulls over and stops the car.

SANDI: What are you doing?

(*Matt grabs Sandi's face and plants a kiss on her lips. Sandi kisses his neck and makes her way down to his crotch.*

Matt sticks his hand behind her back and unhooks her bra. She is about to unzip his pants when they hear footsteps, and a light in the distance interrupts their foreplay. (An ARIZONA POLICEMAN approaches their car and stands next to the driver's side window.)

SONIA FLEW

Melinda Lopez

When Sonia learns of her son's decision to leave college, enlist in the military and fight against terror in Afghanistan in the weeks following 9/11, memories of her own childhood overwhelm her. She struggles to reconcile being forced as a young girl to leave Cuba at the dawn of Fidel Castro's rule with her own responsibilities as a mother facing uncertainty. Sonia must find a way to come to terms with her past, her lost parents, her own children and her adopted country—or risk losing everything that she loves. Set between post-revolutionary Cuba and post-9/11 America, SONIA FLEW telescopes the large cultural and political forces of a historic moment to examine their impact on the intimate lives of ordinary men and women. What do we owe our parents? Can we forgive the past? This poetic and urgent play bridges time and culture in a drama about the cost of forgiveness.

- **How do you identify yourself?**

  M. Lopez: Cuban American.

- **Zak and Jen are fearful of their mother's reaction to Zak enlisting in the military. Why?**

  M. Lopez: I imagine Sonia as an incredibly accomplished, no-nonsense, take no prisoners kind of Latina. She is a lawyer and can argue well on any subject at a moments notice. She is a force. And they know her politics, which unlike the caricature of Cuban American political life, is very liberal (I know MANY Cuban Americans who are very liberal politically.) Jen knows Zak is going to get creamed in a debate with his mom. But Zak has also grown up—and 9/11 has fundamentally changed his understanding of his place in the world. This is a Zak who is different from the one who left for college in September.

- **Zak and Jen have a very special bond. Can you elaborate on that?**

  M. Lopez: I don't have a brother. I have always imagined what that would be like. My perfect brother. And so, perhaps I have created the idealized bond of what I wish I had. A sibling who always has my back. I also imagine that for children in an interfaith marriage, they get a lot of conflicting messages from their parents—and they have to turn to each other to stay 'sane.' I also think that's why this decision by Zak hurts Jen so much. Because he hasn't talked it over with any of them.

- **Where can we find the full text of the play?**

  M. Lopez: It's published through Dramatist Play Service and available on Amazon. It's also (about to be at this moment) published in Spanish—along with my play, BECOMING CUBA. The publisher is in Cuba, but I will work to have scripts available here. Check my website: www.melindalopez.com

CHARACTERS
ZAK: 19, brother.
JEN: 17, sister.

IN THIS SCENE
Minneapolis – Christmas. Zak is looking for the right moment to tell his mother he has joined the military.

(Please overlap dialogue. Pace is very fast throughout.)
JEN: You can't tell her now. You can't possibly tell her now. She's wired.
ZAK: I told you.
JEN: I think it sucks.
ZAK: No but really…
JEN: Sucks sucks sucks.
ZAK: Don't hold back.
JEN: What about school?
ZAK: I'm not ready.
JEN: You're ready for war but not school?
ZAK: It's hard to explain, but basically.
JEN: It's really done?
ZAK: Done.
JEN: It's for like, what, a few years?
ZAK: Five to start…
JEN: Five years?
ZAK: I'll come home…

JEN: In a body bag.

ZAK: I'll finish school then.

JEN: Mom is going to freak.

ZAK: I won't even get posted anywhere. It'll all be over already.

JEN: This sucks.

ZAK: Look, this guy came to talk to us—

JEN: A recruiter?

ZAK: A soldier, okay?

JEN: Nazis.

ZAK: And he just made me think a lot-- I mean, we have it good over here, you know, and I wonder all the time, about—you know, who pays for this? I mean—

JEN: The guy with the medical degree, asshole.

ZAK: I don't mean Dad, asshole, I mean, who pays, you know? Who keeps it together? Who keeps us safe?

JEN: Zak.

ZAK: No, shut up—I'm not brainwashed. I give a shit. Don't you? Shouldn't we? What did we ever do for it? You and me, Jen, what did we do for it?

JEN: Are you on crack? Because you can't actually sign if you're on some kind of—

ZAK: It's my time, Sissy. It's my time. I can't sit around.

JEN: Just finish school.

ZAK: It's done.

JEN: Done?

ZAK: On Monday, it'll be done.

JEN: Monday?

ZAK: That's when I sign the contract.

JEN: Monday's Christmas Eve—

ZAK: I have to tell mom. Do you think she'll be okay?

JEN: It has to be rescinded if you're not...*corpus delecti* or something.
ZAK: *Compos mentis,* dumbass.
JEN: Don't do it.
ZAK: The Few. The Proud.
JEN: The Brainwashed.
ZAK: Help me with Mom.
JEN: She'll be okay. Mom's always okay. What about Dad?
ZAK: He knows.
JEN: Okay, she won't be okay about that.
ZAK: She'll be okay. Are you okay?
JEN: I think I really hate you right now.
ZAK: I'll be fine.
JEN: Not for you, for me! How am I going to stand living here without you?
ZAK: You've done okay so far.
JEN: Yeah, but Brown was some place I could visit. Meet guys, drink beer. Now you're going to freaking Afghanistan or something.
ZAK: They're still burning, Jenny. The towers. I went, you know, and they're still burning.
JEN: Why does it have to be you?

the living'life of the daughter mira

Matthew Paul Olmos

In a Neonatal Intensive Care Unit, the premature baby Mira looks to her Labor/Delivery nurse as a mother figure while she tries to survive her challenging first weeks. Elsewhere in the hospital, her teenage mother and uncompromising family clash over who is fit to even raise a child. Meanwhile, Mira's father struggles to keep a promise made to his daughter nine months earlier on a mysterious beach, in an aging Chevy Blue Cassanova van.

- **How do you identify?**

    M. P. Olmos: A playwright, of Mexican descent.

- **Lazaro has a distinct voice; what drew you to write a character like him?**

    M. P. Olmos: Lazaro is inspired by the men in my family. My father's name is Lazaro, Laz for short. The character is written for these men who weren't given the proper tools to care for their families, but for whom family is the most precious part of their lives that they'd do anything on the Earth for.

- **Can you elaborate about the plasticity of the time and space of the play?**

    M.P. Olmos: The story of the play really is a premature baby somehow watching her parents struggle with even how to deal with this child while still in the NICU; so time and space are sort of lifted up out of reality for hope of what could be, before returning to the difficult reality of teenage pregnancy.

- **In this scene it is clear how impactful the father-daughter relationship is, and yet they are the same age. How do you suggest actors approach this?**

    M. P. Olmos: This play is in some ways a poem to my mother, a Labor/Delivery nurse who spent her life caring for teen mothers; it is also written for those in my family who had children very early, so this idea of children having children is big theme. So acting in that context, there is an awareness of both characters that they seem not so different in age, so I think it is intended to play with the thought, "What are we doing in this situation even?"

- **Where can we find the full text of the play?**

    M. P. Olmos: www.mathewpaulolmos.com

CHARACTERS
LUNA/MIRA: female, Hispanic, can play around fourteen, but also late teens Mysterious; not passive; a certain charm.
LAZARO: male, Hispanic, can play late teens, but seemingly older a charisma and romance to him.

IN THIS SCENE
A beach not unlike Baja California, but really anywhere possibly the 1980's or early 1990's, but really anytime. Lazaro meets his daughter Mira.

(Mid-scene) Lazaro and Mira on a beach, by a beat'ass, blue Chevy van with chipped paint, and a crack across its windshield.)
LAZARO: Who'd uh thunk it?
MIRA: Thunk what?
LAZARO: Me an yer mom, makin'somethin'honest to God beautiful.
MIRA: Honest to God beautiful is what makes a boy wanna...be in the van of a Chevy with a girl?
LAZARO:...look...just to be...for your sake...your...mother an me...we ain't...look I thought the two of us was supposed ta get up'close an never get un'close. But—
MIRA: But what.
LAZARO: Well, es only been handful uh months, but I can see her curious'ness go. An so I planned this whole trip way the hell down here. But last night, even after she

wanted the van of my Chevy, I know I ain't no future uh things for her.

(Lazaro puts his Tecate down, he looks at Mira closely)

But if this is you here, what me an her created last night, then me an yer mama was always meant to be here. On this beach. With my Chevy blue Cassannova. An you.

(Beat. Mira tries to peek inside the van)

MIRA: What does she look like. Like right now.

LAZARO: ...sweaty. Heat worked last night afterall. Her sideburns, you know sideburns, they stuck to her cheek. She got dark, dark hair, almost black. She small, don't take up much blanket, but she flops in her sleep. An there's a lil'dent of a scar left on her forehead, think it was a chickenpock she picked before it were ready to go. An can you hear that?

(They listen; sounds of a delicate snoring are heard)

MIRA: You like listening to her sleep, I can tell that you do.

LAZARO: ... she got like a little whistle in her nose.

MIRA: Does that mean I'll have a whistle in my nose too?

LAZARO: After I hear you sleep for the first time, mija, I'll let you know if you do.

MIRA: How long do I haffta wait?

LAZARO: For what?

MIRA: For you to hear me sleep.

LAZARO: Uh...let's see...

(Lazaro checks an imaginary watch)

....about a day under nine months.

MIRA: She doesn't know I'm here yet, does she.

LAZARO: If she knew you were here standing, mija, she'd be so excited; she'd hold around you an never be capable ta let go.

MIRA: Can I ask something?
LAZARO: I don't know much, but okay.
MIRA: What's your name?
LAZARO: Lazaro; everybody call me Laz tho'.
MIRA: Laz, how come what you said, how come es not you an her an the future uh things?
LAZARO: ...love is like...a lotta stuff.
MIRA: Stuff?
LAZARO: Es like on trash day, how all the little trash cars, they go all over the city—
(Mira stares)

You've no idea what I'm talking about. *(pause)* So... there's like these little red trucks, and once a week they go all over the city picking up stuff that people don't want no more. An then they take it to this even bigger trash truck that pushes all the shit inside. And where does the bigger trash truck take it to?
LAZARO: Lookit you, all smart an whatever. I dunno where the hell you get that, but okay. (pause) So the bigger trash truck take it to a place called The Dump. An all that is is this big ol'hole or like—
MIRA: Laz?
LAZARO: Yea, mija?
MIRA: What's The Dump got to do with me?
LAZARO: Sometimes, when those little red trash trucks drive up to the bigger trash truck, I seen them only half full. Me, if I was a trash driver, I wouldn't want to drive around half-full, I would stay driving thru the streets until my truck was all the way overflowing.
MIRA: I don't understand.
LAZARO: See, when your Mama ride around in my van of this Chevy, mija, she don't feel all the way full with me.

MIRA: ...

LAZARO: What is it, wha's that look?

MIRA: I thought, I thought cuz here I am standing...that you an her...

LAZARO: It's not so many times we get to choose in this life, mija. Most of the time we just get no say.

MIRA: So why am I talking to you?

LAZARO: ...I dunno, I got no fuckin'idea—Sorry. Prolly shouldn't talk like that around you.

MIRA: Maybe you actually shouldn't talk around me.

LAZARO: Wha's that mean?

MIRA: Are you really gonna be here a day under nine months to meet me for reals? Is she really gonna stay only half-full for all that time?

LAZARO: Hey. Maybe this hasn't ever happened before in the history of the universe. Maybe not one other father and daughter have ever...maybe that's how special it is we created you; that you an me get to know each other before—

MIRA: Before we never know each other?

LAZARO: Hey.

MIRA: Sorry.

LAZARO: Don't apologize, just...believe in me, ehh?

MIRA: Maybe if you didn't just drive around with her, maybe if you tried harder to be full with her—

LAZARO: Mija, me an your mama a half-full van of a Chevy couple an tha's it.

Heart Shaped Nebula

Marisela Treviño Orta

Heart Shaped Nebula is a cosmic love story that explores the mysteries of the universe and the human heart. On the anniversary of a tragic accident, Miqueo travels to the desert town of Tonopah, known for having the darkest skies with an abundance of stars. He has come to let go of his grief, but the Universe seems to have other plans. In comes Amara, a rebellious teenager who is more than she appears to be.

- **How do you identify yourself?**

  M. Treviño Orta: I identify as a Latina, a Tejana, a Mexican American, a feminist, and as a playwright.

- **What drew you to Greek mythology and astronomy?**

  M. Treviño Orta: My fourth grade English teacher had us reading Greek mythology all year. I was really drawn to the stories, perhaps because they were trying to make sense of the world--why the sun rises, why the seasons change. But I think I was especially drawn to them because so many constellations are connected to Greek myths. My father was an Earth Science teacher at my local Jr. High. We'd sometime use the telescope he had at the school to look at the moon and stars. And our family was very into astronomical events--watching lunar and solar eclipses, meteor showers. The first time I saw the Perseid meteor shower it was truly spectacular. Like nothing I've seen since. If I hadn't become a writer I think I would have gone into the hard sciences like astronomy or geology.

- **We love how you captured the young voices of these lovers. What is your advice to the actors?**

  M. Treviño Orta: These are two individuals who know each other very well--they've grown up together as neighbors and playmates. But in this scene they realize that they both have romantic feelings for one another. So there's a mixture of playfulness and sarcasm because of the familiarity and then shyness because they are not very experienced when it comes to love. Have fun with the teasing. And look for the moments that build toward their realization that love between them is a possibility--it's like stepping on a frozen pond, testing the ice tentatively and realizing what's beneath you is solid.

- **Where can we find the full text of the play?**

    M. Treviño Orta: The play can be found on the New Play Exchange.

CHARACTERS
DELILA: 18, suffers from an irrational and severe fear of the dark.
MIQUEO: 36 years old, never got over the loss of his fiancé. In this scene he is 18 years old

IN THIS SCENE
Nighttime. Central Texas*, a space of memory, a rooftop of a house.
Delila and Miqueo open their books to study.

NOTE*
Miqueo and Dalila should not have any stereotypical "Texan" accent. They grew up in Central Texas and don't have any discernable accent, drawl or twang.

PRONUNCIATIONS
Character names are Spanish in origin and therefore have Spanish pronunciations.
MIQUEO - mee-kay-oh, DALILA- dah-lee-la.

[This scene has been edited for purposes of this publication.]

MIQUEO: *(Slightly uncertain)* Dalila?

DALILA: Hmmm?

MIQUEO: I've been meaning to say, well, I'm, uh, sorry about you and Javier. And... well, if you need anything, I'm here.

DALILA: You know about that?

MIQUEO: The whole school knows.

DALILA: I should have told you.

MIQUEO: No, hey, it's your business.

DALILA: But we don't keep secrets from each other. We never have. You should've heard it from me. I don't know why I didn't tell you.

MIQUEO: Look, it's all right. I get it. Nobody wants to admit they've been dumped right before prom.

DALILA: Whoa-ho-ho...Who said I was dumped?

MIQUEO: Javier said—

DALILA: I broke up with him and he's saying—Typical.

MIQUEO: What's "typical" is you dating a guy like that.

DALILA: A guy like what?

MIQUEO: Ya know...beneath you.

DALILA: "Beneath me?" What is this, high school or a caste system?

MIQUEO: You know what I mean. You always seem to go for guys who aren't good enough for you. They don't see the real you. All they see is a beautiful girl, uh, and you are, but you're more than that.

DALILA: *(Teasingly)* Miqueo, are you blushing?

MIQUEO: *(Slightly embarrassed)* No! Of course not.

(Dalila smiles to herself and taps on the astronomy book.)

DALILA: Page 176, please.

(Dalila fiddles with her star wheel. Miqueo considers the condition of the book.)

MIQUEO: Geez. This is getting pretty beat up.
DALILA: It is five years old.
MIQUEO: Uh, newsflash: most books have something called a shelf life. You're too rough on it.
DALILA: So the pages have earmarks. So the cover has stains. Those are signs that this book is loved.
MIQUEO: So you don't want a new one?
DALILA: No way. It's got sentimental value. You gave it to me. It was the best birthday gift I got that year. Probably the best I've ever gotten, period.
(Dalila opens the book and reads the inscription.)
DALILA: "Happy birthday, Dalila. This book will help you find something beautiful in the dark so you don't have to sleep with the lights on anymore." And it worked.
(Dalila hands the book back to Miqueo.)
MIQUEO: Not completely. You still sleep with a flashlight on.
DALILA: So what? You snore.
MIQUEO: Not all the time.
DALILA: Oh, yes you do.
(Miqueo reads the inscription.)
MIQUEO: Soooooo you think an astronomy book is the best gift I've ever gotten you?
DALILA: Yeah.
MIQUEO: 'Cause, it's coming up again. Your birthday. And I found these really amazing glow- in-the-dark paints.
DALILA: I'm not the artist, Miqueo, you are. What am I gonna do with paint?
MIQUEO: It's not what you would do with them, it's what I would do with them. How would you like the Milky Way in your bedroom?
DALILA: Seriously? You're gonna actually paint something? For me?

MIQUEO: Seriously. Would you like me to?

DALILA: I'd love it. Thank you.

They hug. It lasts a little longer than it should. Both of them realize this as they come out of the embrace, sweetly sheepish.

MIQUEO: It'll be great. I promise.

DALILA: Bring the night sky in.

MIQUEO: Something beautiful in the dark.

DALILA: Like a star.

MIQUEO: Like a comet.

DALILA: Like a nebula.

MIQUEO: Like an eclipse.

DALILA: Like a constellation.

(Dalila points up. Above them the stars that make up the constellation of Gemini appear.)

MIQUEO: ...Dalila, you're the center of my universe.

DALILA: The center of the universe is a black hole.

MIQUEO: Don't joke. I'm serious.

DALILA: I know. Miqueo, you know why I broke up with Javier, don't you?

MIQUEO: *(Sarcastic)* Really? You're gonna talk about another guy?

DALILA: I broke up with him because he doesn't really get me. Not like you do. You're the only one who really gets who I am. Both here.

She points to her heart.

DALILA: And here.

(She points to her brain. Miqueo leans in to kiss again and their respective flashlights roll off their laps and down the side of the roof. One falls off entirely, the other lands in the rain gutter.)

Comida De Puta (F%@king Lousy Food)

Desi Moreno-Penson

Sex, magic, and spoken-word poetry illuminate this dark, erotic tale of Phaedra on the gritty streets of the Bronx. A bodega owner's new wife becomes strangely obsessed with her husband's son, the lunch counter boy. Driven by lust, she invokes the vengeful power of the Santeria Gods who set off a vicious chain of events that no one can stop.

- **How do you identify yourself?**

    D. Moreno-Penson: I self-identify as a second-generation "Bridge and Tunnel" *Nuyorican* (Puerto Rican born and raised in New York City). A "BoroRican" is another word that I've used at times.

- **Alcidia and Sotero are attracted to one another. What are all the obstacles, supernatural or not, that keep them apart?**

    D. Moreno-Penson: Sotero and Alcidia are hampered by three main obstacles: Laluz's "unnatural" obsession with her stepson and her personal dislike of Alcidia causes her to use Santeria in order to keep them apart. Sotero's father *Viejo* considers Alcidia to be a "loose" woman and encourages his son to use her sexually, which confuses and upsets Sotero, causing him to lash out at Alcidia, attempting to rape her. And finally, as both Sotero and Alcidia are socially awkward teenagers, neither of them have the language nor emotional maturity to fully express themselves to each other.

- **You set this play in the Bronx. Can you illuminate how this community informs/ influences the play? Is this play reflective of your own experience?**

    D. Moreno-Penson: COMIDA DE PUTA (F%&king Lousy Food) is a modern, gothic adaptation of Euripedes' HIPPOLYTUS and Racine's PHAEDRA. It is the second play in a cycle of plays I'm currently writing called *Nuyorican Gothic* – highly theatrical, fantastical plays featuring gothic themes, heightened, poetic language, and set in the Bronx featuring Nuyorican (Puerto-Ricans born and raised in New York City) characters. The dynamic, primal beauty of the borough is presented as a gothic and urban world. Sounds convey the roughed-up, desperate language of the streets from the use of pedestrian noise: the distant barking of a dog, a car screeching to a halt, scratchy static emanating from a flickering light bulb, strange and secret things that take place between characters on the streets, behind closed doors, and between themselves and their Gods.

As a playwright I am fascinated by the effects of post-colonialism on second and third-generation Latinos/as; most chiefly Puerto Ricans. There are many people in the country that believe Puerto Ricans are not actually American citizens, but immigrants. With the ongoing controversy that continues to dog the immigration/racial issue in the country, colonialism perpetrated upon any cultural group will create the likelihood of deep, psychological scars.

As such, it is a subject worthy of continued discourse and examination. As I see gentrification as the new form of colonialism, it is a main component of the play. COMIDA DE PUTA captures communities, customs, people, places, and languages that are rapidly vanishing from its Bronx setting as a result of this. The play also portrays African/Latino cosmology as a counterpoint to Greek mythology, thereby recalling the original Greek setting of the story in which the whims, boons, and demands of capricious and self-serving Gods are deeply entwined with people's daily lives and actions.

- **At the end of this scene is Alcidia being manipulated by Santeria? What advice do have for the actress playing Alcidia?**

    D. Moreno-Penson: In the last scene of Act One,

Sotero's stepmother, Laluz is so overcome with jealousy over Sotero's feelings for Alcidia, she viciously entreats the Goddess Oya to do away with her. Oya, in her dark aspect, agrees by taking Alcidia's inhaler in order to "curse" her. Then at the end of her scene with Sotero, Alcidia suffers an asthma attack. The audience should most likely assume this has been manipulated supernaturally, which is why in the stage directions, I chose to include either a strange light, or an ambient sound to accompany Alcidia's attack. However, Alcidia herself would not be aware of this. I would advise the actress playing her to play it as naturally and honestly as possible.

- **Where can we find the full text of the play?**

    D. Moreno-Penson: The play is unpublished, but those interested in reading the entire script would be able to download it from my profile page on the New Play Exchange.

CHARACTERS

ALCIDIA: Latina, 17-19 years old. Manny's younger sister. Pretty. Free-spirited. Foul-mouthed, flirtatious, and street-wise. Will also play the Yoruba Goddess, Oya.

SOTERO: Latino, 18-20 years old. Viejo's son. Handsome. Works the bodega lunch counter. Romantically interested in Alcidia. Insecure, stubborn, sensitive, easily angered. Will also play the Yoruba God, Elegua.

IN THIS SCENE

In an earlier scene, Sotero hears from his father, Viejo that Alcidia went to a disreputable tattoo parlor in the neighborhood, further enhancing her "bad" reputation. When Sotero demands to see the tattoo, a defiant Alcidia angrily mocks him for his cowardice, provoking an attack. At the start of this scene, Sotero is angrily jumped by his friend, Manny, in retaliation for sexually assaulting his sister, and is left sprawled on the street. Sotero never fights back, instead, passively accepting his beating. Alcidia questions him for this, which gives Sotero the chance to finally reveal his feelings for her.

(Manny exits. Sotero looks over at Alcidia. She does not look at him. Another awkward beat. Sotero rises uneasily, chuckling. Alcidia notices.)

ALCIDIA: What's so funny?

SOTERO: I always figured Manny had a little A.D.H.D in him. Now I see I was right. ALCIDIA: How come you didn't fight back? When he was beating on you…you just stayed down and took it. You could beat the shit out of him if you wanted to…why didn't you?

SOTERO: 'Cause I deserve it.

(They look at one another. Another short beat.)

ALCIDIA: *(turning her back to him)* I want to show you something.

(She takes off her jacket and hands it to Sotero; then she begins to pull up her sweatshirt. Sotero is alarmed by this.)

SOTERO: What are you doing?

ALCIDIA: Do you see it?

SOTERO: *(he does)* Yeah…yeah, I see it. *(Peering at it, closely)* But it don't look like a bee—

ALCIDIA: That's 'cause it's not, stupid. It's a firefly. Okay? A firefly. *(Pulling the sweatshirt top down)* I got it for my Abuelo.

SOTERO: What do you mean?

ALCIDIA: When Manny and I were little, our Abuelo used to take us to City Island during the summers. We always went to this ice cream place for sundaes. They were the best sundaes in the world and we'd wait all week for them. But Abuelo worked as a cab driver every day, even on Saturdays, so we didn't get to go until late, when the sun came down. They always kept their back door open and I used to go outside...and that's when I'd see them... hundreds of them...all those bright, tiny lights going on and off in the dark! Abuelo said that fireflies were just like regular flies except they had tiny, little flashlights attached to their tails...! *(Laughs)* I didn't believe him 'cause that wasn't special enough for me, you know...I wanted more...I wanted magic. So, I used to pretend they were fairies. And when they glowed like that, it was 'cause the fairies were saying hello to me. *(Scoffs)* I know it sounds fucking stupid—

SOTERO: No, I think it's beautiful. *(A short beat; plaintively)* You were right about me ... I am scared, Cece. I'm scared all the time. I get scared and then I get mad.

ALCIDIA: Why?

SOTERO: *(Sardonic chuckle)* 'Cause I'm just like my Pops, you know? He gets mad all the time, too, 'cause the bodega's not doing good, 'cause he's sick, 'cause he hates the greenmarket people, and Laluz is too old to get pregnant... *(Short beat; sheepish)* ...Laluz kissed me... she kissed me and I liked it... It made me feel sick 'cause I liked it. Then I saw you...and I got mad 'cause I wish it coulda been you I was kissing instead of that trick.

ALCIDIA: *(taken aback)* Holy shit. Does your Dad know?

SOTERO: Naw. *(Short beat)* I can't go back to the bodega. I don't know what I'm gonna do, but I can't stay here.
ALCIDIA: *(firmly)* Then don't. You could move back to the Heights. Move back in with your grandmother.
SOTERO: *(after a beat; laughs)* Are you fucking serious?
ALCIDIA: Hell yeah! You got along with her before, right?
SOTERO: Well, yeah, but—
ALCIDIA: So, you move back in with her. And while you out there, you get a job, you start saving money, and you start taking classes…your Pops won't be able to say shit; you're legal. That means you can go wherever the fuck you want. There are programs, there's financial aid…you were a good student in high school… *(Short beat)* Sotero, you're not your Dad, okay? Fuck your Dad. Fuck Laluz. There's no reason for you to stay here and be miserable and die. That's the mistake everybody in this fucking neighborhood makes… why should you do the same?
(Sotero looks at her, admiringly.)
SOTERO: Wow. Sounds like a plan.
ALCIDIA: *(scoffs)* Yeah, you say that now, but you won't do shit. You'll stay here, and keep working at the bodega, and you and Manny will go back to being friends—
SOTERO: What if I told you I stayed friends with Manny just so I could be close to you?
(Alcidia is startled by this, but quickly catches herself and resumes her tough-girl stance.)
ALCIDIA: I'd say you full of shit.
SOTERO: That's not nice.
ALCIDIA: *(shrugs)* Well, the world's not a nice place, what can I say?
SOTERO: *(short beat)* Let me see it again, Cece. Please. Let me touch it.

ALCIDIA: What?

SOTERO: The firefly.

(No response from Alcidia, but she doesn't move away from him.)

SOTERO: I want to see it glow brighter and brighter beneath my hand

Until it explodes

Until I can see the starbursts behind my eyelids.

Until my hands feel like they're in a cold, glass bowl of electricity

Of pure light.

When you showed it to me, I felt dizzy

Like I was drunk all of a sudden…but I don't drink; except for the wine I have at church on Sundays, and that don't count, 'cause it's holy.

That's how I feel when I'm with you, Cece

Like my blood's been spiked with holy wine

I know you not like the other shortys around here. The ones I don't wanna have anything to do with. The ones like Laluz. You're different. You're beautiful, strong… and I think if I can touch you…maybe I won't be scared anymore. I can be strong, too.

(Sotero leans over and gently kisses her. It doesn't take long for the kiss to become more passionate. A more vulnerable and insecure Alcidia makes a half-hearted attempt to pull away from him.)

ALCIDIA: N-no…we can't do this. I don't want you to kiss me.

SOTERO: *(holding her close)* Are you sure? I can feel you trembling. That tells me you like it.

ALCIDIA: That's 'cause you're scaring me.

SOTERO: *(smile)* Pero you not scared of anything, Ma. That's why I like you. ALCIDIA: I should go home.

(Sotero kisses her again. Alcidia responds and their lips stay locked for a long moment until we see that Alcidia's body has begun to shake and she begins to cough uncontrollably. Perhaps at this point, there's even a small light change or some sort of an eerie sound to suggest that something supernatural is taking place. Alcidia A begins breathing rapidly, almost hyperventilating and her body slowly slumps down to the ground, as a frightened Sotero continues to hold her fast.)

SOTERO: Cece…what's wrong? What is it? Are you okay? It's okay. Just keep breathing. Keep breathing.

ALCIDIA: *(barely able to get the words out; indicating her jacket)* M-my inhaler… get…get my inhaler…!

(Sotero immediately searches the pockets of her jacket for her inhaler, tossing everything out in the process.)

SOTERO: *(frantic)* I don't see it. I don't see it. It's not in here…! Does Manny have it? Cece…listen to me… does Manny have your inhaler?

(Alcidia is unable to answer him and looks as though she has passed out. Now in a complete panic, Sotero yells across the street to Manny.)

SOTERO: Manny! Yo Manny! Something's wrong with Cece; we gotta get her to the hospital! Bro, come on… forget the fucking pizza and get your ass over here! NOW!

El Che

Marcelino Quiñonez

El Che explores the life of Che Guevara, one of the most iconic figures in Latino culture. Ernesto 'Che' Guevara fought alongside Fidel Castro from 1956 until 1965 and was a significant contributor of the Cuban Revolution. Che was murdered in Bolivia in 1967 after a failed attempt to stir a revolution in that South American country. His Guerrillero Heroico (Heroic Guerrilla Fighter) image has inspired millions after his death, including many Mexican-Americans in the Chicano Movement of the 1960's in the United States. Today, Che is a symbol of rebellion and revolt against imperialism around the world.

- **How do you self-identify?**

    M. Quiñonez: Mexican, Mexican-American and as Latino.

- **Why did you decide to write about Che?**

    M. Quiñonez: Che's life has become a myth. While many revere and defend his actions, others despise and detest his very existence, sometimes equaling him to a mass murderer on the loose. *El Che* deconstructs the mythical figure and presents a man with all his flaws. The play explores his relationships. A common thread in Che's life is departure. He was a man who was constantly finding his next adventure and often times leaving behind the ones he loved, including two wives and five children.

- **In the scene below, Che is leaving his second wife Aleida. How does this scene move the play forward?**

    M. Quiñonez: In this scene Che clearly reveals the heartache, and pain he felt and left on others. Ultimately, we have a love scene. Both characters are firm in their positions and at the same time, lament the situation they must now confront as husband and wife. There are sprinkles of tenderness and moments of agony scattered throughout the scene. It is an impossible love. Che is fueled by his ambition to change the world and Aleida's suffering is more than any country could feel.

- **Where can we find the full text of the play?**

    M. Quiñonez: *El Che* is part of a published anthology titled *Latina/o Heritage on Stage: Dramatizing Heroes and Legends*, which can be purchased online:

    https://www.amazon.com/Latina-Heritage-Stage-Dramatizing-Legends/dp/1427655464.

EL CHE

CHARACTERS

ERNESTO 'CHE' GUEVARA: A passionate soldier. He is blinded by his idealism and tries to convince anyone who will listen to join his revolution. He hates imperialism, loves poetry, and is a great listener. He is in his 30's.

ALEIDA MARCH: An intelligent, practical, and pretty Cuban woman. She is respectful and sincere. She is in her late 20's.

IN THIS SCENE

March 1965. Sounds of birds chirping at night and sounds of children asking not to be put to sleep. Che enters the scene pacing. He eventually sits and looks around the empty kitchen. He takes out a letter and a cassette tape from the pocket of his jacket. He looks at them and then he puts them both inside his jacket. Aleida enters from the children's bedroom.

(The set is the inside of a home. A table with a tablecloth will suffice and a few empty mugs of coffee to decorate the home. The sounds of birds chirping at night should be heard. Sounds of children asking not to be put to sleep)
(Che enters the scene pacing; he sits down and looks around the kitchen, it's empty. He takes out a letter and tape and looks at them both. He puts both inside his jacket.)

CHE: Did you listen to the speech I gave in Algeria?

ALEIDA: It was printed in La Grama. I was happy you spoke up.

CHE: "Madmen always tell the truth." How can Algeria, Asia and the Latin American countries escape imperialism if nominal socialist countries play the same rules as the Yankees? Fidel wasn't happy. He said I need to know when to keep my mouth shut. He said I spoke for Cuba without asking Cuba! *(Raising his voice)* He's always spoken to me like that. I know Cuba, I work with the farmers, I see the numbers in the office. I volunteer my Sunday's cutting sugar cane. I know what I'm talking about.

ALEIDA: You're going to wake up the kids, don't scream.

CHE: Aleida, this is my house, don't tell me I can't raise my voice.

ALEIDA: You can scream all you want. I just don't want the kids to wake up. You heard how long it took me to put them to sleep. Did you scream at Fidel? Está loco.

CHE: Si, está loco. *(Off-stage we hear the sounds of a seven-year-old boy talking)* Camilo? Did you hear papá telling your sister to go to sleep? Ay, ay ay- Camilo is going to be trouble.

ALEIDA: I guess Aliusha is not the only one who missed you.

CHE: Now is not the time to prick my emotions. I can't have Fidel scolding me over the trip and my wife painting a picture of guilt over my children. I'm doing what I was meant to do Aleida; you know that better than anyone.

ALEIDA: I've known it since the day I met you, I don't know why I argue with myself.

CHE: It's because you're a woman, arguing is how you breathe. You understand the truth and then you contradict it.

ALEIDA: Ésta bién, I contradict the truth because it's a false one.

CHE: It's not false, it's always been the same, you just like going in circles. I haven't changed one bit since you met me Aleida. My stomach is bigger, that's it.

ALEIDA: You're right, you're the same adventurer I met in the Sierra Maestra, only now you have five kids instead of one and they're big enough to know you exist.

CHE: Aleida, I'm always going to exist. If I'm here one day or one decade, I'll always exist.

ALEIDA: I forgot you're never going to die, forgive me. *(Beat)* Would you like some coffee?

CHE: How am I going to get any sleep if I drink coffee now? *(Beat)* I keep playing my conversation with Fidel in my mind over and over. I've been with him the last 48 hours. ALEIDA: I was at the airport when you arrived. I saw Fidel's men take you after you kissed me.

CHE: I agree with him. *(Beat)* This isn't working, Che in Cuba. There's nothing else for me to do here. I've taken this revolution as far as I can, given my position as a foreigner. *(Pause)* In three weeks, I am leaving for the Congo.

ALEIDA: The Congo? What for? You just got back. You agreed to this life six years ago.

CHE: This isn't a diplomatic visit. I'm going to go fight with the Congolese; they're ready to liberate themselves. I can help launch their revolution.

ALEIDA: *(Upset)* You can't do this.

CHE: You shouldn't scream the children are asleep. Why are you becoming hysterical?

ALEIDA: Because you're leaving! Because you have four kids in this house who need you!

CHE: I have a whole country in the Congo who needs me! I have an imperialist system that's destroying humanity. I can't sit here ideally and just watch. Why are you making me go in circles?

ALEIDA: *(Screaming)* I'm not making you do anything. I'm reminding you of what's in front of you. If you leave and liberate the Congolese, what's going to happen next? There's always going to be a country that needs to be freed, it'll never end!

CHE: Fidel has been in active talks with the people from the Congo for months now, they need a leader and I'm the most qualified.

ALEIDA: Does Fidel always tell you what to do? He brought you to Cuba and now he's sending you out. Everyone says, there can only be one leader here. He's threatened by you.

CHE: I expect that garbage from the Yankees, but not from my wife. He's sending me because he knows I'm not happy here.

ALEIDA: What about your kids? Have you thought about them?

CHE: Aleida, the kids have you, your parents, Miriam, they have the state. Everything we've fought for in the Revolution, this is the pay off. Aliusha, Camilo, Celia, Ernesto and even Hildita, are not only mine, they belong to everyone. My children and you will be fine because I've already fought for you. You've already fought for them!

ALEIDA: And I'll continue to do so.

CHE: It's cold in here. Maybe you should make some coffee. *(Aleida does not respond or move)* Forget it, I'll make the café. I get back from my trip and my wife can't make me a cup of coffee. *(Mockingly)* "All he did was sit and read and play chess, he never did his part!" Why are you smiling?

ALEIDA: I'm not smiling, that's the last thing I feel like doing.

CHE: Two sugar spoons right?

ALEIDA: Three.

CHE: You're the reason I have to cut sugar canes on Sundays.

ALEIDA: You go and cut those canes because, "the revolution needs it. If Cuba is to sustain itself, we all need to do our part. This is the invention of the new man. I am doing what humanity was unable to do since the beginning of time." Did I get every word?

CHE: All you need now is a beard and my beret and no one would know the difference. You already have the belly after the four kids. *(Beat)* Drink your coffee, its warm; it'll calm you down. *(Aleida sips her coffee)* How does it taste?

ALEIDA: It's fine. You're not going to convince me you're right just because you made me a cup of coffee.

CHE: I'm not trying to convince you to change your mind; I just need you to understand me. *(Aleida does not respond)* I recorded some Neruda poems for you and I wrote a letter for the kids. Once I leave, you can open both. *(He reaches in his jacket and gives her both.)*

ALEIDA: In your absence I get Neruda.

CHE: He's better than me. *(Beat)* I want you to take the kids to the city more often; I want you to enjoy the ocean, the crowds and the clouds. I want you to get that history degree you've always wanted.

ALEIDA: All your wants seem really simple, but you're forgetting the most important element: you.

CHE: It's been done before.

ALEIDA: Don't compare me to anyone else!

CHE: You're not going to hear anything new tonight. It's impossible to be both a solider and husband. I can stay with you for as long as you'd want and then what? I would have lived my entire life unfulfilled. We'd both be miserable in the end.

ALEIDA: You're never going to change. You'll always be unfulfilled because you have no limit.

CHE: Aleida, I promise you, you will be my last thought.

ALEIDA: You're right; Neruda is better than you. I'll start thinking of how I can tell the kids you'll be gone again.

MOTHER LOLITA

Guillermo Reyes

The play, set in 1994 Los Angeles, centers around a high-energy apartment complex that is ruled by a sexy Hispanic siren named Lola. This fast-paced new comedy brings us murder, music and redemption in the aftermath of the '94 quake.

- **How do you identify yourself?**

    G. Reyes: Chilean-American, Latino, Latin-American, U.S. Latino, all of these might apply.

- **Lolita and Capo are both immigrants but they are both vying for status. Can you illuminate on the perceived class structures and national identities?**

    G. Reyes: Lola is a Chilean immigrant of Italian (Sicilian) descent and she sees herself as unique and special. Her Italian background is important to her because she also comes from a privileged family. Why she lives in a run-down Hollywood building and works as a landlady is one of the mysteries that is uncovered in the course of the play. If she's so privileged, why is she living this way? There was a fall from grace in her past as she escaped from her family after a harrowing incident, but she's got too much pride to share her past. This type of class distinction is important to certain types of upper class elite Latin Americans and setting herself apart from the "average immigrant" becomes important and plays a crucial part in the way she sees herself and the way she condescends towards Capo. Capo, in turn, has to navigate the negativity towards working class immigrants not just in Lola's attitudes but in the society around him which views immigrants as something that needs to be eliminated. California may have changed its attitudes since then but in 1994, voters approved of the anti-immigrant measure, Proposition 187. These issues surround their relationship, but the bottom line is that Capo is an attractive man and Lola enjoys his company. She has trouble falling in love but part of the journey of that story is that, by the end of the play, she's able to accept him as he is. Even in a dark comedy like this,

Lola can begin to appreciate someone not just for his looks but for the positive things he can bring to her life. A hopeful romantic attitude takes over somehow by the end of the play, but only after a convenient murder.

- **The comedic rhythm and tempo drive the scene forward. How do you recommend actors approach your text?**

    G. Reyes: Yes, pace and delivery are important. I'd be careful with stereotyped accents. If the actor has a natural accent, he/she should use it, otherwise, avoid sounding superficial or silly. The temptation always exists to make fun of the characters and play them as fools and their accent as something to laugh at. Comedy's a difficult art form for a reason. I'd simply accept the fact that Lola and Capo are deeply attracted to each other and that there's a cat and mouse game that needs to be played between them constantly. It's not until the end of the play that Lola can learn to appreciate what Capo's bringing into her life. Another side to Capo is that he's actually an educated man. He just happens to be a Salvadoran refugee who has to make a living the only way he can for now, and sees himself in love with Lola. If she uses him and dismisses him as a "stud," she's missing out on another more "civilized" side to him.

- **Can you tell us how the novel, *Lolita,* or other sources sparked the plot twists in this play?**

    G. Reyes: There's a complicated set of cultural attitudes surrounding the name "Lola" and "Lolita." The novel was published in 1955 about a man's obsession with an underage girl who's also responsive to his seduction. But the name was already suggestive in and of itself and in Latin American culture, it had become a standard go-to name for that type of underage seductive personality. I come from Chile, a country in which the word "Lola" and the male equivalent "Lolo" are used for both underage and oversexed young women and men. People use it constantly, "Look at that Lola and the way she walks." Whether the novel and the film made it more popular, it's possible, but the slang was already there in Chile and a verb, "pololear" means to date and presumably to go beyond a date, which acknowledges underage sexuality. I was just re-imagining a woman who's become a mother and who sustains that level of appeal as "Mother Lolita," and besides, I've got an odd imagination. I wrote an entire autobiographical book detailing my strange relationship with my mother and my "stepfather" or stepfather figures. I get the feeling both Lolita and Capo are stand-ins for my own psychosexual development, so 'nough said. It's by no means autobiographical (my own mother never killed anyone, thank goodness) but it's a dark comedy for a reason.

- **Where can we find the full text of the play?**

    G. Reyes: It is being published by a small independent publisher, but until then, it's available by emailing me, Guillermo.reyes@asu.edu, and it's also available under the NNPN new plays website. Alexander Street Press has an entire collection of my plays online which includes this one, but it's an earlier version of the play.

MOTHER LOLITA

CHARACTERS
LOLA (LOLITA) ALESSANDRO: 35, Chilean woman of Sicilian descent, youthful, sensual, was teenage mother to her only son, Xavier, speaks with accent.
CAPO: 25, Salvadoran man in love with Lola, a "reluctant" stud, man with muscles and superior intellect. He says he was going to be a teacher in El Salvador, but his past is a changing story.

IN THIS SCENE
In the aftermath of the '94 quake which has unsettled all their lives, tenants of the Hollywood Pit Gardens are either sleeping in the courtyard, or are crowding up themselves in small apartments, administered by the regal, strict Mother Lolita. Her affair with the Salvadoran immigrant Capo has become strained because Capo insists he wants to move in with Lola as her lover. She doesn't do lovers. But he insists. Her son is coming back from a correctional facility and this will create the inevitable conflicts between mother, spoiled son and her lover.

CAPO: We have to talk, Lola, inside.
LOLA: I go inside, you don't follow! I have to prepare.
CAPO: Why? Prepare for what, for whom---I mean if it's not for me, Lolita?
LOLITA: Remember, I'm Signora Alessandro. Only my son call me "Lolita" and you are not my son---
CAPO: Yes, everyone in this building know what I am to you.
LOLITA: What? All right, inside! Nobody talk about my private life in the courtyard of the Hollywood Pit Gardens. ....inside!

143

(Capo and Lolita enter their apartment)
LOLITA: What you doing? Trying to ruin my reputation, mopping man!
CAPO: Your reputation? What does it matter now herein the Hollywood Pit Gardens?
LOLITA: I am a mother and a Catholic woman. Remember that.
CAPO: Yes, but---
LOLITA: I am Signora Alessandro, from distinguished family of Santiago, Chile and Palermo, Sicily.
CAPO: Then what the hell are you doing here if you so high and mighty back there in Sicily and Santiago?
LOLITA: Look, face it, I am upper class.
CAPO: Lola---!
LOLITA: My father said God made the classes separate and unequal. It's in the Bible somewhere. In the U.S., they had slavery. In Chile, we have Europeans on the one hand and Indian peasants on the other. I do not associate with peasants.
CAPO: And last night?
LOLITA: That was sex.
CAPO: Those are all stupid ideas from the Old Country, this is the US, anybody can make it big in America.
LOLITA: You buy any propaganda the gringos give you.
CAPO: I don't risk my life coming here for more of thesame! I've left El Salvador behind.
LOLITA: Then be happy with one night here and there.
CAPO: And what are you....?
LOLITA: Oh, just checking life insurance papers, you never know. I want my child protected.
(starts to leave again)
CAPO: Wait, wait. One thing, Lola, just one thing. Look,

I don't want to live down there no more, in that basement---

LOLA: You complaining again? I set up traps for the mouses, right?

CAPO: You mean "mice."

LOLA: Don't correct me, teacher.

CAPO: There's eight guys living down there now, in a two-bedroom apartment.

LOLITA: I got eight in a one-bedroom apartment in 5-D. Those people choose to live like that, I just collect rent.

CAPO: The owner ever complain?

LOLITA: He trust me---

CAPO: Maybe he shouldn't trust you so much then.

LOLITA: What you mean by that?

CAPO: It don't matter. Look, after what happened last night. It's time we lived together---*(tries to hold her)*--You're my woman now! And I'm your man.

LOLITA: That's not how it work here in California. I am like the earth, I don't stand still.

CAPO: I don't care. It's time to make a home.

LOLITA: You? Make a home with me?

CAPO: It's time you admit it, I've brought a little bit of happiness to your life---

LOLITA: You are only a man with muscles.

CAPO: I don't even like muscles---

LOLITA: But you got 'em, baby.

CAPO: I got 'em by accident then, construction work, physical labor! One day I'll go back to work on my teaching degree and gladly lose these muscles---

LOLITA: You be no good to me then!

CAPO: People gonna think you using me for my---

LOLITA: I have nothing else to get from you. You're a fine thing who bring me a bit of flirtation, and last night, some mighty pleasure.
CAPO: You admit it.
LOLITA: True. At night, you are like a hungry wolf, but in the day you turn back into...a man.
CAPO: Then while I am good, I stay!
LOLITA: In the basement.
CAPO: No, up here with you!
LOLITA: My son's coming back today.
CAPO: Your son?
LOLITA: Yes, from jail. Or is it Yale?
CAPO: Jail or Yale? Which?
LOLITA: Both. Kicked out of Yale, spent year in jail. My accent make them sound alike.
CAPO: Don't you mean "juvie"?
LOLITA: I don't know! But they take shoplifting very seriously in Connecticut.
(She has walked out by now and they continue the conversation as she steps out into the courtyard)
CAPO: Now where are you going?
LOLITA: None of your business. I am mother first! You hear me? Mother first, landlady second, woman last! I go! And when I come back, I want to see those windows sparkling clean, I also want your smelly socks out of my apartment!
CAPO: You can't kick me out, I haven't even moved in yet!
LOLITA: Fine, keep it that way. Good day, señor profesor!
(She exits).

THE SWEETHEART DEAL

Diane Rodriguez

It's 1970 and the world for Latinos is rapidly changing. With Cesar Chavez leading the largest Chicano social movement of the century, farmworkers and their families are struggling to survive. In Obie Award-winning writer/director, Diane Rodriguez's play, *The Sweetheart Deal*, we find the young couple Mari and Will leaving everything behind to volunteer for the United Farm Workers union working for the underground newspaper, El Malcriado. In the midst of this tumultuous moment in American history and torn between family loyalties and upholding a social movement, they struggle to be the change they want to see.

- **How do you identify yourself?**

    D. Rodriguez: Professionally, I identify as a theatre artist since I direct, write, perform and produce. I have made my living going from one to the other and the fact that I can do more than one discipline has served me well.

- **What should we know about this brother/sister relationship?**

    D. Rodriguez: At one point Mari and Mac were close because they are very much alike. Both have the potential to be leaders, both have a kind of charisma that makes them popular. They were raised in a working class family and both made a point of getting away from the environment in which they were raised.

- **Mari says the war changed Mac-- does he suffer from PTSD? If so, how does it manifest?**

    D. Rodriguez: Mac does suffer from PTSD but in the 50's and into the 60's soldiers returning home had to manage on their own. He has blackouts, paranoia and probably if we dig deeper has flashbacks. He depends on Will, Mari's husband for support when they return from Korea but Mari gets in the way and he resents her for a lifetime. It's as if he is locked in time and continues to relive those moments of his return.

- **What advice would you give to the actor playing Mac?**

    D. Rodriguez: Mac is not a one-note character. There is nuance there as he is trying to come to grips with his betrayal of his father as well as his sister. Truly, his blackouts surprise even him, but to no avail, no one in his family believes him and he is forever in defensive mode. An actor playing Mac should explore his vulnerability.

- **Where can we find the full text of the play?**

    D. Rodriguez: The play can be found on the New Play Exchange.

CHARACTERS
MAC: Mari's brother, 40's, troubled.
MARI: 30's, big hearted, a realist, a fighter

IN THIS SCENE
Will, Mari's husband has been severely beaten up by some growers and their goons at a ranch where Will went to serve court documents. He believes he sees Mac sitting in his truck watching but doing nothing to stop the beating. Upon hearing this, Mari confronts her brother.

(Mari kicks Mac who is under a truck, fixing it.)
MAC: What?
MARI: Get up.
MAC: God damn it. That hurt.
MARI: Will said he saw you at the ranch when he got beat up and you didn't do a thing to stop it.
MAC: What the hell are you talking about?
MARI: He saw you sitting in a truck watching as he got beat up and now he's in the hospital.
MAC: Mari, go home before things really start to get rough. These people play dirty.
MARI: How could you, Mac?

MAC: Why are you always blaming me for shit?

MARI: Because, somehow you're always to blame.

MAC: You're in over your head. Man, Will could'a married anyone and he picked you. Unbelievable.

MARI: You lie. You're a *vendido*. You're working for the growers.

MAC: No seas *pendeja*. Even if I wanted to sell out, no one's buying.

MARI: You said you were going to quit the teamsters.

MAC: You think it's that easy? You think I love living in *Del-ahno*, the crotch of the universe? You think I love tumbleweed rolling across my lawn, the aromatic smell of rotting row crops after harvest. I'm making a living. How much you getting paid?

MARI: You're such a hypocrite. You were a cop, a public servant. A peace keeper. What happened to all that?

MAC: I'm making a living doing this. It's not that hard to figure out, *sonsa*. You know how hard it was being a cop on that police force. The only brown man trying to prove that I was worthy. I had served my country-and that didn't mean a goddamn thing to them-all those accusations- that I was using too much force. They were jealous of me, and you and *toda la familia* believing them.

MARI: Something happened to you in Korea, Mac. You need help.

MAC: I was fine. Will was taking care of me until you got into the picture and broke us up.

MARI: I didn't break you up.

MAC: How could I have even known where Will was going yesterday? He had already dropped me off.

MARI: You followed him. It's not that hard to figure out considering your history.

MAC: Don't start. Don't start bringing up the past, bringing up Pop.

MARI: Who's talking about Pop? Oh, my God. You haven't changed.

MAC: ……That was an accident……

MARI: ……you knew his balance was…..you hit him, bad. And you were his favorite. Do you know what that did to him?

MAC: ……He was always sick. He was weak…..

MARI: ….He was your father, my God…. And now, Will? We've been here before, Mac. Same place. Same topic. Repeating ourselves.

MAC: This is bullshit.

MARI: You know, after the thing you had with Pops, he told us he never wanted to be left alone with you. I wanted to press charges so bad but I did nothing because Dad didn't want me to….. but with Will, I'm not going to let this one go.

MAC: I blacked out. I told all of you. But this thing with Will, I didn't touch him and that's the truth.

MARI: You didn't touch him but you watched him. You're dangerous, Mac. So now, I'm watching you, too. Be careful.

(She exits)

Los Dreamers

Mónica Sánchez

Los Dreamers, is a story of resistance and persistence. "Scoobi" is an undocumented-law-student-love-child of the Zapatista rebellion of 1994. "Petra," her mother and former revolutionary, is also undocumented. "Dylan" is Scoobi's all-American ticket to citizenship. "Roko" whose undocumented soldier-life was taken in Afghanistan, haunts his would-have-been bride. On the heels of Scoobi's marriage-of-inconvenience to Dylan, this odd quartet navigates personal and political borders under the constant threat of deportation.

- **How do you identify yourself?**

  M. Sánchez: I'm a long-time theatre artist. For 30+ years, I've followed my bliss—towards a life in the theatre, and the theatre of life. I'm originally from New Mexico. My mother is first generation Mexicana and my father was begot from generations settled and indigenous to the geography of this state. Call me mestiza; Chicana; Latina; New Mexican--Mónica.

- **In this scene time is fluid, the scene begins in the present but shoots backward and then forward. How should the actors approaching your text handle these transitions?**

  M. Sánchez: Yes, this scene begins in the present at a medical office. Together they summon their common history. They remember the moments of Roko's surprise visit, still speaking in past tense until they are inside the memory, *living* it, as opposed to *remembering* it. We witness their final reunion until Scoobi's line: "You were supposed to pull out," in effect, pulling us out of the moment of implied intercourse and back to the present. In short, there are clear transitions in the text that should be supported by clear physical actions.

- **Can you speak to us about the style of the piece and how that might influence the intimate moments in this scene?**

  M. Sánchez: *Los Dreamers* is not realism. It lives somewhere between hyper-reality and the space of dream and memory. The stakes are high in this scene. Roko is fighting for his very life-- what's left of it: the unborn child. Scoobi is fighting for her freedom and her choices: to put an end to Roko's haunting and to continue the work she's committed to. The style of this play and this scene allows for a polarity of emotions and dynamics; the more one commits to the big moments, the deeper one can mine the smaller, more intimate ones. For example, Scoobi is driven to a frustration beyond words; all she can do is scream. Roko matches her emotional lexicon until they are spent. Stillness and silence create the ineluctable space for them to come together. If we were to continue this moment, we'd see that it leads to the conception of the child. But we don't. Scoobi tugs us back to the present. We should however have no doubt that this is not just a make-up-kiss, it is a life-changing inciting incident.

- **Where can we find the full text of the play?**

    M. Sanchez: The play can be found on New Play Exchange.

CHARACTERS
PENELOPE: (aka Scoobi) ...The daughter. Grounded, pragmatic. 20's. A dreamer.
SOLDIER: (Ricardo aka Roko) ...The ghost of Scoobi's lover. Prepossessing. 20's. A dreamer.

IN THIS SCENE
Scoobi has come for an abortion. Roko invades the space to convince her otherwise. Scoobi struggles to keep her resolve in the present. Roko fights to rekindle the past. His tactic is to coax her back to the last moments they were together; to the moment of conception. This is his "last stand" to remain alive through their unborn child. For Scoobi, this scene is an exorcism of Roko's ghost as much as it is the abortion. They are each contending with time as much as with each other.

(*A medical office. Scoobi sits on a table, places a sheet over her lap and lays down supine, head downstage. Her legs are spread, knees bent, feet in metal stirrups. The Soldier appears.*)
SOLDIER: Scoobi, no.
SCOOBI: Go away.
SOLDIER: Scoobi, no. Don't do this.
SCOOBI: Go. Away.
SOLDIER: Please Scoobi.
SCOOBI: Oh my god, not now, you can't be here now. You can't be here anymore!
SOLDIER: Scoobi, babe--
SCOOBI: No!
SOLDIER: Scoobi, don't this do this. Don't kill me twice.
SCOOBI: I didn't kill you. You killed you. I told you not to go. I begged you not to go.
SOLDIER: I know. You were right. You're always right. But not now. Please. This is us Scoobi. We made this, me and you--
SCOOBI: I told you not to go. You ruined everything.
SOLDIER: No. I ruined a lot-- most things. But not this. Scoobi, please babe! That's me, still inside of you. That's a piece of me that's going to love you forever, please Scoobi--
SCOOBI: Stop.
SOLDIER: Don't you know how beautiful our kid will be?
SCOOBI: Stop.
SOLDIER: What if it's a girl Scoobi?
SCOOBI: Shut up.
SOLDIER: How could you do this to our little baby girl? Scoobi, I saw, I saw it on NOVA on PBS, our little girl's inside of you, right now her little fin hands are there,

holding onto her lifeline, caressing it, holding on to us.
SCOOBI: Go away!
SOLDIER: We made a little astronaut Scoobi. How can you cut the tether? How can you send our little soul out into orbit like that?
SCOOBI: How could you send me out? Fuck you, I'm lost, I'm orbiting....
SOLDIER: Scoobi, I'm sorry--
SCOOBI: ...in the deepest darkest, coldest, loneliest, inner space.
SOLDIER: Scoobi, it was gonna work. What else could we do? I enlisted. I finally had a job, a legit job. I sent you everything I made. I was almost done. I had benefits, credit, I was gonna get my papers, for us!
SCOOBI: Oh, by the way, you got them. First Lieutenant Ricardo "Roko" Tovar, citizenship granted! Posthumously.
(Beat.)
SOLDIER: Yeah, bad timing huh?
SCOOBI: Insult to fatal injury.
SOLDIER: We shoulda got hitched before I went in...like you said.
SCOOBI: I can't even say "I told you so!"
SOLDIER: Uh, you just did? Never mind.
(Beat.)
SOLDIER: Scoobi, I knew it when it happened.
SCOOBI: SHHHHHHHHhhh--
SOLDIER: It was when I came home on leave, during Ramadan. They cut a bunch of us loose.
SCOOBI: I didn't think I'd see you for at least another six months.
SOLDIER: I'd already talked to your moms, to the Van

Southerlyquelachingadas, who you were supposed to babysit for that weekend.

SCOOBI: When I got home, I saw your truck--

SOLDIER: I watched thru the vertical blinds as you came to the door and--

SOLDIER:	SCOOBI:
Stopped.	I stopped.

SCOOBI: It was like...I could see the door, breathing.

SOLDIER: I held my breath.

SCOOBI: Every day I wished, I dreamed about opening the door and finding you there waiting for me. And now. There was your truck. I could feel you. I wanted you, I needed you to be there and if you weren't...if you weren't there...I'd--

SOLDIER: The door opened.

SOLDIER:	SCOOBI:
And there you were.	And you were there.

SCOOBI: I--

SOLDIER: Couldn't talk! Shit, how I'da liked to freeze that moment; for the first time ever you didn't know what to say!

(Scoobi just shakes and nods her head.)

SOLDIER: I picked you up. Like a bride. And I carried you to my truck.

SCOOBI: It didn't seem real...I buried my head in your neck and I could smell you. It was you, all your smells combined to smell like you. The way any hint of garlic creeped through your pores, the smells of the sun on your skin, onions growing near a ditch, like pecan trees in the spring before they know there're pecans, like a mustang in heat--what's so funny?

SOLDIER: Nothing. *(laughing)*

SCOOBI: What?

SOLDIER: Nothing!

SCOOBI: What's so funny?!

SOLDIER: Nothin--"like a mustang in heat!" Ay que poetic! ...Hey, come here.

(Scoobi's feelings are hurt.)

SOLDIER: Come here.

(She does.)

SCOOBI: Stinky!

SOLDIER: I found a place where we could put a tent.

(Soldier throws the sheet over the table creating a tent.)

SCOOBI: And there we were.

(They both crawl inside/under.)

SCOOBI: How long?

SOLDIER: Tomorrow.

SCOOBI: You go back tomorrow?!

SOLDIER: I got five days furlough. It takes three just to get here and back.

SCOOBI: Don't go back.

SOLDIER: Scoobi, your dad was a soldier--

SCOOBI: My dad was a revolutionary! Not a pawn for the empire!

SOLDIER: Okay I won't go back. I'll just go to jail. Is that what you want?

SCOOBI: Aaaaaaaaaaaaaaaaaaaaaaauuuuuuuuuuaaaaauauuu aauauaauuaaauauaauauauau!!!!!!

(Primal scream)

SOLDIER: Oh Scoobi, I missed you too!

(Scoobi screams again. Soldier screams. Scoobi screams back until her air runs out. Soldier screams back until his air runs out.)

(Beat.)

(Scoobie, now calm as glass. A moment. Their eyes glued. Kiss super glued. Then Scoobi peels herself away and returns to the table.)

SCOOBI: You were supposed to pull out.

SOLDIER: Yeah, tell that to the Commander in Chief.

(Scoobi is not amused.)

SOLDIER: I know. I couldn't. I didn't. It was the last time for me Scoobi. I'm not sorry.

SCOOBI: You can't stay. Any part of you.

SOLDIER: But--

SCOOBI: Everything's already so hard! They're rounding us up Roko, they're sending us away! I have to finish school, I'm so close now, but I can't with a baby! Not with your—I'm, I can't tell you what I'm doing, but it's important. A lot of us are working, planning, organizing. I won't detour like my mom. I can't--

SOLDIER: Not even for me?

SCOOBI: You're dead!

SOLDIER: Penelope.

SCOOBI: Ricardo. You're dead.

Fade

Tanya Saracho

When Lucia, a Mexican-born novelist, gets her first TV writing job, she feels a bit out of place on the white male-dominated writer's room. Lucia quickly becomes friends with the only other Latino around, a janitor named Abel. As Abel shares his stories with Lucia, similar plots begin to find their way into the TV scripts that Lucia writes. *Fade* is a play about class and race within the Latinx community, as well as at large, and how status does not change who you are at your core.

- **How do you identify yourself?**

    T. Saracho: I was born in Sinaloa, Mexico and came to the U.S. by way of Texas. So I'm a Mexican national, but I've been here long enough to feel acculturated -- although, not quite long enough to feel assimilated. However, if you call me a Latinx, that's cool too.

- **What inspired you to write about the intersectionality of class and race within the Latinx community?**

    T. Saracho: This play sprouted. At first, I started writing it to fulfill a theatre writing workshop requirement as I was ending my first year in Television but as I kept hearing pages, I realized I wasn't writing about my experience, but about how, as immigrants, we trap and reenact the class and gender roles we import from our native countries. Also, unbeknownst to me, the play became about betrayal, accidentally. So, like I said, it sprouted.

- **The scene is about assumptions, on both Abel and Lucia's part. What's the unspoken?**

    T. Saracho: Both characters have made instant decisions about one another – as explored in this scene – and untangling those misconceptions is what the play is about.

- **Where can we find the full text of the play?**

    T. Saracho: Samuel French.

CHARACTERS
LUCIA: 28, Mexican-born, acculturated. When in Mexico one would call her a "Fresa" but here, she's just an Americanized Mexican who navigates the code- switching between Spanish and English as well as the rest of her (globalized) generation. (This is the "Tuitear" and "Googolear" Generation.)
ABEL: Early 30's, born in the U.S. Mexican-American but quite Mexicanized. Born and raised in LA, proud of his Mexican heritage. Got a little bit of a chip on his shoulder. Oh, by the way, don't ask about his tattoos because it really bothers him to talk about them, okay? Just don't. He gets grumpy.

IN THIS SCENE
The time-- Like, right after Trump got elected. And all scenes take place during the night time, after work hours. An office in a Film Studio. One of those generic itinerant writer's offices in the writer's building where coat after coat of paint covers up years of nail holes and career disappointment. The place has seen decades of bad writing, receding hairlines and frantic all-night writing sessions.

NOTE * denotes an OVERLAP. The following line of dialogue is meant to start when an * appears in the text. THE OVERLAPPING IS VERY IMPORTANT. It just sounds like people do when they normally interrupt each other. It's not necessarily trying to talk over one another -- although sometimes it is.

163

(Abel goes to leave again, but Lucia interrupts his exit again.)

LUCIA: Hey, wait. Hold on. The other day, I'm sorry if I -- did I offend you with the whole Spanish thing?

ABEL: I wouldn't say you offended me, no. Not offended.

LUCIA: I, what then?

ABEL: You nothing.

LUCIA: Oh, good then. I just... I wouldn't want to offend you. You're like the only, well, you're the only other... one of us I ever see around here so I wouldn't want to, you know...

ABEL: Everyone on the cleaning crew's "one of us," so.

LUCIA: Right. But you're the only one who's talked to me. That's why... well, the whole Spanish thing. Don't you think we sort of have to claim these spaces? We're in Trump's America, we have to be militant about speaking our mother tongue whenever the hell we want--

ABEL: Our "MOTHER tongue?"

LUCIA: You know what I mean.

(Beat)

LUCIA: Well, I'm just glad I didn't offend, that you weren't offended.

ABEL: Yeah. I wasn't.* You can't help where you're from.

LUCIA: Good. I'm glad. *(beat.)* Wait. *(beat)* What did you say? *(beat)* Did you say, "I can't help where I'm from?" What is that supposed to mean?

ABEL: You're Mexican, right?

LUCIA: Yeah.

ABEL: From Mexico. Born there?

LUCIA: Yeah?

ABEL: Raised in a specific kind of way.

LUCIA: What do you mean?

ABEL: The way you talk.

LUCIA: What, like I have an accent?

ABEL: No, I just recognize the way you talk. In Spanish. I waited tables for a while and the kind of Mexicans that would come in, you always knew what kind of table they were going to be, because their little fresita accent.

LUCIA: You're calling me a fresa?

ABEL: Not as an insult. Just what it is.

LUCIA: I'm so not a fresa! I have to have a job, first of all,* my daddy didn't set up some trust fund for me --

ABEL: I'm just saying that you can't help where you're from.

LUCIA: Where I'm from? Where are you from?

ABEL: Here. El Sereno.

LUCIA: Oh. I thought you were Mexican.

ABEL: Yeah, I am. But I was born here. My grandparents are from Guanajuato.

LUCIA: Not even your parents? Your grandparents are the Mexican ones.

ABEL: We're ALL the Mexican ones.

LUCIA: Right, but that makes you more like... Mexican-American.

ABEL: No. I'm a Mexican who happened to be born in El Sereno. Just by accident.

LUCIA: Ah.

(Tense-ass pause.)

ABEL: Does stink like corn nuts in here.

LUCIA: Sorry.

ABEL: You don't have to say sorry* to me.

LUCIA: Hopefully it'll dissipate now that you're taking the trash. Thank you.

(Abel starts to go. Lucia's like, "shit, it does stink in here.")

She goes to see if she can open the window.)
ABEL: You wanna crank the window?
LUCIA: Yeah, I think* I'm going to open it.
ABEL: It has sort of a... there's a little trick to it. You want me to crank it open for you?
LUCIA: No, I don't need you to "crank" it for me,* thank you.
ABEL: Ok, but they're from the 40's when this studio got built so they're a little tricky.*

You just gotta crank it.
LUCIA: I got it. Thanks.
ABEL: Well. Give a holler if you need my help.
LUCIA: I'm fine.
(Abel's like "suit yourself She-Rah," and bounces. Lucia starts to hit the pane with her shoulder. After a while, Abel comes back.)
ABEL: You sure you don't need help cranking it?
(She hits it.)
ABEL: Te digo que tiene maña.
(The Spanish makes her stop and look at him.)
LUCIA: Well, look at that. He does speak Spanish after all.
ABEL: Hey, I never said I didn't speak it. I just wasn't gonna answer you with it only cuz you had decided for both of us that we were gonna speak it. *(beat)* You gonna let me crank the window open for you?
LUCIA: Yeah. If you stop saying "crank."
ABEL: Look. It's cuz this is how you open it. You were pushing it and you have to do it like this.
(Yup. He old-school cranks it.)
LUCIA: Well, now I know. Thank you.
ABEL: You gotta get old school with it.
(She cracks a smile at "old school.")

Destiny of Desire

Karen Zacarias

In Karen Zacarías's hilarious, provocative and revolutionary send-up of the telenovela genre, women take power over their futures, their families, and their destinies. Love and betrayal overflow amid a vibrant cast of classic Mexican telenovela characters, with nods to Shakespeare's comedies and Brecht's epic theatre. Two girls—one rich but sickly, one poor and healthy—are switched at birth by a scheming beauty queen. Eighteen years later, things fly apart when the two women meet, become friends and fall for men they are forbidden to love.

- **How do you identify yourself?**

    K. Zacarias: I was born in Mexico and moved to the United States when I was ten years old. I consider myself Mexican-American/Latinx/ American.

- **What inspired you to tell a story in a 'telenovela' format?**

    K. Zacarias: As Latinx theater artists, many of us have an ambivalent relationship to Telenovelas. Love them or hate them, they are the biggest creative export of the Americas and the most popular form of entertainment in the world. Theater Critics often use the word "telenovela" to describe the work of many Latinx playwrights and actors and it's always used derogatively, dismissively and incorrectly. So I decided to purposely write an unapologetic telenovela for the stage that hopefully takes this populist genre to high art. Telenovelas are a very specific genre, with archetypes and conventions that should be examined, honored, and tested.

- **You give very specific directions in the introduction to the play, "Once they enter as Characters of** *DESTINY OF DESIRE***: they are always truthful, committed, and in the moment when in a scene. No camp. No fake Spanish accents. (*real ones are fine)… Communicating without explaining. Heightened but centered." You also contextualize the work as Brechtian. These are great guidelines to help the actor and director. Can you elaborate on your impulse to place them in the play directions?**

    K. Zacarias: In a comedy, tone is everything! *Destiny of Desire* is not a farce nor a parody; it is subversive, exuberant, and sly comedy that only works if the actors seriously commit to the truth of what is happening to their characters. The Brechtian frame gives political context and theatrical contrast to the heightened storyline. Elegance, precision and honesty are key to the pace, tone, and success of the piece.

- **You incorporate music in the play; the characters sing where they need to express themselves with song. In this scene Fabiola sings a Tango. Why a Tango?**

    K. Zacarias: The "melo" in melodrama is about music; Brecht also used songs in his Epic Theater so *Destiny of Desire* has both songs and musical underscoring. *Destiny of Desire* employs musical forms like Classical, R&B, Pop, and honors many Latin American musical traditions such as Salsa, Huapango, Bolero, Ranchera, Cumbia, and Tango. Usually a Tango is a sexually charged dance between an older powerful man and a younger more submissive woman. In this Tango, Fabiola turns the tables on the genre, and uses the Tango as a personal anthem to her psyche.

- **Where can the play be found?**

    K. Zacarias: I have been doing rewrites on *Destiny of Desire* through productions at Arena Stage, The Goodman Theater, South Coast Rep, and Oregon Shakespeare Festival. At this moment, the play is so new, it is still not published. For more information on the script or agents please visit www.karenzacarias.com.

CHARACTERS

FABIOLA CASTILLO: 38 years old, the beauty Queen wife of Armando Castillo.

SEBASTIÁN JOSE CASTILLO: 37 years old, Armando's estranged son from a former marriage.

IN THIS SCENE

The play opens with Fabiola giving birth to a sickly child but secretly switching her for another as to not upset her powerful older husband Armando Castillo. In this scene, we learn that Fabiola is in love with Sebastián, her husband Armando's banished son from a former marriage (aka: her step–son).

(A Hotel Room. SEBASTIÁN is getting dressed. FABIOLA opens the door to his hotel room and rushes in.)
FABIOLA: Oh, Sebastián!
SEBASTIÁN: Fabiola!
FABIOLA: You cannot be here in Bellarica.
SEBASTIÁN: Fabiola...you should not be in my room.
FABIOLA: This is too dangerous.
(beat)
I have missed you so much!
(She takes off her jacket)
SEBASTIÁN: Our last meeting in Monterrey was three months ago.
(She pounces him on the bed and mounts him. He wants to resist but the resolve is difficult)
FABIOLA: But if Armando finds you here, he will destroy us.
SEBASTIÁN: I know. Fabiola...I cannot go on like this any longer.
(FABIOLA pulls off his belt) (Beat)

FABIOLA: What are you saying?

SEBASTIÁN: Fabiola, we need to end this.

FABIOLA: You said I was beautiful.

SEBASTIÁN: You are as beautiful as ever.

FABIOLA: Touch me. Feel me. My skin, my lips, my body are all yours.

(She ties him with her belt)

SEBASTIÁN: I cannot deny the desire I feel for you but I want something more.

FABIOLA: One day Armando will die and everything will be ours.

SEBASTIÁN: I do not want my father to die. Not anymore. I have not been home since he threw me out for my drinking and gambling.

FABIOLA: Go to Monterrey! Wait for me at our favorite hotel. I will find a reason to travel there tomorrow.

SEBASTIÁN: I want to come home, Fabiola. Today... I caught a glimpse of what my life could be... If I made a change.

FABIOLA: Me too. I love you.

(Stops her)

SEBASTIÁN: This is not how love feels.

FABIOLA: Another woman? Who is it? I will kill her.

SEBASTIÁN: I do not know her name. But with her, I felt a moment of innocence and grace. And I realized then how I have longed to be a better man. And the first step is to end this and make peace with my father.

FABIOLA: After Armando disowned you and threw you out on the street?

SEBASTIÁN: I will ask his forgiveness. I have a plan involving online technology that will generate new revenue streams for the Castillo Casino. My father may be proud but he still wants to be rich.

FABIOLA: Oh Sebastián, for years you asked me to run away with you. I was stupid to say no.

SEBASTIÁN: Fabiola, you were right to refuse me. We were young and angry.

FABIOLA: I was seduced by an older man and suddenly married with a baby. And then I met his handsome son, only a year younger than me.

SEBASTIÁN: You were like fire, beautiful and dangerous. I burned for you.

FABIOLA: I fell deeply in love with you.

SEBASTIÁN: It is time to set ourselves free of the past.

FABIOLA: Oh Sebastián, one can never be free of the past.

(FABIOLA sincerely cries for a moment)

SEBASTIÁN: I have never seen you cry.

FABIOLA: My heart aches for you.

(beat.)

But, nothing this good can last forever.

SEBASTIÁN: And it will destroy us if we keep on. Think of my father. Think of your daughter.

FABIOLA: *(Bitterly)* Pilar Esperanza.

SEBASTIÁN: My little sister. She was three years old the last time I saw her.

FABIOLA: Pilar is 18 and a thorn in my side.

SEBASTIÁN: I would love to see her again.

FABIOLA: Promise you will never betray our secret to Armando.

*ACTOR (ARMANDO): 68% of married women, in the United States say they would have an affair if they knew they would never get caught. Chicago is in the United States.

FABIOLA: When he loves, he loves, but when he angers... God rest Sofia's soul.

SEBASTIÁN: My father did not kill my mother. He loved her dearly.

FABIOLA: I hope you are right.

SEBASTIÁN: I will never let any harm come your way, Fabiola.

FABIOLA: Thank you.

SEBASTIÁN: Forgive me.

FABIOLA: Goodbye.

(She smiles sadly. She exits. The door closes behind her.)
(Music)

FABIOLA'S TANGO (PAIN MAKES ME BEAUTIFUL)

>YOU LEFT ME
>I WILL NEVER FORGET
>YOU LEFT ME
>I WILL NEVER FORGIVE
>I'LL MAKE sure YOU REPENT
>YOU FOOLISH BOY
>I'M NOT YOUR TOY
>I'LL DRIVE YOU TO YOUR KNEES
>I WILL IGNORE YOUR PLEAS
>GO AHEAD SAY GOODBYE
>WE WILL SEE WHO SURVIVES
>BECAUSE
>PAIN MAKES ME BEAUTIFUL

Scenes For Two Females

QUALITY: THE SHOE PLAY

Elaine Avila

Roxanne is the manager of Tremendulo boutique, one of the most exclusive shoe shops in the world. Pippa aspires to be her protégé—helped only by her uncanny gift to channel fantasies behind shoes (from gladiators to astronauts). A dark, comic struggle for power, Quality explores the relationship between commerce and art, the legacy women pass down to each other, and how the world is serving the very wealthy.

- **How do you identify yourself?**

    E. Avila: Portuguese. Azorean. Canadian. American.

- **Can you describe the power dynamics between Pippa and Roxanne?**

    E. Avila: In the opening of the play, I describe Roxanne as "radiant with confidence, a lioness on her plot of land." She has all the power: she assesses Pippa from head to toe. Pippa aspires to be employed by Roxanne, at one of the wealthiest shoe boutiques in the world. Pippa is desperate for a job. In the scene below, Pippa has been hired, and has been learning from Roxanne for two weeks, and is starting to gain power. Roxanne is giving Pippa a reward for receiving training well. Roxanne is letting Pippa see the new collection before anyone else.

- **Can you speak to the humor and tempo in this scene?**

    E. Avila: I've had the good fortune to see this scene performed in London, England; Albuquerque and Santa Fe, New Mexico; Panama City (in Spanish); Edmonton, Alberta; San Francisco; Bellingham and Los Angeles. There is lots of humor! This is a silly scene (many productions have called it the "shoegasm" scene), but the characters take the situation very, very seriously. It works best if the actors explore both a slow and a quick tempo. Sometimes Roxanne luxuriates, sometimes she expects Pippa to be able to respond very rapidly. Pippa is 100% with Roxanne in parts of the scene, but begins challenging her in other parts, and her tempo reflects this.

- **Where can we find the full text of the play?**

    E. Avila: It is available in *Jane Austen, Action Figure* *and Other Plays*, published by NoPassport Press (available online, many places, internationally), and also through the Playwrights Guild of Canada.

CHARACTERS
ROXANNE: Manager of Tremendulo Shoe Boutique.
PIPPA: Hoping to be employed
(Actors of any ethnicity can play these roles).

IN THIS SCENE
Tremendulo Shoe Boutique, The City. Tremendulo shoes are extreme works of art that cost as much as shoes can cost. This is Pippa's second week on the job and the new collection has arrived.

Two weeks later. Roxanne, happily humming "These Boots Were Made for Walking."
(Pippa enters.)
ROXANNE: I love Sunday mornings. Divinely quiet. Everyone's at brunch, church, or recovering from a hangover. Time for your reward. What do you have there?
PIPPA: My Italian isn't the best, but-- are they-- from the shoe factory?
ROXANNE: Which means?
PIPPA: It's the Spring Collection?
ROXANNE: Yes. My clever girl. Go ahead. Rip them open. Wait. Take a moment. Remember, no one has seen these designs. We'll be the first ones. (*Pippa begins to open*) No. Not yet. One more deep breath. Until we can't stand

it another moment. Now. Now. Rip. Show me one. Ah. What's it called?
PIPPA: Stimulate.
ROXANNE: Hmm. Stim-u-late. Mmmph. Maximo has outdone himself.
PIPPA: That is your idea. He is using your ideas.
ROXANNE: I know. So what? Next.
PIPPA: This one is" Mount" ...
ROXANNE: Oh. Maximo. I love it when you go all the way. God the arch. It's so sexy--the bravado in showing so much instep—mmph. This one has to go in the window.
PIPPA: What do we do with the old ones?
ROXANNE: Throw them in the back. Next.
PIPPA: No-one wears them?
ROXANNE: No.
PIPPA: They never go on sale?
ROXANNE: Of course not. That would be lowering our market worth. Pippa, please, another pair...
PIPPA: Blush.
ROXANNE: Ah. To come back to simplicity, open-heartedness, tenderness. After feeling jaded...that is true mark of his artistry. Do several all at once--oh god, I can't stand it. (*She unwraps them too.*)
ROXANNE & PIPPA: Oh. Oh. Oh. Ah. (*Roxanne and Pippa rests, satiated.*)
ROXANNE: Pippa, be a dear and put Arouse, Envy, and Titillate in the window, would you? (*Pippa does so, with reverence. Pippa and Roxanne bask in a mutual glow.*)
PIPPA: Do you remember what you said? About high heels—women being too timid.

ROXANNE: Yes?
PIPPA: Let's turn that around.
ROXANNE: Sell them on boldness.
PIPPA: Defiance.
ROXANNE: The sexiness of their walk.
PIPPA: The line of their body.
ROXANNE: Can't get that with flats. Let's practice. Think of your clients...which one is most timid?
PIPPA: Art history professor. I had one yesterday.
ROXANNE: Did she buy anything?
PIPPA: No. But she wanted to.
ROXANNE: How could she? On her salary. An inheritance?
PIPPA: No. She's the type that eats ramen. Saves up for a spectacular splurge. Once in her life.
ROXANNE: Let's get inside her head. I'll kick us off. "I am forty-five years old, somehow I missed dating. Busy in my art historical enclave, I came to know more about painting techniques of the Renaissance than about people."
PIPPA: "I have to commute two hours into the city, and still my apartment, that I can barely afford, is 25 square feet..."
ROXANNE: "I got thinner and thinner, my body "
PIPPA: "a wiry artistic extension of myself "
ROXANNE: "Silhouetted against the smart classroom projections"
PIPPA: "My voice disembodied in the dark,"
ROXANNE: "wispy grey hair "
PIPPA: "Unseen "
ROXANNE: "Flattened against the wall at art openings, smiling wanly at my more famous students" We'll get her into heels.

PIPPA: Three-inch minimum.

ROXANNE: Let's sell her. I want to do a tag team with you.

PIPPA: What do I—

ROXANNE: We play off of each other. Put the shoes there. We'll pretend it's her. Right. The watcher gauges how it's going, then moves in, we switch.

PIPPA: Signorina, may I be of assistance…

ROXANNE: She's frightened. Too much. Excuse my employee. Great glasses. I love your hair.

PIPPA: You look strong enough to tower—

ROXANNE: To saunter—

PIPPA: To sashay—

ROXANNE: All those people watching you all day, how lovely it would be to feel that every piece of your ensemble is impeccably in place--

PIPPA: She's scared—how do you know people watch her—

ROXANNE: Didn't you speak at the Blick opening? Weren't the appy's divine? How could I forget a woman of your wit --

PIPPA: --and grace?

ROXANNE: Want to try something bold?

PIPPA: How about…" titillate"?

ROXANNE: Too sexual, you're scaring her.

PIPPA: "Command."

ROXANNE: Too much.

PIPPA: She brushed against the Louis XIV fleur de lis slippers—3 inch heels—just like French royalty.

ROXANNE: Good. These will make her feel substantial. Her grey hair celebrated, powdered, piled upon her head—I know. Let's channel them together.

Quality: The Shoe Play

PIPPA: Touch them. Aren't they supple? Impeccable construction. (*Pippa channels*) "I leave my four-poster bed and slip into my brocade dressing gown—"

ROXANNE: (*touching shoes*) I'm there. "My entourage racing after me as I make my very important meetings regarding the commissioning of important playwrights and their tributes to me,"

PIPPA: "everyone hanging on my every word, my slightest displeasure—"

ROXANNE: "Power, arbiter of all culture. Deciding what shall happen. What shall be eaten, read, viewed, loved—"

PIPPA: "adored by the wealthiest in my realm."

ROXANNE: "Everyone follows me. I am the Queen."

PIPPA: So what if they cost a month's pay?

ROXANNE: They are worth it.

PIPPA: Too high? They are designed like a cathedral. Perfectly balanced. You could stand in them all day.

ROXANNE & PIPPA: "Uh…I'll give them a try."

(They break into peals of laughter.)

ROXANNE: That was great.

PIPPA: Link her pain to a fantasy, and you have the key to her heart.

ROXANNE: Precisely.

PIPPA: Oh, Roxanne, you've climbed inside my head and thrown out all the junk. Redecorated.

Fabulous Monsters

Diana Burbano

Set in L.A. 1977. When punk rock exploded in L.A., Sally and Lou were there: feminists, Latinas, queens of noise. One went pop, one stayed punk, but sparks from their tumultuous friendship remain. Decades later, can they overcome old wounds, forgive each other, and rock as hard as they ever did?

Diana Burbano

- **How do you identify yourself?**

    D. Burbano: A nerd. A punker. A romantic. A deep feeler. An immigrant and an American.

- **Kady is impulsive. Why is she in love? Is it the music?**

    D. Burbano: Kady is in love with the idea of what rock and roll used to mean. She's been raised in an age of auto-tune and fakery, so to be in the presence of someone who is raw and real is a real turn on.

- **Music plays a central role. What artists should the actors listen to?**

    D. Burbano: Oh this is my favorite question! Joan Jett, Patti Smith, Tina Turner, The Runaways, X, Blondie, Bikini Kill, Siouxie Sioux, Lou Reed, Lucinda Williams, Poly Styrene, Pussy Riot, Le Tigre Sleater-Kinney and Linda Ronstadt.

- **There is an age divide between Kady and Slade, what is your advice to the actors playing them?**

    D. Burbano: Slade while seemingly cool, is uncomfortable and not open about her feelings, while Kady has a fluid and open sexuality and as she says in another part of the play, "labels are for blue jeans".

- **Where can we find the full text of the play?**

    D. Burbano: The play can be found in the New Play Exchange.

CHARACTERS
KADY: 16-20. Pretty, complicated and ambitious teenager. Half-Latina.
SLADE: Older than Kady. Punk rocker. Androgynous. Angry. Latina.

IN THIS SCENE
In this scene Kady has secretly followed Slade to her AA meeting, hoping to speak to her alone. In the previous scene Slade abandoned her old bandmate, Kady's mom, in the middle of trying to reform their 70's punk band.

(Kady is waiting outside, texting furiously. The phone pings and hoots. She carefully arranges herself in the lens and takes a pouty selfie. Slade comes out, sees Kady, watches her.)
SLADE: Are you more or less vain than the average teenager?
KADY: *(Jumps)* I'm not vain! I'm maintaining an online presence.
SLADE: I see.
KADY: I'm trying to build my fan base.
SLADE: What are you doing here?
KADY: I want to talk to you. I want to apologize for how everything went down yesterday.
SLADE: How'd you track me down?
KADY: I googled AA meetings near your house.
SLADE: What the fuck ever happened to "anonymous?"
KADY: Are you pissed?
SLADE: Always. I walked all over town last night. I'm sad at how cleaned up Hollywood is. You can't even pick

a fight with a bum for fun anymore. Although, I'm so fucking old I'd probably break my wrist punching him.

KADY: Must be fun to be in a fight.

SLADE: It's a rush. When it's not just you getting beat up.

KADY: Who beat you up?

SLADE: Is your phone off?

(Guiltily turning it off)

KADY: Yes.

SLADE: My dad used to whale the shit out of me. First for being stupid and doing badly in school, then for not being girly enough. I always wished I had the balls to punch him back, but he was still my Papi.

KADY: My stepdad would never hit me.

SLADE: One of the first shows we ever played, I called a guy a cocksucker 'cause he was saying disgusting things about Lulu. And called me an ugly dyke. He was in the front row, so I whacked him as hard as I could with my guitar. I probably coulda killed him except I was drunk and my aim was off.

KADY: Weren't you scared?!

SLADE: Nah. The guy jumped on stage before the bouncer could get there, and hit me, and I hit him back and then it was like high school, just rolling around trying to hurt each other. But I hit him first. And it felt good.

KADY: I'd be scared of breaking something.

SLADE: I was already pretty broken— So.

KADY: Can— Can we go somewhere and talk?

SLADE: Right here seems OK.

KADY: *(Deep breath)* —I've been in love with you since I was 12!! My stepdad put Greed and Gluttony on his old record player, I had to go over right then to see what it was. He showed me the cover. It was crazy. I looked at you, looking so mean and hard, and your eyes were so deep. And it was like, I KNEW you. That music looked into my soul.

SLADE: At 12?

KADY: Absolutely. It was the first time I— *(Blushes furiously)* You so knocked me out. Dad gave me the LP. And I read everything I could about you.

SLADE: I'm, god, I'm. I'm old.

KADY: I don't care. *(Kisses her. Slade pulls away)*

SLADE: Stop. I'm barely hanging on to sobriety as it is.

KADY: *(Calmly moving forward. She grabs Slade's's fidgety hands)* What made you stop using?

SLADE: I don't know. It calls to me. All the time. But so does playing guitar. There's no great defining moment. I couldn't look at myself anymore. So I quit. Got an asshole for an AA sponsor. Pretend to pray to god for acceptance. It works OK.

KADY: But if you don't believe in it?

SLADE: Mostly I like being around people more fucked up than me. Makes me feel good.

KADY: I'd love to meet Nigel

SLADE: Terrible idea.

KADY: Well— I want to go to your place.

(Kady looks pointedly at Slade. She leans in for a kiss. Takes a beat. Leans in again.)

SLADE: *(Stops her)* Does your mom know?

KADY: That I'm in love with you?

SLADE: That you're gay.

KADY: I'm not.

SLADE: You're not?

(Slade releases her hands.)

KADY: I'm not. I'm in love with YOU. Today.

SLADE: Today, you're in love with me.
KADY: Yes. I am.
SLADE: And tomorrow?
(Kady kisses Slade very hard.)
KADY: Can I go home with you?
SLADE: Oh my god. I REALLY don't understand kids today...
(Slade kisses Kady cautiously)
SLADE: Lulu.
KADY: Whatever. She won't know.
SLADE: *(Closes her eyes and breathes in.)* You smell like... dirt and lavender. *(Looks at Kady)* I'd have to have a heart for you to break it.
KADY: How come you never hooked up with—-? ARE you gay?
SLADE: I'm a guitar player. The axe rests on my pubic bone so when I play, I'm making love.
KADY: I couldn't care less if you were a boy or a girl or a guitar.
SLADE: Nigel was the same. (She kisses *Kady*) Beautiful. Shit. Teenagers. Why do you have to be so beautiful?
(Kisses her harder. Kady melts into Slade as Slade's eyes are closed, Kady pulls out her iPhone, and takes a picture.)

LA RUTA

Isaac Gomez

To the U.S.-owned factories in Ciudad Juárez, Mexico, *La Ruta* is just a bus. But to the hundreds of women who live, work and often disappear along the route, it's so much more than that. Inspired by real testimonies, and using live music to evoke factory work and protest marches, *La Ruta* is a visceral unearthing of secrets buried in the desert and a celebration of the Mexican women who stand resiliently in the wake of loss.

- **How do you identify yourself?**

  I. Gomez: I'm a Mexican queer man from the far West Texas Border (El Paso, TX / Ciudad Juarez, Mexico). I'm a writer. I'm a brother. I'm a godfather, uncle, cousin. I'm a partner, I'm a best friend. I'm a teacher. I'm a creator. I'm a world builder. I'm a border baby. A *pocho*. Growing up in El Paso/Ciudad Juárez, your feet are planted in two places at once and the people in these cities know you better than anyone else in the entire world because the rest of the country is trying to pretend like you don't exist. Like you don't matter. Like a bridge or a wall is enough to say "you are here" or "you are there" but when you are in a border city, you are everywhere. And it's this amorphous way of living that has not only shaped the person I am today, but the kind of art I make and the characters who live in my plays; they're strong to their convictions but incredibly indecisive all at once — much like me, and much like the people I know and love.

- **What inspired you to write a play about the women of Juarez?**

  I. Gomez: Being born and raised in its sister city (El Paso) we used to visit my cousins in Juarez often. It wasn't until I was well into my twenties that I first heard about the missing and murdered women of Ciudad Juarez, the feminicide that's been going on since the early 1990's. When I confronted my mom about this, she told me it was something everyone knew. Everyone... except me. And it was the first time I was confronted with the idea that, as a man, this was something I didn't *have* to know about. So I didn't. And I hadn't. And for the next few years, I'd interview women in Juarez, spending time with them, hearing their stories, falling down the rabbit hole of violence and crime, and creating artistic works that would put these women and their experiences front and center – something surprisingly rare in artistic works centering on the missing and murdered women of Juarez.

- **From the real testimony, what was your process in honoring the voices of these women?**

I. Gomez: The Mexican women in my life are my greatest influences. They are my muses, they are my mentors, I owe everything I am to them. Growing up, I would spend hours in the kitchen with my mother, her sisters, and my grandmother cooking, cleaning, listening to the latest gossip and soaking it all in. Hearing their fights with their husbands and with my brothers, always doing the best they could even when it felt like it wasn't enough, all while making *tamales, tortillas, pan dulce* and more. When there was no one to take care of me while I was on vacation from school, my mother would bring me to work with her at Walmart supercenter. And I would spend hours upon hours at her side, listening to her navigate the world as a Mexican woman without an education working her way up the latter at one of the largest retail stores in the country. Almost all of my plays feature Latina women at the center of my narratives. And they push against the stereotype one often sees in theater, film and television that positions them as over-sexualized, or as maids or domestic workers. The Mexican women in my plays are complicated, nuanced, messy, powerful, beautiful, holistic women with some of the strongest desires, fears, hopes, and ambitions, much like the Mexican women in my life. My plays are my love letters to them, my gift, and the one thing I can give back for all they've given me. The women in Juarez live fervently in my spirit.

- **Where can we find the full text of the play?**

    I. Gomez: Currently, the play is not published but will be receiving its world premiere at Steppenwolf Theater Company, opening December 2018.

CHARACTERS
IVONNE: A mother, 30's
YOLI: A friend, 26

IN THIS SCENE
Following the disappearance of Yolanda's daughter, Brenda, Ivonne runs away from Juarez in hopes of escaping the horrors that have forced her to be complicit in the kidnapping and murders of these women in the worst possible ways. Yolanda is in the nearby deserts, handing out fliers of her missing daughter. She bumps into Ivonne and has a lot to confront her about. They haven't seen each other in two years, and Yolanda is convinced that Ivonne has something to do with Brenda's disappearance and is determined to find out what in the only way a mother knows how.

NOTE
A "/" indicates the start place for the following line.

LA RUTA

Ciudad Juárez, Mexico.
(A WOMAN with a shawl wrapped carefully around her head is seen kneeling by these crosses. She holds a deep red rosario in her hand, and she is praying.)

IVONNE: *(mid-prayer)* Santa Maria, Madre de Dios, Ruega por nosotros, pecadores, Ahora y en la hora de nuestra muerte, Amen.

She starts over.

Dios de salve Maria -

Beat

Wait. How many was that?

She counts the beads.

Shit. I lost my fucking place. Damn it this always happens. Why do they put so many god damn beads on this stupid thing if –

To the sky.

Perdoname Señor. It's just, I can't, there's no way of.

Beat.

It's just a lot of beads. That's all.

Beat. She stands. For the first time, she notices how many crosses there are.

I don't remember there being this many of you.

She reads a name on a cross. She knows exactly who this is. She traces the letters of a name with her fingertips.
(Yoli enters carrying an abundance of fliers.)
There is a picture on each one.

YOLI: Discúlpe señora? Have you seen my –

Ivonne is startled. She looks at Yoli. Dead silence. This lasts for an uncomfortably long time. Really, really, really long. Beat.

Beat.
Beat.
Beat.
After a moment, Yoli slaps Ivonne across the face. Hard. Ivonne does not move. Yoli slaps her again, even harder. Still, Ivonne is motionless. Yoli is about to go in for a third slap before Ivonne grabs Yoli by the wrist to stop her. Yoli pulls away.

YOLI: What the /fuck are you doing here?

IVONNE: Yoli I was just passing /through –

YOLI: Don't say my name you selfish, selfish excuse for a woman.

You don't get to say my name not now not ever.

A moment.

Were you. Were you praying?

Yoli laughs. It starts off small but then builds to an uncontrollable, uncomfortable laughter.

You were actually praying!

She continues to laugh. Ivonne stands there, motionless.

IVONNE: I pray all the time, Señora.

YOLI: How strange.

IVONNE: Why's that?

YOLI: I don't know, you tell me.

A moment.

IVONNE: Yoli... I'm not the /one -

YOLI: You were the last person to /see her.

IVONNE: I don't think I was, /actually.

YOLI: You took her to Centro and she /didn't come back.

IVONNE: I didn't take her she left /herself.

YOLI: You were the last person she was /with.

IVONNE: You don't know that for /sure.

YOLI: Don't tell me what I do and don't know. I am her mother. I know everything.

Beat.
Beat.
Beat.

IVONNE: You cut your hair. It looks nice.

YOLI: What are you doing here, Ivonne?

IVONNE: Picking up a couple of thing I left /behind.

YOLI: I don't mean Juárez I mean here.

Refers to the crosses.

What are you doing here?

IVONNE: I can give you a million reasons Yoli but none of them will ever be good enough so why even try.

YOLI: Because you owe me that much, that's why. So you'd better try, you'd better fucking try, WHY ARE YOU HERE.

IVONNE: To pay my respects. To the dead. The missing. The ones left behind.

I was hoping there'd be a cross for Brenda, /but...

YOLI: Say her name again and I will kill you myself.

IVONNE: She meant the world to me too /Yolanda.

YOLI: God you haven't changed one bit /have you?

IVONNE: You have no idea what I've been through so / don't talk to me like you get me, okay?

YOLI: What you've been through? What YOU'VE been / through?

IVONNE: Yes, what I'VE been through. It's not so black and white.

YOLI: Yes, it is! You know what happened to her. You saw her last. It's that simple. No other way around it.

Beat.

Now. If I were you I would pack up my shit and head in the other direction Ivonne. You're not welcome here.

IVONNE: Is that a threat?

YOLI: Es una promesa.

IVONNE: I'm not afraid of you, señora.

YOLI: Oh you poor little thing. I'm not the one you should be afraid of. There are monsters out there in the desert, Ivonne. You were gone for two years. You think you can just leave and everyone would forget who you are and what you owe? Not a chance.

IVONNE: ...

YOLI: Your disappearance was your conviction, Ivonne. It doesn't take much for the truth to reveal itself. Even if it has to be squeezed out of you like water.

IVONNE: You don't know the truth.

YOLI: And your little friends?

IVONNE: They're not my /friends.

YOLI: The ones you left to clean up your mess? Word on the street is they're pissed. They want answers. They want/ you.

IVONNE: You think you've got this whole thing figured out.

YOLI: I've got a pretty clear picture.

IVONNE: Okay so where's Brenda then, huh? If you've got a crystal clear image of how all this works then, please. Explícamelo. Where is she now?

Yoli rushes Ivonne, tackles her to the ground. Straddles her and wraps her hands around her neck.

YOLI: Tell me where she is.

IVONNE: Yoli... I can't... No puedo respirar.

YOLI: Where is she.

IVONNE: I don't... I don't...

YOLI: WHERE IS SHE DAMN IT?
IVONNE: I don't know!
YOLI: TELL ME!
IVONNE: It... it... It was my family... or yours.
Yolanda releases her. Ivonne coughs intensely.
YOLI: What?
IVONNE: It was my family or /yours.
YOLI: No.
IVONNE: And if it were you, you would have done the same /thing.
YOLI: No. You're lying.
IVONNE: Yolanda, por favor, don't make this harder than it /has to be.
YOLI: I don't believe you, I /don't.
IVONNE: Don't make me say it, Yolanda, you can't even imagine it nobody /can.
YOLI: All I do is imagine, Ivonne. I'm alone. All the time, thinking and thinking and thinking and thinking, there's nothing you can say to me that I haven't already imagined myself just say what you need to say, SAY /IT.
IVONNE: I WATCHED AS THREE MEN GRABBED HER AND PINNED HER TO THE GROUND!
YOLI: Who? Pinned who to the ground, my Brendita?
IVONNE: *(shaking her head)* No...
YOLI: Then who?
Beat.
Who. Who. Who who who who
IVONNE: *(losing a piece of herself)* My... sister...
Beat.
YOLI: Erika?
Ivonne breaks.

Oh Ivonne.

No. Oh no.

A moment.
Ivonne pulls it together for a moment. She is very still. This is very still.

IVONNE: One of them ripped off her favorite blouse with his hands. I remember it because I gave it to her on her birthday, it was white. The other one grabbed a plastic bag from the trash can. I could barely see her eyes. They looked me straight in the eyes and said "this is what you get for being a bad girl, you get to watch." He pulled down her pants, he spit, he shoved, he... I could feel my skin my fingernails clawing deeper and deeper into the bedpost trying to scream trying to help but they tied me the other side of the room so I couldn't stop them. There was a curling iron sitting, sitting on the ... I've never heard her scream like that before. Next thing I know, we're in the back of a van. It's blue. We drive for a while before the back-door swings open and I can feel the breeze and the hot summer sun and like a pile of trash, they throw her body in the desert, slam the door shut, and drive off. They dropped me off at the S-Mart by the bridge. And told me to call them tomorrow.

Beat.

But I went to your house instead. I wanted to tell you, wanted to scream, wanted to take you with me, but all I could do was put up fliers with you, Yolanda, I was scared.

YOLI: Ivonne. I'm so... I'm so sorry.
  She reaches for her. Ivonne pulls away.
IVONNE: I don't need your pity, señora.
YOLI: Is there... what can I ...

IVONNE: I needed you to be there for me, I needed a mother.

YOLI: I couldn't protect you, Ivonne, there's no way I / could've.

IVONNE: But you can tackle me, threaten me, try to squeeze the air out of me and feel pretty good about all that? You think because you know the truth now that you can walk away from all that, start over, start fresh, well it doesn't work like that Yolanda because you still don't even know the half of it. Trust me. I know what it's like to have someone ripped from your arms, Erika was my everything. So don't go acting all motherly all of a sudden, trying to fix this, trying to tell me what's the truth and what isn't because the truth is that I'VE LIVED A LIFE OF FEAR AND PAIN AND I WILL DROWN YOU IN IT! I WILL FLOOD THIS ENTIRE DESERT WITH IT!

Beat.

I'm not the monsters who took your daughter, señora. As much as you'd like me to be? I'm not.

Beat.
Beat.
Beat.
Beat.

YOLI: I can't live my life thinking that something like that happened to mi Brendita, Ivonne. So I'm asking you. Please. If you know. Tell me. Where is my daughter.

Beat.

Please. Please.

IVONNE: I wish I knew.

Lights shift.

MARIA! MARIA, MARIA, MARIA

Lisa Loomer

The play follows the on-stage and backstage life of a multi-ethnic television sitcom, "All in the Multicultural Family."

Lisa Loomer

- **How do you identify yourself?**

  L. Loomer: I am a writer. I also identify as American, Latina, and as a woman…

- **This play is set during the time of the OJ civil trial. How do you recommend actors now and in the future approach these themes?**

  L. Loomer: The play is about stereotyping in Hollywood—and in the culture at large. I think the situation is very different now on TV. So view the play as part of our history. But do revisit it, because, of course stereotyping and prejudice do persist.

- **In the preface of the play you describe the tone as "sitcom big overtly bright—as seen on TV." What conventions of this tone still apply to the reality of this scene?**

  L. Loomer: Sitcoms are not as big and bright these days. But the first scene still needs to be exaggerated in tone, it's part of the satire.

- **Where can we find the full text of the play?**

  L. Loomer: My agent, Beth Blickers at APA, represents the play.

Maria! Maria, Maria, Maria

CHARACTERS
MARIA: 30. A smart, passionate Latina actress who plays a stereotypical Latina spitfire/mom in a sitcom.
PATRICE: 25. A Yale educated African-American actress who plays Maria's badass black daughter in the same sitcom.

IN THIS SCENE
These actresses play roles in a sitcom called "All In The Multicultural Family." Backstage, they are discussing the plans the (white) producer and writers have for their characters in the show.

(Maria head backstage to the make-up room. Patrice follows. Maria sits in front of the mirror, removes her bad dye-job burgundy wig revealing her long black hair.)
PATRICE: Maria. Can I talk to you a moment?
MARIA: I know. It's Friday night. You probably have a date—
PATRICE: *(Upset)* It's not that.
MARIA: What's up?
PATRICE: Well… I'm pregnant.
MARIA: Pregnant! Are you sure?
PATRICE: Of course, I'm sure. It says so right in the next scene.
MARIA: Oh right—I forgot, what with la migra and all—
PATRICE: I don't need this, Maria. Not now. This can't be good for my career.
MARIA: Tell me about it. I've been pregnant a hundred times. They make you fat. They put you on welfare. And then! They find you a husband. Well, maybe not you, because you're black—

PATRICE: I'll bet they don't even know who the damn father is.
MARIA: Well, there's only one thing to do. Go to the producer. They think it's such an edgy show, ask him for an abortion.
PATRICE: Are you kidding? I can't talk to J.G. He's totally intimidated by me. He wants to kill me in a drive-by and have you adopt an American-Indian. I can't die in a drive-by after the first season, Maria—
MARIA: Jesus.
(A P.A, VLAD, enters with pages and hands them to the women. He is so shy about his English that he never speaks, so he can be played by an understudy.)
MARIA: What's this? New pages?
(Vlad nods.)
MARIA: Thanks, Vladimir.
PATRICE: Thanks, Vlad.
(He nods and leaves.)
PATRICE: *(As she reads)* I hate these last-minute changes. Always something...
MARIA: What is it? Changes in the last scene?
PATRICE: In the *next* scene. Seems the last part of that *last* scene was just...

(Incredulous) a dream.

MARIA: A dream?
(Maria reds her new pages)
PATRICE: Looks like the INS didn't really break in at all.
MARIA: Of course, they broke in! It's on tape! It was the only real moment in the whole show—
(Maria looks through the pages.)
PATRICE: But now it was a dream. It wasn't the INS... *(reading script)* It was a couple of delivery boys from Thrifty's.

MARIA: It was the damn INS, girlfriend—you saw them.
PATRICE: Well, actually I didn't. I was out copping drugs and getting pregnant. It says here it was just a couple of guys—
MARIA: Sure, sure—
PATRICE: A couple of guys... (*reads on*) delivering your medication.
MARIA: Medication? I don't take medication. There's nothing wrong with me. Unless...(*Panicking*) You don't think they're trying to get rid of me? I mean—

Just because I improvise a couple of lines? Oh God. They hate me. They want to cancel my contract. What's wrong with me? (*Searches script*) Why the hell do I need medication?

PATRICE: (*reading script*) Because you're paranoid.
MARIA: Paranoid!? I'm paranoid?
PATRICE: Not you, Maria. *Maria.*
MARIA: Don't you see what they're doing, Patrice? The writers are giving <u>her</u> medication to get to me! What are they giving us?
PATRICE: (*Checks script*) Prozac—
MARIA: Prozac.
PATRICE: (*shakes her head*) White people. What do you expect?
MARIA: Well, we'll see about that Prozac! And we'll see about that pregnancy of yours too...

TO THE BONE

Lisa Ramirez

A contemporary American drama written in the tradition of John Steinbeck's *Of Mice and Men*, which gives the audience a close up look into the lives of the invisible work force that puts food on our tables. The play examines the very nature of equality and justice in contemporary America through the eyes of five Central American women whose migration to the U.S. in search of a better life brings its own test of the human spirit. Ramirez spent six months interviewing immigrant poultry workers in the Catskills of upstate New York.

- How do you identify yourself?

  L. Ramirez: Latina writer/actress/activist.

- Lupe and Carmen come from two different worlds. In this scene they discover a friendship. **What is it that ultimately bridges their cultural divide?**

  L. Ramirez: A soul connection of art/poetry.

- **Carmen has recently arrived in the U.S. and has been working in the chicken plant so that she can send money to her mother who needs medical treatments. Lupe has been in school at the local community college. How does this moment before affect their physicality and energy levels throughout the scene?**

  L. Ramirez: Carmen is seated and still. Lupe has more energy.

- **Where can we find the full text of the play?**

  L. Ramirez: The New Play Exchange.

TO THE BONE

CHARACTERS

LUPE: Salvadorian, 20 years old. She is studying political science and law at the community college. She works at the local clinic for school credit. She listens to and writes her own Hip-Hop. She was born in the US and her mother holds the lease to the small house they live in.

CARMEN: A young Honduran woman, 19 years old. Carmen is Reina's niece. She has just arrived in the U.S. for work. She is undocumented.

IN THIS SCENE

Lupe and Carmen are outside a small house. Carmen has been in the US for two weeks and is working at the chicken plant. Lupe has her iPod on and is dancing B-girl style. She tries out a few moves.

(Lupe and Carmen are outside the house. Lupe has her iPod on and is dancing B-girl style. She tries out a few moves)

LUPE: You like Hip-hop?

CARMEN: Hip-hop?

LUPE: Hip-hop music?

CARMEN: Uh- it's okay.

LUPE: Ok? Just okay? If you think it's just okay- then you haven't heard the real shit! Who do you like?

CARMEN: I don't- I don't know?

LUPE: You don't know? You don't know? You gotta KNOW! In Hip-hop a point of view is- like ESSENTIAL! You gotta have an opinion!

CARMEN: Okay.

LUPE: Here sit down. Sit over here- right here. Lemme blow your mind open Carmen! Lemme change your

Lisa Ramirez

LIFE! Right here- right now! You ready?
(Lupe busts a couple of moves)
CARMEN: Okay.
LUPE: Me? I like political Hip-hop. You know- music that takes a stand? Tells a story? Not just 'booty' this and 'coochee' this- or 'bi-yatch' that- you know? I like La Bruja- Rebel Diaz- Rosa Clemente- the Hip-hop activist. You know any of them?
CARMEN: Uh- no.
LUPE: That's cool- that's cool. I even write my own shit. You wanna hear it?
CARMEN: Uh, I think so.
LUPE: Okay- okay- okay-
(Lupe grabs a notebook out of her bag. She paces around until she finds the page with one of her new songs)
Okay- okay- a little background? This here- this is about- FREEDOM- and- and- gettin'- OUT from like- UNDER- you with me?
CARMEN: Okay?
LUPE: But like- it's NEW. I'm still workin' on it. So don't JUDGE- okay?
CARMEN: Okay.
(Lupe warms up for few seconds)
LUPE: Okay- okay- okay- ready?

(Lupe starts moving B-girl style) ALl I wanna do - is get out of this zoo

It's just a one way street - it's time to get a clue

Say you think it's not - think it's all you got

Stick around too long girl - your dreams will drop

TO THE BONE

Mama always told me - there'd be days like this

She sacrificed her life - so that I would not miss

Opportunities that come - with liberty and trust

Only to find out - that the dream is a bust

Freedom flee-dom - is my only hope

A le-ga-cy - that I wear like a coat

Freedom flee-dom - rainin' down on me

Oppression is - the opposite of free

(Whispering)

freedom flee-dom - is my only hope

A le-ga-cy that – I wear like a coat

freedom flee-dom - rainin' down on me

oppression is - the opposite of free

(Pause. She looks at Carmen)

You like it?

CARMEN: Wow. Lupe!
LUPE: It's about freedom- right? Personal freedom.
CARMEN: Right.
LUPE: You like it?
CARMEN: That was great.
LUPE: Thanks.
CARMEN: It's like poetry. A little bit. I like poetry.
LUPE: Yeah? You like poetry?
CARMEN: Yes.

Lisa Ramirez

LUPE: Who do you like?
CARMEN: Who?
LUPE: Like- which poets?
CARMEN: Oh- you wouldn't know them.
LUPE: You ever- you ever write any?
CARMEN: Uh, what?
LUPE: Of your own?
CARMEN: What?
LUPE: You know. Poetry like?
CARMEN: Maybe.
LUPE: Maybe?
CARMEN: Sometimes.
LUPE: I knew it! Do some!
CARMEN: No Lupe.
LUPE: Come on Carmen!
CARMEN: It's okay.
LUPE: It's not okay- I showed you!
CARMEN: Now?
LUPE: Hell yeah!
CARMEN: I have never-
LUPE: Do it!
CARMEN: Okay. Only a little bit.
LUPE: Seize the moment girl!
CARMEN: Okay. Okay. It goes- it goes like-

'in the

silence

of dawn

my face

> lined
>
> with pillow'
>
> Keep going?
>
> 'if i could only read
>
> this map
>
> i could fly away
>
> before the birds
>
> cry'
>
> Okay- that's all- that's all-

LUPE: That was- that was-
CARMEN: That's all for now.
LUPE: That was DOPE Carmen!
CARMEN: I don't know.
LUPE: Well- you SHOULD know! That was- WOW!
   (Lupe looks at Carmen. After a moment she reaches into her backpack and pulls out a notebook)
LUPE: Here- for you.
CARMEN: What's this for?
LUPE: It's for you. To write your thoughts down. Your dreams. Whatever. More poetry maybe? An empty notebook is- anything you want it to be- right?
CARMEN: Wow Lupe.
   (Lupe reaches into her backpack and takes out a pen)
LUPE: And a pen!
CARMEN: Thank you. *(Slight pause)* Lupe- what do you do?
LUPE: What do you mean?

CARMEN: I know you work at that clinic, but-
LUPE: Oh- I only work at the clinic during the day. But- I go to school at night- you know- part-time?
CARMEN: And what are you studying- at school?
LUPE: Oh- I want to get into law- be a lawyer- or something like that.
CARMEN: Wow Lupe!
LUPE: But like- not like one of those corrupt mofo's right? Like- a lawyer for the PEOPLE- you know? Like people who are too scared to stand up for themselves. Or- like they can't- you know- for whatever reasons. Take those bad boys DOWN- you know?
CARMEN: Yes. *(Slight pause)* That's what I want to be. A student? That is my dream. To study- to learn.
LUPE: It's okay- but I really wanna move to the city. Go to NYU. But- it's like hella expensive yo.
CARMEN: N-Y-U?
LUPE: New York University? That's where the real shit happens. *(She yells)* MAN-HAT-TAN!!!
CARMEN: You're so lucky.
LUPE: I guess. I just wanna GOOOO. You know- 'FLY AWAY' like your poem?
(Lupe makes an arm gesture)
CARMEN: Aw Lupe.

Luchadora!

Alvaro Saar Rios

Imagine the Chinese legend Hua Mulan set in the world of lucha libre—Mexican wrestling. The discovery of a worn pink wrestling mask prompts Nana Lupita, a Wisconsin grandmother, to share her tale about growing up in 1960s Texas. As her tale unfolds, Lupita's life as a teen tomboy comes alive—bike riding with her friends, working at her father's flower stand and watching lucha libre. When a World Championship match is announced, Lupita anticipates seeing it until she discovers her ailing father is one of the wrestlers. With the help of a magical mask maker, Lupita secretly trains to take her father's place. She soon finds it difficult keeping her secret from her friends and, most importantly, her father.

- **How do you identify?**

    A. Saar Rios: I'm Mexican-American. I also identify as brown and Texican (Texas Mexican).

- **What drew you to the world of Lucha Libre wrestling?**

    A. Saar Rios: I grew up watching wrestling as a kid. One of the reasons I loved it was because it is a world of tradition, masks and secrecy. Once I realized these same elements are what make great stories for the theatre, I knew I had to write about it.

- **In this scene Lupita is beginning to learn the wrestling techniques and traditions. Do you have any advice on how the actors should approach the athleticism of the scene?**

    A. Saar Rios: Overall I would say treat this scene the same way you would treat a combat scene in a play. Make sure you and your partner are safe about all the movement choices. Focus on what looks theatrical and less on what is real. Remember, it's still a play.

- **Where can we find the full text of the play?**

    A. Saar Rios: The award-winning play is published by Dramatic Publishing Inc.

LUCHADORA!

CHARACTERS
THE MASK MAKER: Older Latina; any body type; doesn't look like a wrestler.
LUPITA: Latina teenager.

IN THIS SCENE
At the end of Act I, The Mask Maker reluctantly agrees to help Lupita find a trainer so Lupita can secretly prepare to take her father's place in a wrestling match. Lupita is so excited to start her training that she doesn't sleep well the night before. To make matter worse, her old, unreliable bicycle causes her to shows up late for training.

(An empty room. The Mask Maker appears.)
(Lupita appears out of breath.)
THE MASK MAKER: Mañana! [Tomorrow]
LUPITA: You want me to come back tomorrow?
THE MASK MAKER: That is what mañana means.
LUPITA: I don't understand. Did the trainer not show up?
THE MASK MAKER: Yes, the trainer showed up on time.
LUPITA: Where is he?
THE MASK MAKER: Not he. She.
LUPITA: She?!?! What do you mean? Wait! No way. You're going to be my trainer? Oh man, now I really can't wait to do this.
THE MASK MAKER: Do you have a watch?
LUPITA: Yes.
THE MASK MAKER: Learn how to read it.
LUPITA: I know how to read it. It says "7:02."
THE MASK MAKER: Training started at 7am.

219

LUPITA: I'm only a couple of minutes late. My bike chain--
THE MASK MAKER: My time is muy importante, Lupita. Until you respect that, we won't start. I'm giving you one more chance. If you are late again, training will cease.
(The Mask Maker leaves.)
LUPITA: *(To Audience.)* Day two. Señora! Estoy lista! [I'm ready.]
(The Mask Maker appears.)
THE MASK MAKER: Lupita, it's 5am. The sun is still sleeping.
LUPITA: I didn't want to be late.
(The Mask Maker lays out a mat.)
THE MASK MAKER: Let's get started. Lupita, we have one month to get you to the level of El Hijo. Show me what you know.
LUPITA: Right now?
THE MASK MAKER: No. Mañana. Of course now!!!
(The Mask Maker charges Lupita. Lupita runs.
The Mask Maker stops. Lupita stops.
The Mask Maker charges again and Lupita runs.)
THE MASK MAKER: You are aware this is not wrestling.
LUPITA: I'm just a bit nervous. I need a minute.
THE MASK MAKER: Go outside.
LUPITA: Outside?
THE MASK MAKER: Apurate! *[Hurry.]* But stay where you can hear me.
(Lupita runs offstage.)
THE MASK MAKER: Now, take a deep breath, hold it for five, and let it out. Then, come back.
(Moments later, Lupita re-enters.)
LUPITA: Hey. That worked.
THE MASK MAKER: Good. Let's try this again.

(The Mask Maker charges Lupita again. Lupita dodges her and quickly puts The Mask Maker in a bear hug.)

LUPITA: What do you think about that?

(The Mask Maker stomps Lupita's foot. Lupita howls. The Mask Maker goes around Lupita and kicks out the other leg. Lupita falls. The Mask Maker pins Lupita. One, two, three.)

THE MASK MAKER: *(Getting up)* We have a lot of work to do.

LUPITA: You cheated.

THE MASK MAKER: El Hijo will do worse. He'll bite you. Poke you in the eyes. He'll even try to unmask you.

LUPITA: If he pulls off my mask, I'll still beat him.

THE MASK MAKER: If you are unmasked, the match is over. And when El Hijo realizes you are not a male, he will humiliate you in that ring until he gets what he wants.

LUPITA: To wrestle my father.

THE MASK MAKER: Always protect your mask. By what you've shown me, it's obvious you don't know how to wrestle. So we'll have to start with the basics. A great luchador learns how to fall before they learn anything else.

LUPITA: Fall? You mean like this?

(Lupita falls on the mat.)

THE MASK MAKER: That's not falling. That's...I don't know what that is. Push me.

LUPITA: Push you?

(The Mask Maker pushes Lupita.)

THE MASK MAKER: Orita! [Now]

(Lupita pushes The Mask Maker. The Mask Maker hits the mat and writhes in pain.)

LUPITA: Señora! Are you OK? I didn't mean to--
THE MASK MAKER: If you believe it, then the audience will believe it. That's falling.

(The Mask Maker gets up.)
THE MASK MAKER: Your turn.

(Lupita falls.)
THE MASK MAKER: Otra vez. [Again]

(Lupita falls.)
THE MASK MAKER: Again.

The Hours Are Feminine

José Rivera

1960. Two immigrant families—one Italian American, the other Puerto Rican—move to Long Island. Racism and differing languages keep the neighbors apart, until an unexpected friendship offers an opportunity for kindness and a new sense of home.

- **How do you identify yourself?**

    J. Rivera: As a writer. I'm very proud of my Latino heritage and try to celebrate it as much as possible in my work but I'm a writer first and everything else second. If you were to ask me what kind of writer I am, I would say I'm a Puerto-Rican American writer.

- **What drew you to write about the immigrant experience of the 1960's?**

    J. Rivera: My parents came to the U.S. in 1959 when I was four years old, so that experience is embedded deeply in my memories and in the memories of my mother who told me many stories about that time period. Virtually everything in the play is true, from my father's job at the diner, to the Italian family we lived with, the Hurricane Donna. It was a pivotal time in my family's life we were transitioning from our Spanish-only, Puerto Rican-centrist existence to partial assimilation in the U.S. culture.

- **Can you elaborate on the construct of language in the play? You state: (Characters speaking a SECOND LANGUAGE speak with HEAVY ACCENTS, indicated in the text by "quotation marks.")**

    J. Rivera: That's an acting note. The idea is when Spanish-speaking characters are speaking to each other, we understand that they're speaking Spanish though the audience hears them speaking in English. Because they're speaking their first language to each other, we don't hear them with an accent. When a Spanish-speaker speaks to an English-speaker, they're speaking in their second language and so it's in an accent. The ideal production would be bi-lingual.

- **Mirella and Evalise discover their friendship in this scene. What advice would your give the actors?**

    J. Rivera: I would say, take your time. There's a lot of emotional and cultural distance between the two women, so a quick friendship would not be plausible. Let there be real suspicion and hostility from Evalise – these will be the obstacles both women will have to overcome in order to make the friendship possible. Once they click with each other, then the women are completely enthralled with each other and all their barriers drop.

- **Where can we find the full text of the play?**

    J. Rivera: The full text is not available at this time.

CHARACTERS
EVALISSE: 28, Puerto Rican, a mom.
MIRELLA: 49, Italian, a wife (speaks with an Italian accent – lines "in" indicate accent).

IN THIS SCENE
Having been the victim of sexual assault and violence by her landlord, Evalisse is heard crying from her home. Mirella is married to the landlord's son—she hears her cries across the way.

(Mirella and Evalisse look at each other and don't know what to say to each other at first.)
MIRELLA: "I love that color on you."
EVALISSE: Thank you. It's the first dress I ever made. It's a little lopsided.
MIRELLA: "You make your own clothes? That's fancy!"

EVALISSE: My mother taught me how to use a sewing machine. It's about the only practical thing I know how to do. But Fernan is so stubborn, he won't let me use it to make money.
MIRELLA: Well, I got no work skills whatsoever! "I don't make, I don't cook, I don't clean, I don't fix, I don't drive."
EVALISSE: Really? I thought American girls could do everything.
MIRELLA: "Everything, yes. They're lucky. But Italian girls can love really good. We are experts for love. The best for the world."
EVALISSE: *(smiles)* No, no, Puerto Rican girls are the best lovers in the world. There's not even a second place.
MIRELLA: "My old boyfriend, the Cuban, was very happy on top of me!"
EVALISSE: Ugh! Cubans! They're nothing but atheists and communists! What do they know about love?
(Evalisse crosses herself.)
(Mirella laughs. Then looks at Evalisse a long, critical moment.)
MIRELLA: "Why did you come here?" Of all places on earth ... nothing to do, no one interesting to talk to, it's so *dead* here ...
EVALISSE: Cities scare Fernan. The chaos and guns, the drugs and filth. Fernan didn't want to be afraid for me and Jaivin all the time. So he told me we were going to an island full of flowers and trees and peace and quiet. I'll tell you -- this doesn't *feel* like an island.
MIRELLA: "But didn't you like where you were from?"
EVALISSE: What were we supposed to do? Stay back there and starve?
MIRELLA: So you guys are just like the Italians -- and everyone else!

EVALISSE: (not understanding) Nobody had work or money -- so everybody left. Fernan's family, nearly all his brothers and sisters left. Ten of his brothers live in the Bronx.

MIRELLA: Ten siblings? Damn! Long nights with nothing to do, huh? "And you? Do you have a million brothers and sisters?"

EVALISSE: Just a brother who ran away from home and disappeared in the city. No sisters.

MIRELLA: "Oh, I could not live without my sisters. I have three. I'm the oldest but I was the last to get married. The sad part is they're all married to jerks in California and Florida."

EVALISSE: You must miss them.

MIRELLA: "I just want them to get divorces and come back to Brooklyn."

EVALISSE: No -- divorce is a sin.

MIRELLA: No -- divorce *lawyers* are a sin! I dated one when I was temping in a law office.

EVALISSE: Why did you wait so long to get married?

MIRELLA: "I -- *promised?* Uh, with a *ring?* On my *finger?*"

EVALISSE: Engaged.

MIRELLA: "Yes! I was *engaged* three times to three stupid men! A lawyer, a cop, a taxi driver." Each time, I descended the social ladder, like a regular buffoon! "Then I meet Little Anthony two years ago, and I like him, and he's smart and not too crazy, and I not getting younger and his father has some money, so why not?"

(Off Evalisse's skeptical look.)

"There's a thing in Little Anthony. Maybe in all men. It's like a damaged thing, do you know what that is ... ?"

EVALISSE: I know, I know that thing ...

MIRELLA: "It's what makes him so tender. And makes me want to have his fourteen children one day. The thing that's most different from his father."

EVALISSE: *(beat)* His father -- Mafia?

MIRELLA: *(laughs)* Charlie in the Mafia? Girl, those people have *standards*! Charlie's too stupid to be in the Mafia!

EVALISSE: *(not understanding)* "Stu-pid?"

MIRELLA: "Believe me, the first time I met Charlie I didn't like him. Charlie owns building for black people -- oh, the things he says about those people is sick for the people to live in them, dirty all the time."

EVALISSE: *(low)* -- and they very, very bad his buildings. Rats and I met Charlie.

MIRELLA: "A big pain in the ass."

EVALISSE: Then why are you living with him?

MIRELLA: "Not my idea! I love the city. I love crazy people and the noise and people moving fast and it's fun, oh it's so fun. Charlie says to Little Anthony: 'I'm lonely. Come to Long Island. Brooklyn is dying because of the black people and the -- uh, the -- other people --'"

EVALISSE: Us. My people.

MIRELLA: "'Bring wife for the summer,' he say."

MIRELLA: I said: 'screw that!' But Little Anthony is too big and strong and he says, 'we're going to Long Island for the summer!' So now I'm standing here talking to you."

EVALISSE: Your Spanish is getting better.

MIRELLA: *(liking her more and more)* "Spanish and Italian are like sisters. But sometimes I get masculine and feminine all wrong in Spanish!"

EVALISSE: There are a lot of crazy rules in Spanish. Things that don't make sense. *Day* ends in "a" but it's masculine. *Hand* ends in "o" but it's feminine. And *time* is masculine but the *hours* are feminine.

¡CURANDERAS! SERPENTS OF THE CLOUDS

Elaine Romero

¡CURANDERAS! Serpents of the Clouds features a young Latina doctor who makes a spiritually transforming journey to Mexico where she meets an eccentric "curandera" (a female folk healer), confronts her truth hidden in an ancient Aztec scroll, and discovers her own innate gift of healing.

- **How do you identify yourself?**

  E. Romero: I'm New Mexican, Latinx, Latina, Chicana, Chicanx, Mexican-American, Mexican, Sonoran, Tucsonan, Arizonan, Californian, Oregonian, Chicagoan . . . Though identity remains an important conversation, I am pushing this conversation further nowadays. This often becomes the first and last conversation. How do we transmute that?

- **These are two healers but they approach healing in different ways. Why did they have to meet?**

  E. Romero: I wrote this play staring at the Codex Boturini, which tells the story of the journey from Aztlán to Tenochtitlan. That journey became the topography of the play (I place Aztlán in the U.S.). Their shared journey springs from a spiritual plain not a physical one. Images of a woman crying on a rock from a deep place inside her soul told me Victoria's story. A broken tree spoke to me of Paloma's pain. When I gazed at the Codex they became human beings, heading south toward Mexico, away from home, but somehow toward themselves. They meet each other as they are fleeing. They catch one another in the act. They meet so they can confront each other, so that the person they are each deep inside must be called out forever. Their story is not one of coincidence, but of destiny.

- **Is Victoria ashamed that she doesn't speak Spanish?**

  E. Romero: Yes, but on some level, as the play reveals, she knows it. She knows more than she says or thinks she knows. Language is sneaky that way. It's a lot easier to say one does not speak Spanish than to try to describe a shade of partial fluency, or high-level comprehension. Spanish gets stuck in people's throats for many reasons.

- **Paloma sees right through Victoria. Does Victoria have a *susto*?**

    E. Romero: Yes, Victoria has *susto*. Her soul has, indeed, separated from her body, an illness caused by fright. In the journey of the play, Paloma finds herself compelled to heal. Victoria must rid herself of her *susto* to live. They need one another to get past a critical moment, which could be the end of them both.

- **Where can we find the full text of the play?**

    E. Romero: WOMEN PLAYWRIGHTS: THE BEST PLAYS OF 2000, D.L. Lepidus, Editor, Smith & Kraus, 2002.

CHARACTERS
PALOMA: A Latina curandera, a folk healer, in her early forties.
VICTORIA: A pocha. A young doctor in her twenties.

IN THIS SCENE
On a train to Mexico, two women meet for the first time. One wants to talk, one wants to be quiet. They do not divulge that they are both running away from something back home. Both healers in their own right, the young one is a newly minted doctor and the other woman is a traditional curandera who doesn't know if she can keep on healing others.

Elaine Romero

(Victoria sits in a window seat, leaning against the window somewhat dreamily. She hears the sounds of rain splashing against the window. A woman enters.)

VICTORIA: Ouch.

(Victoria shakes her finger in pain. Paloma quickly grabs Victoria's finger and does a quick little soba—massage to heal the finger. It is a healing moment. Victoria looks at her finger, surprised and relieved.)

What'd you do? *(Denying the healing)* It must not have been that bad.

PALOMA: *(Belated)* Perdóneme.

(Victoria nods, moves closer to the window.)

Mire nomás a todos esos tontos empapándose. Tengo el último boleto.

VICTORIA: *(Bad Spanish)* No entiendo.

(Victoria gives Paloma a blank look. Paloma excitedly taps her feet on the ground; she energetically leans back, arms outstretched, drinking in the joy of her seat. This woman causes a tornado wherever she goes.)

PALOMA: A veces la gente no sabe cuando quitárseme de enfrente.

VICTORIA: I know you people have different space bubbles, but Christ.

PALOMA: Perdone usted. Aren't you a Mexican?

VICTORIA: *(Embarrassed)* You speak English.

PALOMA: I don't know nothing about no space bubbles, and all that fancy stuff, but I do know when you have to get going, you have to go.

VICTORIA: Yeah, right. Well, I'm just gonna drift off here for a second.

PALOMA: Where are you gonna drift off to?

VICTORIA: So, if you could refrain from engaging me in

conversation, I'd appreciate it.
(Paloma shakes her hand as if to say this woman thinks she is too big a deal.)
PALOMA: I won't say a word. Shhh.
(Paloma zips her mouth shut. Victoria closes her eyes, enjoying a moment of peace.)
Didn't your parents teach you Spanish?
(Victoria is startled.)
VICTORIA: *(To herself; reflective)* My Spanish is lost somewhere in my cells.
(Paloma starts munching down a bag of chicharrones, fried pork rinds.)
Would you mind?
PALOMA: I don't know. It's a public place, public train, public bathroom.
VICTORIA: I came here to think. I just need some peace and quiet.
PALOMA: You came to México for peace and quiet?
VICTORIA: Be careful. I understand some Spanish.
PALOMA: *(Continuing)* Between all the babies crying, mariachis playing and little old ladies gossiping until their teeth fall out, I don't think you're gonna find no peace and quiet here.
VICTORIA: You don't understand. I'm going through a hard time. I just finished medical school.
PALOMA: You finished medical school, but you can't learn Spanish?
VICTORIA: It's very stressful.
PALOMA: Excuse me for being born. If you don't want to share no air . . .
VICTORIA: I don't mean that.

(Paloma blows on her. Victoria smells the stench. She brushes Paloma's breath out of her face.)

Christ, what'd you eat for breakfast?

PALOMA: Garlic cloves and rattlesnake pills. They're good for the blood.

VICTORIA: *(Doubling over)* My God, I think I'm gonna be sick.

PALOMA: They drive away all sorts of nasty diseases and creepy witch doctors. Have you ever smelled a brujo up close? ¡Híjole!

VICTORIA: Can't say that I have.

PALOMA: They make pigs smell like perfume. And they're always trying to kiss me with their pinche bad breath. But I know what they really want. They want to steal my power.

VICTORIA: Are you a witch or something?

(Paloma takes a map out of her bag.)

PALOMA: Where are we anyways?

(Paloma in a quick few seconds has entangled herself in the map, even ripping it in a few places.)

VICTORIA: Here, let me see that. What are you looking for?

PALOMA: I always find where I am anyways. Or people find me. They just drive up and ask me, "May I help you?" See, the power draws them. The world takes care of curanderos, healers, because we take care of the world. *(With a tinge of sadness)* That's what the people say. *(After a second)* One man gave me a ride all the way to Houston, and it was four hours out of his way. For nothing more than for me to cure a viejita, a little old lady. And she lived for four more years to the date, one year for every hour he went out of his way.

VICTORIA: Charming story.

PALOMA: God helps us when we're willing to make a sacrifice. Like that stranger made a sacrifice and he didn't even know it. Most sacrifices are like that. They don't happen in the mind. They happen in the heart. *(Another tinge of sadness)* Los dioses listen to the heart.

VICTORIA: Did you say gods?

PALOMA: I meant God.

(Paloma makes a quick sign of the cross, and then she chews her finger.)

VICTORIA: I was beginning to think you weren't even Catholic.

PALOMA: Have these things happened to you? People coming to you when you needed them? Even when you didn't want them to?

VICTORIA: No one's ever driven me to Houston for no reason.

(Paloma motions her disapproval.)

PALOMA: I had a reason.

VICTORIA: Oh, that's right. You were going to heal somebody.

PALOMA: Yes, I was.

VICTORIA: You can't heal anybody. Well, not unless it's some trumped up folk disease like the evil eye.

PALOMA: Mal ojo.

VICTORIA: I read an article about that in medical school. Do you really think a baby will get sick if someone admires it too much? C'mon.

PALOMA: Or susto, illness from fright. I bet you don't believe in susto either.

(Paloma looks Victoria straight in the eye as if she is peering into her.)

It's when something so upsetting happens to a person that their soul leaves their body. It can even lead to death. You can tell if someone has susto because their nose feels soft como algodón, like cotton.

(Paloma does the susto diagnosis on Victoria's nose. Victoria recoils.)

And to bring that soul back, you have to say the Apostle's Creed three times, clap your hands, and say that person's name.

(Paloma releases one very haunting cupped clap.)

VICTORIA!

VICTORIA: *(Defensive)* How'd you know my name?

PALOMA: It's carved in your eyes.

(Paloma snaps her fingers. Paloma drops her hand, frustrated.)

No More Maids

Anne García Romero

In Los Angeles, two Latina actors meet in the waiting room as they prepare to audition for roles as maids on a new television comedy. Together, they fantasize about playing biologists or nineteenth century poets... anything but maids. While in the audition room, they confront the Latina casting associate and the three hatch a plan to start their own production company.

- **How do you identify yourself?**

  A. García Romero: I am a bicultural Latina playwright.

- **One of the things we really love about this scene is that these actors are really talented and it strikes to the core of Latina stereo-types in Hollywood. Sure, they can play a maid or a gang member, but they know that they are much more. What inspired you to write the play?**

  A. García Romero: Latina actors need to continue to receive more opportunities to exhibit, explore and celebrate the wide range of their talent and craft. In Chicago, the Broken Nose Theatre Company invited me to contribute to their Bechdel Fest, a yearly festival where playwrights write ten minute plays that pass the Bechdel test: female characters must talk to each other about something other than a man. So, I set out to write a play for two to three female characters. Next, at that time, I saw a production of a play which featured a woman of color as a cleaning lady, working for an Anglo family. While I admire all that domestic workers contribute to this country, I felt very frustrated that in the twenty-first century, certain playwrights were perpetuating the stereotype of the maid of color on stage, while their Anglo counterparts played professors, actors and other professionals. These stereotypes not only severely limit opportunities but they perpetuate narrow and inaccurate cultural views. So, I set out to write a play that celebrates what Latina actors can do, explores how Latina actors comprise a culturally complex community and exhibits how we need to finally move past stereotypes in television, film and theatre toward more complex representation.

- This scene resonates with the working actor and the struggles of multi-racial and multi ethnic Latinx identity. What advice do you give to the actor as they dive into the transformations? What styles should they be exploring?

    A. García Romero: This scene necessitates swift transitions, linguistic precision, and comedic collisions between diverse realities. As Raquel and Cynthia first practice their audition scene, they experiment with heightened dialects and comedic sensibilities. They wonder how far they can push these stereotypical characters from this new sitcom, Barrio to the 'Bu. When they connect with each other over their casting struggles, they employ a more naturalistic tone as they confess the difficult realities they face as Latina actors. When they transform to play biologists, they explore the precision and intensity of scientific language. As they shift to play nineteenth century poets in Cuba, they delve into poetic specificity and a heightened period tonality. The intersections of these four diverse realities create an overall comedic sensibility. However, the actors must commit to each reality with sincerity, so that the comedy arises from the collisions of their desires.

- **Where can we find the full text of the play?**

    A. García Romero: *The Best Ten-Minute Plays of 2016.* Hanover, NH: Smith & Kraus, 2016.

Anne García Romero

CHARACTERS
RAQUEL FERNANDEZ: 20s, actor, Latina, Puerto Rican-Mexican-American.
CYNTHIA SOMOS: 20s, actor, Latina, Cuban-Norwegian-American.

IN THIS SCENE
(Present. Los Angeles. Casting office waiting room. And various other realities.) Raquel and Cynthia have arrived to audition for the roles of maids in a new television pilot, Barrio to the 'Bu. They befriend each other in the waiting room where they decide to run lines before their audition. The women soon explore their dreams of an acting life where there are no more maids.

(Lights rise on Raquel and Cynthia in the casting office waiting room. They each hold audition scripts and rehearse a scene from a television pilot. In the scene, they are maids.)
RAQUEL: Ay, my back is like killing me, María. Why do we got to scrub the floor so much?
CYNTHIA: La señora likes it like totally spotless, Anita.
RAQUEL: That old lady is like so uptight.
CYNTHIA: Look, Anita, I like helped you get this job. Do not like mess it up for us.
RAQUEL: I know, María. I am like sick and tired of the gang life. La vida loca is like driving me crazy.
CYNTHIA: I prayed for you like every day for like eight years. I like lit candles for you.
RAQUEL: And like I'm totally grateful but like my pinche knees are like killing me.
CYNTHIA: You'll like get used to it, a'ight?
RAQUEL: I like kinda miss my homies back in Whittier.
CYNTHIA: That's why you like gots to work with me far far away in Malibu.

RAQUEL: The 'bu. You're my boo, in the 'bu.
(Cynthia throws her script down.)
CYNTHIA: Boo in the 'bu? Who even talks like that?
RAQUEL: Okay, I will admit the writing is pretty lame. What's with all the 'likes'?
CYNTHIA: And so stereotypical. Do I look like a stereotype?
RAQUEL: Well um...no offense. But, you don't exactly look like these roles.
CYNTHIA: What is that supposed to mean?
RAQUEL: I mean...I dunno. Forget it.
CYNTHIA: And do you look like these roles? I'm not aware that all Latinas have to look a certain way.
RAQUEL: Um...Are you Cuban?
CYNTHIA: On my mother's side.
RAQUEL: And your dad's side?
CYNTHIA: Norwegian. *(beat)* And you?
RAQUEL: Mexican mom. Puerto Rican dad.
CYNTHIA: And these characters are supposed to be from the 'hood. Did you grow up in the 'hood?
RAQUEL: I grew up in the suburbs of Chicago.
CYNTHIA: And I grew up in Kansas City. *(beat)* I don't think that all Latina characters on television need to come from el barrio. No offense at all to el barrio, but it's not the only place we live, you know?
RAQUEL: Yeah. Sorry for asking you all that. I'm just kinda nervous. *(beat)* I'm Raquel.
CYNTHIA: Cynthia Somos.
RAQUEL: Somos? Meaning "We are"?
CYNTHIA: Okay, it's a stage name because I have this super long Norwegian last name and there's just no way...I thought Cynthia Somos...has a ring to it, right?
RAQUEL: I mean I haven't met any Cuban-Norwegians before.

CYNTHIA: You know, with scripts like this, we should start writing our own material.

RAQUEL: I dunno. My life is pretty busy. I work in a law firm to pay the bills. Legal secretary. They let me leave for auditions. So I don't really have time to be writing scripts.

CYNTHIA: I mean what roles would you write? *(beat)* No more maids. *(beat)* What role do you wanna play? Go.

(Lights shift. Lights rise on Raquel and Cynthia wearing black horn-rimmed safety glasses and lab coats. They are biologists.)

RAQUEL: The results show high levels of acute toxicity and we need action levels.

CYNTHIA: The amperometric titration may have failed.

RAQUEL: Did you check the aqueous solubility?

CYNTHIA: Our lab assistant did that.

RAQUEL: *(bossy)* That grad research assistant needs to step up her game if we're going to land another National Science Foundation grant.

CYNTHIA: I don't like your tone. You are not my boss. We're both at the same level.

RAQUEL: What about the bioaccumulation?

CYNTHIA: I told you, we will recarbonize.

RAQUEL: If we are going to make advances in the field, we will have to recarbonize.

CYNTHIA: The polio vaccine wasn't invented overnight. We need to help reduce the spread of malaria in the third world.

RAQUEL: I know what it is. You're afraid of failure so you're being mean and impatient. Am I right?

CYNTHIA: No one in my family has ever been a biologist. Sometimes the pressure is just...too much!

RAQUEL: I realize that but we are so close to discovering a new vaccine to halt the spread of infant malaria in Sub-Saharan Africa. So we have to embrace our polycyclical power.

No More Maids

CYNTHIA: Our test tube transformations.
RAQUEL: Our scientific sagacity!
CYNTHIA: Our biological bravado!
(Lights shift to Raquel and Cynthia back in the waiting room.)
RAQUEL: That would definitely be better.
CYNTHIA: Right? I mean when was the last time we saw Latinas playing biologists on television? *(beat)* Um. Never.
RAQUEL: *(re: audition script)* Right. Okay. But. I mean, these roles aren't really that bad.
CYNTHIA: Excuse me?
RAQUEL: Look, I want to work.
CYNTHIA: Yeah, me too. But auditioning for these roles in this pilot is insulting.
RAQUEL: Look, my aunt was a maid for years. It's noble, respectful work.
CYNTHIA: I agree. But do we need more Latina maids on television?
RAQUEL: I need to get some tape for my reel.
CYNTHIA: By playing a maid? *(re: audition script)* Maria the maid is a saint and Anita the new maid used to be a gangster but now she's changing her ways by working with Maria in the house of this rich white family. I mean come on, Maria and Anita, West Side Story names? Oh and did we mention they're well endowed and super hot?
RAQUEL: When *cholas* want to leave the life, it's not so easy.
CYNTHIA: Again, I totally agree. But do we need another Latina gangbanger on television?
RAQUEL: I need my SAG card.
CYNTHIA: I waitress to pay the bills. Alright? I need a TV gig too. *(beat)* But do we need to get one by playing maids?
RAQUEL: What about you? *(beat)* No more maids. *(beat)* What role do you wanna play? Go.

(Lights shift. Lights rise on Cynthia and Raquel holding fans. They are nineteenth century poets in Havana.)
CYNTHIA: *Compañera*, have you heard the good news?
RAQUEL: About *los Soles y los Rayos*?
CYNTHIA: Exactly. The Suns and the Rays...the secret society for liberation from Spain will meet this afternoon and they seek poets.
RAQUEL: I would rather stay home and finish writing my sonnet after my *siesta*.
CYNTHIA: The Spanish must leave. We must write verse that can help our cause.
RAQUEL: But what about your verse, *compañera*? Your octosyllabic ballad with its intricately woven rhyme scheme is not exactly revolutionary in nature.
CYNTHIA: True. I have heretofore applied my poetry to chronicle the wonders of the island. A wave. A cathedral. A *palmera*. A fortress. But can we not use our poetic powers to regain *Cuba* for all?
RAQUEL: I would rather not be political in a group. I would rather be political in my writing but not in person.
CYNTHIA: Can it not be both, *compañera*? I was speaking with *Gertrudis Gomez de Avellaneda* and she plans to be at this meeting.
RAQUEL: Our grand Cuban poetess has returned from *Madrid*?
CYNTHIA: Indeed she has. I do adore her verse. *(reciting)* Pearl of the sea. Star of the west. Beautiful *Cuba*. Your brilliant sky covered by the opaque veil of night while the ache of sadness clouds my face.
RAQUEL: She did so wonderfully capture her last views *de la Habana* as she sailed to *España*. If *Gertrudis* is going to fight for *Cuba* then so shall we!
(Lights shift back to Raquel and Cynthia in the waiting room.)
CYNTHIA: That would rock!

Corazón Eterno (always in my heart)

Caridad Svich

Two almost star-crossed lovers as they meet, fall in love, are separated and find each other again. *CORAZÓN ETERNO (always in my heart)* is a poetic, romantic comedy of love pragmatic and impossible, temporal and eternal.

- **How do you identify yourself?**

    C. Svich: As a playwright and theatre-maker, as an artivist and cultural worker, as a woman and Latinx human being.

- **Why did you name both these characters Julia?**

    C. Svich: I was interested in the mirroring of these two characters as they take different journeys in their lives, but also what joins them, and also that there were comic possibilities too in having them both have the same name. The play, in part, is a romantic comedy.

- **In preparation for this scene the actor will have to do dramaturgical research into the common themes of Hardy and Woolf. Why did you choose these two writers?**

    C. Svich: Thomas Hardy for his explorations of individuals caught by and/or sometimes finding articulation of their passions through connection to other humans and nature. Hardy's work has a deep connection to wildness and the concept of being bewildered by and through desire. In the case of Woolf, her interest in mapping consciousness and in creating spaces for the female and androgynous voice is resonant in terms of the concerns of this play.

- **This scene is about love at first sight. How did developing this as a concept come to be, especially in terms of crafting the characters of Julia G. and Julia I.?**

    C.Svich: I am interested in classic tropes in writing and one of them is the "love at first sight" trope, which you can see in works as diverse as Romeo and Juliet and more. I had actually never written a play with this trope before, and wanted to play with it, in this instance with a same-sex love story at the center. Both Julias in this play meet when they are at a potential crossroads in their lives and as such their meeting feels fated or shall we say destined by the gods. There's humor in this and also that wonderful sense of enchantment that can spirit the play along its tragic and comic narrative lines.

- **Where can we find the full text of the play?**

    C.Svich: You can reach out to me on my website-http://caridadsvich.com/plays/fulllength/corazon-eterno-always-in-my-heart/

CHARACTERS
JULIA I: High school student.
JULIA G: High school student. New to town.

IN THIS SCENE
Julia G. sees Julia for the first time. It is indeed love at first sight. In this first scene of this play we see how the two women are attracted to each other, and how already they behave as if they are inside a narrative too that they are creating.

JULIA G.: From a corner of the park, I see her.
JULIA: I do not see her, at first.
JULIA G.: She is as if lit from within. A vision. Pure and simple.
JULIA: I am standing near a cherry blossom tree.
JULIA G.: She is unlike any woman I have ever seen. As radiant as the natural world itself.
JULIA: I'm a silly girl.
JULIA G.: As she twirls under the tree, swinging her arms, letting her skirt float up,

JULIA: Just barely
JULIA G.: A shower of cherry blossoms falls upon her shoulders. May I help you?
JULIA: What?
JULIA G.: The cherry blossoms have fallen upon you.
JULIA: So?
JULIA G.: Well, it is said that to keep cherry blossoms on your person for far too long can make the gods look unfavorably towards you.
JULIA: I'll take my chances.
JULIA G.: You'd toy with the gods?
JULIA: Why not?
JULIA G.: You're brave.
JULIA: Not really.
JULIA G.: …Strange that I haven't seen you 'round here before.
JULIA: We moved here recently. Me and my dad.
JULIA G.: And your mom?
JULIA: She died.
JULIA G.: Oh. I'm sorry.
JULIA: A long time ago. When I was a baby.
JULIA G.: I'm sorry.
(A moment.)
JULIA G.: I've lived here all my life. I know it may seem like a small town stuck in the middle of nowhere, but there are hidden gems in this city. I could show you.
JULIA: Maybe some other time.
JULIA G.: You're very beautiful.
JULIA: Hmm?
JULIA G.: …What is it you're reading?
JULIA: I'm not.
JULIA G.: Something for school?
JULIA: English lit.

JULIA G.: Thomas Hardy. *Tess of the d'Ubervilles.* I read it in school too. Are you in Osborn's class?

JULIA: Yes.

JULIA G.: She's tough, right?

JULIA: Quizzes every Friday.

JULIA G.: She's worth it, though.

JULIA: How do you mean?

JULIA G.: She wants the best for her students. Besides, she's tough because she has to be. Those guys in admin would walk all over her if they could. The principal?

JULIA: He's weird.

JULIA G.: Such a jerk. Osborn is the real deal. If you keep up with the work in her class, it'll change your life.

JULIA: *(head in book)* I'll remember that.

JULIA G.: ...Hardy's a real beast. Poor Tess. He really puts her through her paces. And it's all because she's a woman.

JULIA: Hmm?

JULIA G.: Every action she takes is determined by the fact that she is bound by society's dictates.

JULIA: But she follows her heart.

JULIA G.: To what end? She's punished for it.

JULIA: She kills a man.

JULIA G.: She suffers for her sins. It's stupid.

JULIA: Okay.

JULIA G.: Anyway, I prefer the modernists. Have you read Virginia Woolf yet?

JULIA: No.

JULIA G.: She's a genius.

JULIA: In what way?

JULIA G.: Every way. She believed women shouldn't have any boundaries. She thought they could do anything.

JULIA: That's debatable.

JULIA G.: Why?

JULIA: My father says…

JULIA G.: Men always say. And they're wrong.

JULIA: …You always say what's on your mind?

JULIA G.: "I detest the masculine point of view. I am bored by his heroism, virtue and honor. I think the best men can do is not talk about themselves anymore."[1]

JULIA: That's intense.

JULIA G.: That's Virginia Woolf.

JULIA: So, what? You're a teacher?

JULIA G.: Oh, no, I'm... Actually, at the moment I'm a messenger. But what I'm really going to be is a writer or a singer or a musician. You see, I write songs. Lots of them. I love music. I've been writing songs since I was a little kid. My mom says I have a knack for it. My mom's great. Really supportive. You should meet her. I think you'd get along. I mean, I don't know you that well – not at all, really - but I can tell, she'd…

HECTOR (VO): Julia? Julia?

JULIA: That's my dad. I should get going. Nice to meet you.

JULIA G.: Julia.

JULIA: What?

JULIA G.: My name's Julia, too.

JULIA: Really?

JULIA G.: Yes.

HECTOR (VO): Julia!

JULIA G.: Could I see you again?

JULIA: Maybe. *(exits)*

JULIA G.: *(to herself)* (She said) "maybe."

---

[1] From Virginia Woolf's *The Pargiters*

Scenes for Two Males

Parachute Men

Mando Alvarado

Parachute Men is an unconventional and quirky comedy about three brothers who suck at being brothers, suck at love and suck at being men. The siblings are reunited when one of them returns home on the anniversary of their mother's passing. Now it's clear that the pecking order has changed and the battle begins to see who can take that baby step into manhood first.

- **How do you identify yourself?**

    M. Alvarado: Mexican-American

- **What drew you to write a story about brothers?**

    M. Alvarado: This story is about my brothers and I. When I was 9 years old, our father passed away and since I was the oldest that made me "The Man of the House." I turned out to be real bully cause I didn't know shit about being "The Man of the House." Years later, as adults, I tried to apologize to my brothers for my ineptitude and cruelty but they didn't blame me for their upbringing. In fact, they thanked me for being tough on them. But, I didn't feel resolved in myself about what I did to them so I wrote this play in a way to say I'm sorry.

- **What advice would you give to the actors, specifically the one playing Eli, and the character's condition?**

    M. Alvarado: Study, study, study, absorb then just be. Try to use behavior as a reactionary response to being unable to express yourself or cope with a specific uncomfortable moment. Play the truth and not the condition.

- **What do you want the actors to know about the emotional challenges of returning home?**

    M. Alvarado: I think the biggest realization for me when I first went back home to South Texas was being able to understand that life moves on whether you are there or not. Home is fluid and it grows and moves on just as you do so to expect it to be what it was like, what you had nostalgically had built up in your mind, is ludicrous and painful. It's never easy to come back to a place you ran away from. But, confronting it is the only way to move forward with your life because you may have physically moved on, but the pain is still there, the act is still sitting in limbo, waiting to be addressed again.

- **Where can we find the full text of the play?**

   M. Alvarado: For productions, they can reach out to:
   Carolyn Daucher
   Office of Melissa Orton at ICM
   65 East 55th Street
   New York, NY 10022
   212-556-5750 (Direct)

CHARACTERS
ELI: Oldest brother
ERIC: Youngest brother

IN THIS SCENE
After having been "welcomed" back by his middle brother, Andrew, in the previous scene, Eric sneaks back into his former childhood home. He's hoping to find life just like he left it only to be surprised that some things have changed and others still remain the same.

(Eric makes his way back to his room. He comes back out.)
ERIC: What's all that shit in my room?
ELI: I built a studio-For what? I needed a place to record. Andrew said to use your room.

ERIC: He did what?

ELI: I got to record my album- Mix it. Arrange it. I got all kinds of equipment-

ERIC: Hey, focus-

ELI: All kinds of instruments. Ready for making music. Going to make a number one album-

ERIC: Shut the fuck up! What did you do to my room?

ELI: I turned it into my recording studio. I'm a professional recording artist. And I need a recording stu-

ERIC: Eli, that's my room.

ELI: You've been gone for 1564 days. Dec 28th. Three days after the 25th.

ERIC: Listen to me. You don't mess with my room.

ELI: Andrew said I could.

ERIC: I don't give a shit what Andrew said. Get your stuff out of my room.

ELI: Why are you being an asshole?

ERIC: Because it's my room. It will always be my room. I can be gone 50 years. It doesn't matter. It's my room. So get your shit out of there. Now!

ELI: Jesus, I will.

ERIC: You need to take your medication.

ELI: You going to hit me?

ERIC: No. Of course not.

ELI: Where am I going to put my recording equipment?

ERIC: That's not my problem.

ELI: Man, you're really cranky. Eric? Eric?

ERIC: What? FUCK! What Eli?

ELI: I'm recording an album. Going to get it played. On the radio. Then, you know, go on tour, go number one on the billboard charts. I'm going to be big time. That's why I needed my recording studio. You want to help me write a song?

ERIC: No.

ELI: I need to find another studio. Maybe build one in the back. I have to have my recording studio. I have to record my album.

ERIC: Eli. Go get me your medication.

ELI: I don't like the pills. They make me feel tired. Eric? Eric?

ERIC: Stop doing that.

ELI: What am I doing?

ERIC: Calling me. Just talk to me. You don't have to call for me.

ELI: I want to make sure you're still here.

ERIC: You see me standing here, right?

ELI: I know. But sometimes I call for people and they don't answer back. So, I want to call out your name and hear you respond. Eric?

ERIC: What!?

ELI: You see. You responded.

ERIC: I can't- I can't- I can't deal with this right now. Just stop calling me by my name. Okay?

ELI: You want to take a shower? Rinse off. Start fresh. I got a new showerhead. It's nice.

(A breath... Eric looks at the guitar resting against the dinner table.)

ELI: After you left. I picked it up. I'm a natural. Like Jimi Hendrix. You sure you don't want to help me write a song?

ERIC: No.

ELI: Okay. If you change your mind, let me know. We can write that number one together. It's gonna be my break. Get me out of here.

ERIC: Where you gonna go?

ELI: All over the great big world like you.

ERIC: It's a waste of time.

ELI: I want to experience life like you did.

ERIC: You want to know about my experiences? In Newton, people were setting up fake donation sites in the kid's names. In Jersey, time after time there were false insurance claims, shady contractors, millions of dollars donated and we couldn't even get gallons of fresh water. I was there to help. Really help. But it's all bullshit. No one really cares. It's like a fad. Disaster. Services rush in. Donations. A concert. Celebrities. Tickets to the Yankees. Pictures on the Internet and then, after the shine has worn off, the people are gone, the money is gone, and Jay Z is gone. And nothing's really changed. And you realize you didn't save shit. People are just a bunch a life sucking viruses that live off each other until there's nothing left and we're all dead.

ELI: People will be nice once they hear my album.

ERIC: When is the last time you saw Dr. Resendez?

ELI: Four months ago.

ERIC: You have to take your pills.

ELI: I will if you stay.

ERIC: Can you be left alone?

ELI: I'm alone in my room.

ERIC: Does somebody always have to watch you?

ELI: I'm 21. I have hair on my balls. I think it's time I watch myself.

ERIC: Good. I'm going to the Ice House for a beer.

ELI: I like tequila sunrises. Cause it's always morning. Morning's make me happy. So will you be back by the morning?

ERIC: Yes.

ELI: I'm going to clean your room.
ERIC: Good.
ELI: I packed everything nice and neat. Your movies. Your books. Your porn collection. Your baseball cards. Your trophies. Your pictures. Your clothes. Your toys.
ERIC: Just make sure you put everything back where it was.
ELI: I will. I'm glad you're back brother.
ERIC: Are you mad at me?
ELI: We have to understand that you're in the wrong skin.
(Eric goes.)
ELI: Good night, Eric. Eric. Eric. Eric. Eric. Eric. Eric. Eric. Eric. Eric. Eric. Eric.
(The phone rings. Eli stares at it.)

Sangre De Un Ángel (Blood Of Angel)

Roxanne Schroeder-Arce

When a mother has had enough of her rebellious teenage son, Ángel, her older son, Juan, and his family offer to take him in. Juan hopes he can guide his brother to make stronger decisions about school and his future. Despite the efforts of a stable home and a loving family, Ángel resists the help, looking to his troubled friends and their gang family for approval. He is lured back to attending school by a caring auto-mechanics teacher who gives him responsibility and the opportunity to rebuild a classic 1957 Chevy. Eventually, Ángel begins to open up to his family and a hopeful future, but trouble follows him home when angry young men come looking for him—with a gun.

- **How do you identify yourself?**

    R. Schroeder-Arce: I identify racially and ethnically as white.

- **What inspired you to write about the story of Adam Chapa?**

    R. Schroeder-Arce: I was in graduate school, working as a drama specialist at Metz Elementary School in East Austin, blocks from Adam Chapa's home where he was killed. Adam's daughter was in one of my second grade classes. Though I didn't know Adam, I was aware of the tragedy from the news, and I asked the classroom teacher about it. Nearly a week after Adam's death, his daughter came back to school during my drama class. The play opens exactly as it happened that day. She and her Mom walked into the classroom and she began telling the story of her father's death to the other children. The way she spoke struck me and the family's story seemed to beg me to share it. I talked with all of the family members as well as the family members of the young men who were arrested in the case. Everyone loved Adam and the more I learned, the more compelled I felt to put his story forward. I couldn't stop writing. The first production of the play was produced by a bilingual youth company in Austin, and Adam's family created an altar for him in the lobby and a chosen family members spoke of him to the audience before every performance.

- **Can you illuminate more about the peer pressure that Ángel is feeling, and the risk factors that influencing him?**

    R. Schroeder-Arce: Ángel is facing a lot of pressure

from his friends to be cool, to spend time with them, to support them, to drink, miss family events, defy his teachers and skip school. These friends are beginning to create enemies with some gang members and the leader of his crew is pushing them to fight back. At the same time, Ángel is also feeling pressure from his brother Juan and his family to be home more, to spend time with his niece and nephew, which Ángel appears to want to do. But his friends tell him that if he doesn't stick with them, the gang is going to go after him. He doesn't seem to have a choice but to stay in it with his friends.

- **Can you elaborate on the relationship between these brothers?**

    R. Schroeder-Arce: Juan is quite a few years older than Ángel and in some ways feels that he needs to step in as a father figure. He desperately wants his younger brother to make good choices and his mother is counting on him to help Ángel to turn around. Ángel is attracted to goodness in many ways and can see where he is headed but he is resentful of the relationship Juan had with their father and of the fact that Juan is putting limits on him that he is not accustomed to.

- **Where can we find the full text of the play?**

    R. Schroeder-Arce: Dramatic Publishing. https://www.dramaticpublishing.com/sangre-de-un-193-ngel-blood-of-an-angel

Roxanne Schoeder-Arce

CHARACTERS
ÁNGEL: Age 17 lives with his brother's family, touch and curious.
JUAN: Age 26, Ángel's older brother, tries to make everyone happy, father to Jaime and Alyssa.

IN THIS SCENE
Ángel listens as his older brother Juan reads a letter from their mother who is in México visiting family. She has entrusted Juan with his brother in hopes that he can turn him around. Ángel has gotten into some trouble with friends at school and he has been warned not to go to school as some gang members may look for him there. One of Ángel's teachers has just come by to see why he is missing school. This is the first and only time in the play that Juan directly confronts Ángel on his behavior, and the first time they have really spoken about the death of their father.

JUAN: *(continuing to read)* It's all making sense to me. I know that you can make sense of it, too. You remember when your father was like this; I'm sure you do. But, Ángel didn't ever see that man. What you said makes sense now. And you are right about him needing to be around a good man. Like you, Juan. I am so happy that he has you. I am beginning to understand why he does what he does. Not completely, but a little. His family was not a family, Juan. Your Papi was all used up by then, and I was too busy trying to make us survive financially. I forgot to get to him, talk to him, figure out who he is. I think it's too late for me, but you... You are just the person to get in there. It's hard for me to need you, so thank you for insisting. I think I need a little more time here, to feel the

Sangre de un Ángel

life which runs through me which I had forgotten. Let me know if you need me there. For now, it's good to be home. Gracias, mi hijo. Todo mi amor a Julia y los niños. Please let me know how Ángel is doing. I do trust that you will make sure that he is okay. Besos, Mami.
(Ángel sighs, unseen and begins to walk away as Juan looks down at paper)
JUAN: Ángel.
ÁNGEL: How'd you know I was here?
JUAN: I just knew. Did you hear the whole letter?
ÁNGEL: Just parts of it.
JUAN: *(short)* Oh.
ÁNGEL: You mad at me?
JUAN: Did you hear that, too?
ÁNGEL: Hear what? I mean about the game. You mad cause I missed another game, or somethin?
JUAN: *(pause, directly)* Why haven't you been in school?
ÁNGEL: What do you mean? *(pause)* How do you know?
JUAN: Mr. Garza came by to check on you, see if you were feeling better.
ÁNGEL: What? Oh. Man, I don't know, Juan. I just... school's not my thing, that's all.
JUAN: Mr. Garza says he really likes you, that you do good work in his class. You like that part of school?
ÁNGEL: Yah.
JUAN: Well, he said he has a really important project for you.
ÁNGEL: What project?
JUAN: He wants you to rebuild some car.
ÁNGEL: *(excited)* The 57? The whole thing? *(remembering that he can't go to school)* It's not really too big a deal.
JUAN: I thought you'd be excited. He sounded like it was a big deal.

ÁNGEL: Well, it ain't really.

JUAN: Angel, I'm trying to be cool with you living here and all, but school is just not optional.

ÁNGEL: Nothing is optional when you're my age, it seems. Everything just happens, and it doesn't matter what you think or want.

JUAN: You have lots of choices, you just need to realize them.

ÁNGEL: I have choices? What choices? Did I choose my parents? Or where I'm from? Or what kind of blood runs through my veins? Did I choose to be born last? Or to be around when everything got so screwed up? Did I choose to hear Papi yelling and crying all night? Did I choose to live here?

JUAN: You're right, Ángel. We don't get to choose what happens to us, but we do choose how we respond. You know: There is no bad thing that doesn't bring something good.

ÁNGEL: Something good, yah, I know. Mami used to say that all the time to Papi. You tell me when the good came to Papi, huh? He didn't wait. Why should I?

JUAN: Will you shut up? Just shut up! Why do you think you're so special, like you're the only one who ever hurts? We all got hurt when Papi died, all of us. Not just you. He wasn't there for you; I realize that. Mami realizes that. But that doesn't give you any right to sit around feeling sorry for yourself. It's true, Papi drowned himself in the bad. When life got tough, he caved. *(no longer teaching, he lets go)* It's true, Ángel. And you get to choose to copy that or learn from that. I can't decide that for you. *(gets up to leave)* I need to put the kids to bed.

ANGEL: Juan, would you bring me to school tomorrow?

JUAN: (not really surprised, but pleased) Sure.

(Turns and pats him on the back. They exit together)

LATINS IN LA LA LAND

Migdalia Cruz

Explores the relationship between the famous Hollywood murders of Ramon Navarro and the Menendez parents and the long lost stories of Latinas/os in 1940s Hollywood. The dark comedy, one that is loosely based on the Menendez brothers' plot to kill their abusive and rich parents is juxtaposed against golden age cinema, drama, and glamour. Cruz brilliantly interweaves scenes in Navarro's mansion in 1944 with the Medina home (representing the Menendez home) in 1989 Beverly Hills.

- **How do you identify yourself?**

  M. Cruz: A playwright of Puerto Rican descent with Nuyorican roots.

- **How much did the real Menendez story and the history of Latinos in Hollywood influence the writing of this play?**

  M. Cruz: My research included reading everything about the Menendez case and watching the same movies and reading the books the brothers read that led them to the murder of their parents. This made me think about the history of the Latino/a in Hollywood, especially the ones involved in murders and suicides. All this led me to the ideas of Hollywood and its racism and how that contributed to the darkness surrounding all the characters/figures in the play. From Ramon Navarro to Lupe Velez to Lyle and Eric Menendez whose father was an important figure in Latino pop management, all these stories helped me come to my own.

- **There is a playful, creative journey that the brothers take that leads them to a moment of intimacy and vulnerability. How should the actors approach this moment?**

  M. Cruz: With honesty, urgency and excitement. Efrain is the younger more fragile brother and Lorenzo is the older more calculated one. They need to find an alibi that gets them out of the house during the murders that they think is the perfect cover so they attend a drag party at Ramon Navarro's house dressed as Lupe Velez and Dolores Del Rio.

- **Where can we find the full text of the play?**

M. Cruz: Please contact my agent: Ms. Peregrine Whittlesey, pwwagy@aol.com.

CHARACTERS
EFRAIN MEDINA: Age 18, a sensitive young man with a secret.
LORENZO MEDINA: Age 21, his ambitious older brother.

IN THIS SCENE
Efrain is still reeling from the impact of his parents' murder. Lorenzo is trying to calm him down and get him excited about acting the part of Dolores Del Rio as his alibi. They are dressing to go to a drag party at Ramon Navarro's house. In the course of comforting him, Lorenzo reveals his true feelings for Efrain.

EFRAIN MEDINA: Wait.
LORENZO MEDINA: Why?
EFRAIN MEDINA: It's about to start.
LORENZO MEDINA: It started years ago.
EFRAIN MEDINA: The lies I mean.
LORENZO MEDINA: I know what you mean.
EFRAIN MEDINA: They're lying there in —
LORENZO MEDINA: The carpets will be ruined but we'll get new carpets. Don't worry. We have to have fun tonight. Everybody has to see us having fun. It'll help when the time comes.
EFRAIN MEDINA: I'm not you.
LORENZO MEDINA: I know. You're Dolores Del Rio, screen siren, seen about town with Orson Welles and others... and beautiful. What movies were you in?

EFRAIN MEDINA: I don't remember.

LORENZO MEDINA: Remember. We went over it. Half the fun is being convincing. You want to be an actor, don't you? This is just the biggest role you ever got.

EFRAIN MEDINA: I did almost get that guest spot on "The Next Generation."

LORENZO MEDINA: Sure you did. You gave a great audition. I helped you, remember? We got the sides and I played the Bajoran beauty Calyx and you were Lt. Sanchez.

EFRAIN MEDINA: That was a great script... *(Acting his audition as SANCHEZ)* I'm afraid I cannot go back with you.

LORENZO MEDINA: *(Acting as CALYX)* But Lt. Sanchez, why? Our planets are in synch now. We could be happy.

EFRAIN MEDINA: Calyx, I'm afraid... I'm afraid I'm — dying.

LORENZO MEDINA: No!

EFRAIN MEDINA: Yes. I have a polyp on my brain that's slowly driving me mad. I must go where I can harm no one. The first phase is violent. I wouldn't — I couldn't hurt you. I would rather die! *(Efrain puts an imaginary phaser to his head. Lorenzo pulls it away.)*

LORENZO MEDINA: You mustn't. I can't go on alone!

EFRAIN MEDINA: I must return to my pod and — fly into the ionic storm field.

LORENZO MEDINA: I won't go on without you!

EFRAIN MEDINA: Yes — you must. You must go on for both of us. One last kiss sweet Calyx.

(They kiss.)

LORENZO MEDINA: *(Dropping the act)* Let's do that part again.

(Lorenzo kisses Efrain passionately. Efrain pushes him away)
EFRAIN MEDINA: I was good, huh? I wonder why I didn't get the part.
LORENZO MEDINA: You should have gotten Dad to give them a call. He always manages to get things done.
EFRAIN MEDINA: I wanted to do it myself, by myself.
LORENZO MEDINA: By any means necessary. Nothing is too much to ask of others or too little to ask of yourself.
EFRAIN MEDINA: I hate that book. He read it to us at least once a week. The Salesman's Bible. I never wanted to be a salesman… I wanted to be a model — or an actor. Whatever… something creative.
LORENZO MEDINA: You can be anything you want to be now.
EFRAIN MEDINA: That's right. I could make myself up, re-create in any form, like that guy on the Next Generation. I'm a morph. *(laughing)* That's why I didn't get that part. I auditioned as the wrong entity. Why is it that it's always people with names like Sanchez that die in the future?
LORENZO MEDINA: Like that chick with the muscles in Aliens 2. Man, was she hot —
EFRAIN MEDINA: — but iced in the end.
LORENZO MEDINA: Dark people never survive. Like on The Equalizer. I hated that show. Too many Spanish women chasing ambulances, screaming "Ay Dios mio! Mi hijo pobrecito! Esomebody ekilled heem!"
EFRAIN MEDINA: Since when do you care about Spanish women?
LORENZO MEDINA: Since I put on this dress. Makes me feel different. Makes me feel very — Lupe, jou no wat I meang?

EFRAIN MEDINA: *(With a smile)* I think I'm ready now. *(In his DOLORES Spanish accented and dignified voice)* Where's that little manstealer?! I'll bite off her hair at the roots. People think I'm quiet and dignified, but I don't let people get away with things.

My Father's Keeper

Guadalís Del Carmen

Tirisio Armando Gonzalez and his wife Juana are the pillars of their community, in Dominican Republic and in their new home in Chicago. But Tirsio's sudden death causes family secrets to come to light. Dealing with the their father's truth and double life, Mondo and Sofía must learn to lean on each other like never before while figuring out how to best honor their father. The Gonzalez family must define what secrets are worth keeping and which ones aren't worth the trouble.

- **How do you identify yourself?**

    G. Del Carmen: I identify as black, Afro Latina, specifically, Dominican.

- **Can you illuminate the musical choices in the scene and why it is so important to each of them?**

    G. Del Carmen: One of my objectives in this scene was to show the joy that both men bring out in each other while also showing their lived cultural differences. I wanted them both to learn from each other and be exposed to each others' worlds without leaving their safe space. Music was the best way of accomplishing this. I chose Juan Luis Guerra's *La Bilirrubina* because aside from it being one of his biggest songs, it expresses much of what Tirsio can't say to Danny, because of the language barrier but also his fear of being too vulnerable with Danny. Danny excites him and brings him joy. Also, any chance I can to showcase classic Juan Luis Guerra jams, I take it and run with it. Jodeci was one of most quintessential R&B performers of their time. As Danny states, "They sing some of the sexiest songs." I think for Danny, living his life as an out man was something he was proud of, so although he would've preferred having a more public relationship with Tirsio, he can't deny his sexual attraction to him…and eventual love for him. But I also wanted to further express how English has many forms and words that are specific to different communities. I wanted to subtly play with code switching from the eyes of an immigrant still learning the language.

- **What are the attitudes towards homosexuality in the Latinx community that the actors approaching this** scene may need to be aware of?

G. Del Carmen: One of the biggest themes I want to explore in this play is that of masculinity and the idea that homosexuality somehow reduces or takes away from a man's masculinity. This is all within gendered norms of course, if we were talking about breaking these norms, we'd discuss how defining masculinity or femininity can be all together damaging for many that don't fall under either binary. But for this conversation, I think understanding that in communities of color, homosexuality is many times seen as a weakening of the home structure. How we define masculinity in Latinx cultures and many times, African American culture, is very toxic. The idea that gay men are not real men, and therefore can't be strong and can't protect others or be responsible for others is rampant. But the religious implications surrounding homosexuality are the most damaging. The idea that hell is the prescription for homosexuality is one of the reasons for intolerance and many times violence towards the gay community. The biggest attitudes towards the homosexuality in the Latinx community, is that it's an abomination, and that it creates men that are unwilling to be heads of households to protect women.

- **Where can you find the full text of the play?**

- **G. Del Carmen:** *My Father's Keeper* can be found on my New Play Exchange profile.

Guadalís Del Carmen

CHARACTERS

TIRSIO ARMANDO GONZALEZ: Late 30's-Mid 40's. Dominican. Afro-Latino (must be black Latino). Mondo's father. Deceased, we see him in flashback scenes.

DANIEL "DANNY" MOYE: Early-mid 30's in flashback scenes. In his mid 50s's in present time. Tirsio's boyfriend. African American.

IN THIS SCENE

Danny is reading the newspaper when Tirsio meets him at their motel room after a long day at work. Tirsio is a very paranoid human being so he feels the most comfortable meeting his boyfriend at this motel almost ten miles away from where he lives and works. It's the early 90's in Chicago. Upon their first meeting, they were awkward and Tirsio's English was thick…and clumsy because of his nerves… They are now rather comfortable with each other.

[This scene has been modified for publication in this book.]

(Motel set. Spring time, 1992. Danny is on the bed reading the newspaper. Sound of toilet flush as Tirsio comes out of the bathroom. He comes toward the bed and snuggles next to Danny. Tirsio's English is better and his accent is less pronounced.)

TIRSIO: What are you reading?

DANNY: Cosmo.

TIRSIO: You are funny.

DANNY: They're still trying to clean up the mess from the flood downtown.

TIRSIO: In my country, the lights go out all the time or we sometimes get bad hurricanes, but we don't shut things down, we work through them.

DANNY: *(mocking Tirsio's accent)* We're not in your country.

TIRSIO: You should try standing comedy.

DANNY: It's stand up comedy.

TIRSIO: *(laughs at himself)* Ah. That makes better sense. *(pause)* Does it say how much longer it will take to clean?

DANNY: They're not sure. There's fish everywhere. They're not even sure if it was a leak or flood. *(pause)* Uh oh.

TIRSIO: What?

DANNY: That means, if it's a leak the city's insurance will cover it, if it's a flood, taxpayers are paying for it.

TIRSIO: I think we are going to pay for it whether it is a leak or a fraud.

DANNY: Flood.

TIRSIO: In this city, it is fraud.

DANNY: Your English is getting better I see. *(puts the newspaper down)* I'm hungry.

TIRSIO: What do you want to order? I can pick up the food.

DANNY: Or, we can go out to eat together.

TIRSIO: Danny, we talk about this/

TIRSIO:	DANNY:
We can not risk of being seen together.	We can not risk of being seen together.

DANNY: Would it really make people suspicious if two friends are having dinner together?

TIRSIO: Somebody who know me can see us.

DANNY: Babe, you ain't the president or some well known celebrity.

TIRSIO: Everybody in my neighborhood know me, and the neighborhood I work in.

DANNY: We are 10 miles away from all that, no one knows you here!

TIRSIO: Somebody is always watching. People come together and connect things.

DANNY: Connect things?

TIRSIO: Yes! They connect the dots and the lines.

DANNY: You are the most paranoid person I know.

TIRSIO: I am serious Danny.

DANNY: Yeah, I know, sometimes too serious. You know what? I don't want to argue about this ok? I've been in a good mood all day.

(Danny gives him a peck on the cheek, then jumps up.)

TIRSIO: What are you doing?

(Danny goes to his bag and gets out a CD. He puts it in the CD player and plays Jodeci's Feenin')

TIRSIO: What is that?

DANNY: One of my favorite bands. Jodeci. My cousin is their manager's assistant. Ooooo-oooo! They make the sexiest songs. This is a rough cut of something they're working on.

(Danny pulls Tirsio off the bed and towards him, they dance. Tirsio is slightly stiff.)

DANNY: Hold up! You are Spanish! Why are you so stiff?!?!

TIRSIO: I'm not from Spain...I want to hear what it says.

DANNY: For what? We're dancing! Just listen to the rhythm.

(Tirsio loosens up. Danny is really feeling the music. Tirsio starts to focus on the lyrics again.)

DANNY: Good Lord!

(sings the lyrics)

I can't leave you alone

You got me feennin'

You got me feenin'

TIRSIO: Fin-eh? What is that?

DANNY: Feenin'…feeeen-iiin…Feening. *(sighs)* It means wanting something really bad, like you're hungry for it and gets you all hot and you lose yourself in it.

TIRSIO: And your blood pressure go up?

DANNY: Um, yeah, sure, I guess that can happen too.

TIRSIO: I'll be right back.

DANNY: Where are you going?

(Tirsio rushes out the door.)

DANNY: He better not walk up in here trynna have me figure out his blood pressure.

(Tirsio rushes back in. He stops the CD and pops in a tape. Juan Luis Guerra's La Bilirrubina plays.)

DANNY: What is that?

TIRSIO: This is a classic album. I listen to it in the car sometimes. This song is about someone's blood pressure going up because they love someone…like your feen-in.

DANNY: You connect some serious dots.

TIRSIO: Dance with me.

DANNY: I don't know how to dance this.

TIRSIO: Merengue is easy. Is all about the hips. You're good at moving your hips.

(Tirsio pulls Danny towards him. Lights fade as they move their hips to merengue.)

The Happiest Song Plays Last

Quiara Alegría Hudes

In a barrio living room in North Philly, an activist-turned-music-professor moonlights as the local soup kitchen queen, cooking free rice and beans for any hungry neighbor. Halfway around the world, her cousin relives his military trauma on the set of a docudrama that's filming in Jordan. With the Egyptian revolution booming in the distance, these two young adults try to sing a defiant song of legacy and love in the face of local and global unrest.

- **How do you identify yourself?**

    Q. A. Hudes: Boricua/Puerto Rican.

- **The play is the third part of a trilogy that follows Elliot's trajectory. What should actors tackling these roles be aware of?**

    Q. A. Hudes: Each of the plays in the group is intended to stand alone and be its own story but together they tell the story of a coming-of-age of an American young man. He is bright, witty, and adventuresome, and also deeply troubled. *The Happiest Song Plays Last* finds him quite a few years out from his military service struggling to get back into civilian life at a moment when he has a wonderful opportunity to go to Jordan and act in a movie. So, it combines some of his past troubles with a moment when he is really poised to overcome them.

- **Where can we find the full text of the play?**

    Q. A. Hudes: The play is published by Theatre Communications Group- www.tcg.org. You can also go to my website www.Quiara.com.

CHARACTERS
ELLIOT: Latino, 20's
ALI: Arab, thick accent, 40's

IN THIS SCENE
January 2011 - Jerash, Jordon. Elliot is filming a movie, Haditha on Fire. Ali is the consultant and gofer on set. It is their day off and Elliot has been invited to his home.

ALI *(Sitting):* You like wrestling?

ELLIOT: Eh. I used to.

ALI: My little boy has Hulk Hogan DVD.

ELLIOT: Old-school.

ALI: You like football? Soccer?

ELLIOT: I don't know shit about football except you kick the ball in the net and yell GOAL!!!

ALI: This is it! You know football!

ELLIOT: No TV, let's just talk. You think this movie's gonna be good?

ALI: Nigel is smart man. Good listener. Not idiot. Sharp like tack!

ELLIOT: It's nice living in the barracks with the guys again. I told Nigel, you want to do it right? These guys can't live in no hotel, they gotta build barracks from the ground up and stay in it. Cuz that camaraderie? You can't get that in normal life.

ALI: Every army, full of many brothers.

ELLIOT: And the adrenaline? From being in a firefight? From going house to house, not knowing if there's a bullet waiting for you on the other side of the door.

ALI: You like this adrenaline?

ELLIOT: It reminds you you're alive.

ALI: Me? Not so good with adrenaline.

ELLIOT: Did you see a lot of action? In the Jordanian army?

ALI: A lot of action. But not Jordanian army.

ELLIOT: I thought . . .

ALI: Iraqi Armed Forces.

ELLIOT: Iraqi?

ALI: Too much adrenaline. Adrenaline all the time. This is why I leave Iraq.

ELLIOT: Wait. How long you been there?

ALI: Five years.

ELLIOT: The way you talk about Jordan. I thought you were born and raised. It's like people in Philly they be talking 'bout cheesestakes.

ALI: Do not tell guys on film crew. Maybe they treat me different. Like I take their job. Maybe they report and my family is sending back to Iraq.

ELLIOT: Does Nigel know?

ALI: Why you think he hires me? You are expert on United States Marines. I expert on Iraq culture. I am telling him, "Yes, Iraqi would do this. Yes, Iraqi would say this. No, wrong wrong wrong." Nigel gives me money so my daughter put in private school.

ELLIOT: How did he find you?

ALI: Craigslist. "Expert in Iraqi culture, no papers necessary, pay in cash." He receives two thousand emails from this ad.

ELLIOT: Damn.

ALI: Many of us here. In Iraq, they were doctor. University Professor. Here, hiding, afraid, learning Jordan accent so nobody notices. I tell my daughter, do not talk at school, only listen, write, nod head yes, shake head no. No talking until Jordanian accent is perfect. My wife? Do you see her hands?

ELLIOT: No.

ALI: Always tremble. I buy her antidepressants, very expensive. She calls her father. "Baba, baba, help me go back to Iraq. Baba help me go home." He says, "No no no, crazy! Help me leave Iraq and come to Jordan."

ELLIOT: Yo . . . half the shit I said on set. During the actors boot camp? Things I said about Iraq, shit I did there?

ALI: Half the time, you speak from heart. Half the time, from other place.

ELLIOT: Yo man if I had known . . .

ALI: My lovely, most people speak from other place one hundred percent!

ELLIOT: Why the hell are you so nice to me? I'm already here thinking, I don't deserve this. A second chance to meet the Arab culture.

ALI: You think you had real first chance?

ELLIOT: Why would you bring me into your home?

ALI: I am like you. We are same. Xerox copy. Optimist. Always laugh laugh good time. Nice person. But inside heart, person who is different.

ELLIOT: You got anyone still there?

ALI: My mother and father.

ELLIOT: You got anyone young there?

ALI: My cousin Nasser, Very short and fat man. Always he wants to play Basketball but he is short and wide like hafilah.

ELLIOT: Bus?

ALI: Good Arabic my brother. He stays in Iraq, to rebuild. Iraqi Nation Basketball Association. He tries to create this. Smart man.

ELLIOT: I got something. If you could send something to him. Maybe he could track down an address and deliver it?

(Eliott pulls a passport from his pocket, gives it to Ali.)

ALI: This is Iraqi passport.

(Silence.)

This is Iraqi person you know?

(Silence.)

285

ELLIOT: He's my first.

(Silence.)

ALI: Why you bring this today?

ELLIOT: Every day. It lives in my pocket. Every day since 2003 it's in my pocket.

(Silence.)

There's an address here, I'm guessing it's his. Maybe your cousin Nasser could go there. I know it's a big country. But if you could send it to him and maybe he could go there and give it back to the family. Give it to his wife and son.

ALI: How you know he has a wife and son?

ELLIOT: After I . . . I seen them . . .

(Eliott pulls money out of his pocket, hands it to ALI.)

How much does it cost to send a package to Iraq? Or actually, to send a messenger? I want to send money so Nasser can get a driver and go to this address.

ALI: Put this money away.

ELLIOT: For you to send the package. You gotta send it secure, it has to make it there.

ALI: You pay, I take you to Petra. You pay, I take you to Dead Sea. This, you do not pay.

(Elliot puts the money back in his pocket.)

ELLIOT: My cousin's address is on the back. That can be the return address in case it doesn't work out.

ALI: You live with this cousin, Yazmin?

ELLIOT: Not but I gave up my apartment to come film this movie so at the moment I have no return address.

ALI: How you know I don't put this in trash can?

(Silence. ALI puts passport in his pocket.)

No forgive. I cannot forgive. But you know real who I am. I know real who you are. Witness for each other.

MEMBERS ONLY

Oliver Mayer

In MEMBERS ONLY, the long-awaited sequel to the ground breaking BLADE TO THE HEAT, 20 years have passed.

It is 1982 in New York City: the golden age of boxing, the dying gasp of disco, and the flowering of identity politics. Pedro Quinn is well past 40 and still fighting, not only for championships but for the right to be himself, on his own terms. He even has a protege, a young female boxer who reminds him of his own youthful fights in an out of the ring. But when a detached retina threatens to end the only life he knows, and when old frenemies Vinal and Sarita want to make a movie about the champion he killed in the ring 20 years ago, Quinn can no longer hide from the ghosts of his past. Nor can he protect those he loves from the specter of hatred, much less the oncoming onslaught of what will soon be named the AIDS virus. He can hide in plain sight no more, and his biggest fight is yet to come.

MEMBERS ONLY is a play about an America of color forging racial and sexual identities to the pulsating beat of Willie Colon and Blondie, on the cusp of discovery, at the edge of a plague.

Oliver Mayer

- **How do you identify yourself?**

  O. Mayer: I'm a playwright first. Next a professor of and friend to young playwrights. Then a poet. *Latinx* actually fits my experience, as I have never felt completely at home within the parameters of a strictly *Chicano* self. In a lot of ways, this personal struggle has kept me writing plays for over 30 years, trying to question and push the boundaries of what we would now call a *Latinx* identity.

- **MEMBERS ONLY is the sequel to your hit, BLADE TO THE HEAT. What inspired you to write it?**

  O. Mayer: BLADE TO THE HEAT was such a life-changer for a lot of us that the characters never quite left me. My wife Marlene Forte always wanted to play Sarita, but 20 years ago we hadn't yet met and she was unable to get an audition at the Public Theater for the world premiere production. A few years back, she reminded me that I could conceivably meet up with the surviving characters again, giving her the chance to finally play the role. That spurred me. But I had another reason. No offense to Kushner's ANGELS IN AMERICA, but I confess I never quite saw myself or my experience in those characters. I knew that the *Latinx* experience with the history of AIDS demanded its own investigation, and I realized that Pedro Quinn was poised to help us understand what it felt like to be of color in 1982 – not to mention being forced to come out to the world at a moment when the stakes couldn't have been higher in the ring or out.

- **What insight can you give us into Quinn and Dr. Cox's relationship?**

MEMBERS ONLY

O. Mayer: Doctor Cox holds a great deal of power in this scene: Quinn needs to pass his physical exam if he ever wants to fight again. Cox is based on several individuals who were on the front lines of AIDS treatment, before AIDS even had a name. I liked the idea that Cox could be friends with someone like Pedro Quinn, and that they could share experiences outside of boxing or medicine. But characters make choices, which in turn cause repercussions that can change the world. I'd like to think that the seeds of change are in this scene.

- **Where can we find the text of the play?**

O. Mayer: NoPassport Press will be publishing MEMBERS ONLY alongside BLADE TO THE HEAT. With any luck, it will be available in time for the world premiere of the play at LATC, produced by Jose Luis Valenzuela and the The Latino Theatre Company.

CHARACTERS
QUINN: Latino. A longtime professional boxer at the highest levels; losing his eyesight; not out but living as a gay man in 1982 NYC; still harboring guilt for killing a man in the ring twenty years ago.
COX: Any ethnicity other than Latino. 30s/40s. A doctor at the forefront of the AIDS crisis who contracts the virus; frequents Xenon's.

IN THIS SCENE
A shirtless Quinn enters through the medical curtain. He wears only the blessed beads. Doctor Cox, joins Quinn.

QUINN: Thanks for fitting me in, Doc.
COX: I thought you were done fighting.
(About to put on medical gloves.)
QUINN: Everything's a fight, isn't it? This one I didn't ask for.
COX: Sure you're ready?
QUINN: I got a puncher's chance.
COX: How you feeling?
QUINN: Old.
(Leaves the gloves aside.)
COX: Old? I just made my peace with Disco, bought a whole new set of clothes, tightened up my Do the Hustle, my YMCA, and suddenly everything's out of fashion.
QUINN: White suit?
COX: Pure John Revolta.
QUINN: Sorry, Old Man! Although that look still works at the Latin clubs.
COX: Salsa gives me a pain in my coccyx.
(Looks in Quinn's mouth)
Where to this time? Vegas?
(Quinn tries to answer, compress in mouth.)
QUINN: Italy.
(Cox checks his eyes.)
COX: Thought you said Vegas. Blink.
(Cox checks his blood pressure).
QUINN: No place for sissies.
COX: Italy?
QUINN: Getting old. *(as Cox examines him)* Tickles.
COX: Cold hands, sorry.
QUINN: Someone oughta warm you up. You know the best thing about getting old?

COX: Sex is hotter?
QUINN: You hit harder. "Sex is hotter?"
COX: Joke. But medically accurate. At least according to my notes. *(takes notes)* How do you still get it up?
QUINN: Ouch!
COX: I mean to fight. To get in the ring. That's a lot of pressure!
QUINN: Pressure is how you know everything is working.
COX: Not everything, Pete. There's a cloud in your right eye.
QUINN: That's old news.
COX: How you going to see the punches?
QUINN: It's not about seeing. It's about feeling. I feel fine. Come on Doc.
COX: I'm not comfortable about this.
QUINN: Nobody's at 100%, not at this age. We do the best we can with what we got. And we use our experience.
(beat)
Please?
(Cox jokingly blesses him with a sign of the cross.)
QUINN: Blessings all around.
COX: Bring me back something from Italy. And don't forget to duck.
(Quinn starts to get dressed. Cox watches.)
COX: Nice beads.
QUINN: Where the beads go, that's where the spirit goes. Aché.
COX: Gesundheit!
QUINN: I said Aché. Life force. Makes us who we are. The power to manifest. It's in the blood. Tremendo aché.
COX: I didn't know you were religious.

QUINN: I keep it hidden under my shirt.

COX: Santería?

QUINN: They're just beads. They're not even mine. Sometimes I wear them for a little extra luck.

COX: What? Like red underpants? Quinn shows him his underpants waistband -- red.

QUINN: I need all the luck I can get.

COX: How are your glands?

QUINN: My what?

COX: *(feels his lymph nodes)* Discomfort?

QUINN: Yeah, now!

COX: Flu-like symptoms?

QUINN: When I get the flu. Why?

COX: Something out there.

QUINN: Like the clap?

COX: We think it's transmitted via shared substances.

QUINN: Drugs?

COX: Or sex. Affected communities include homosexuals, Haitians.

QUINN: You think I'm Haitian?

COX: Wear a condom.

QUINN: Why not a HazMat suit?

COX: Start with latex.

QUINN: *(sees the unused gloves)* Why didn't you?

COX: I know who I'm dealing with.

(The disco ball returns. MUSIC. Disco variety.)

COX: There's a run of patients down at Beekman Hospital, you don't want to be one of them. HazMat ain't too far away. Nurses leave their food outside the hospital room door. If no family comes to bring it inside, the patient starves. No joke.

MEMBERS ONLY

QUINN: I'm not laughing.

COX: You ever go to Xenon's? Dancing like I've never seen. Sweat pouring off bodies, steam coming off their skin. Disco evolving on the fly. People doing performance art on the dance floor, popping, locking, rapping. Something's happening. You should come.

QUINN: Hurts my coccyx, Doc.

COX: I beg to differ, Young Man.

QUINN: When I get back from Italy. We'll dance.

COX: Call it a date. *(about to leave)* Red underwear, huh?

Doctor Cox exits. Quinn is slow to put on his shirt.

KILLING OF A GENTLEMAN DEFENDER

Carlos Murillo

In 1994, the world was shocked when International soccer star Andres Escobar was gunned down in Medellin, Colombia following his disastrous own goal at the FIFA World Cup USA. In 2015, Martín, an ambivalent teaching artist in Chicago is hired to create a play about violence in Chicago with youth from the violence plagued neighborhoods of the city. Caught between his boss' desire for a docudrama and his own belief in metaphor, Martín unearths the Escobar story from the past to tell a city's story in the present. Tragedy ensues.

- **How do you identify yourself?**

  C. Murillo: I am a US born son of a Colombian father and Puerto Rican mother. I grew up in the suburbs of New York City and spent part of my childhood in Bogotá, Colombia and Caracas, Venezuela.

- **Martín offers Ricardo a ride home. What's his motivation to help this student?**

  C. Murillo: Up to this moment, Ricardo has acted as the rabble rouser and call out king of the young actors putting on the play within the play. Martín and Ricardo provoke each other throughout – Martín tries to break through Ricardo's reluctance, hoping to awaken the latent talent he sees in him; Ricardo constantly challenges Martín on what he sees as his hypocrisy in his ideas about the world. Immediately prior to this scene, Ricardo has an acting breakthrough – his raw talent bursts forth, and more importantly, he lets his guard down to show that he actually cares – about the process and about the people he's working with. Martín sees this as a "teachable moment" and seizes the opportunity to encourage Ricardo to reach beyond the limitations imposed on him by circumstance.

- **The scene very much examines power/status and the student/teacher relationship. Is there a clear winner?**

  C. Murillo: I think they both win and lose.

- **Where can we find the full text of the play?**

  C. Murillo: To request a copy please contact my agent, Antje Oegel at AOI International.

CHARACTERS
MARTÍN: early 40's. Caucasian of Colombian and Puerto Rican descent.
RICARDO: 17. Mexican descent, plays many roles in the play.

IN THIS SCENE
The gymnasium, a great rehearsal has just ended and everyone has left.

[This scene has been modified for this publication.]

MARTÍN: Ricardo?

Can I chat with you for a second?

RICARDO: What's up?

MARTÍN: That was really good.

Like, really, really good.

RICARDO: Thanks.

MARTÍN: The energy, the focus, the…

I knew you had it in you.

Pause.

MARTÍN: I just wanna say, um….

I know things sometimes have been…

Tense? Between you and me?

Pause.

I just wanna say it's…

nice to see you really care.

RICARDO: Just doing my job.

MARTÍN: Look:

> I know it might seem like
>
> I've singled you out...?

RICARDO: You're doing your job.

MARTÍN: Let me finish?

RICARDO: I gotta catch the bus –

MARTÍN: I'm hard on you, Ricky, cause

> Sometimes I think I am you.

This freaks Ricardo out a little. Almost takes a step back.

MARTÍN: I don't mean I'm –

> I know that sounds...
>
> What I mean is.
>
> You remind me of me when I was your age.
>
> If I met that version of myself?
>
> I'd grab him by his collar, tell him
>
> "Wake the fuck up."

RICARDO: I am *not. you.*

MARTÍN: I know.

RICARDO: I'm not asleep...

> I'm wide awake.

MARTÍN: You sure about that?

RICARDO: Maybe it's you that's asleep.

Ricardo starts to exit.

MARTÍN: Ricardo –

RICARDO: *What?*

MARTÍN: Sometimes I look back.

    At things I did?

    Things I didn't do?

    When I was your age?

    I think: I'm fucking lucky –

    Cause we're all that close…

    one misstep away from…

    Ricardo starts to laugh.

    What's funny?

RICARDO: Second there?

    I thought we were in one of those stupid ass movies

    Some teacher shows up at some fucked up school

    Thinks they got a magic wand, that just being there…

    Fuck that.

    You have no idea who I am.

MARTÍN: Ricardo – I

RICARDO: I am not you. You are not me.

    You might *think* you know me –

    But I don't pretend I know who you are.

    I have no idea who the fuck you are.

MARTÍN: Let me give you a ride home, we can talk –
    Ricardo starts to walk. He knocks over the giant World Cup trophy.

MARTÍN: Ricardo…
RICARDO: Night, *Marteen*
   He exits.

icarus burns

christopher oscar peña

In the social landscape of the 2008 American presidential election, hope and change are giving rise to dreams. Immigrants, homosexuals, children, and families hoping to thrive are struggling to survive. But the higher they fly, the harder they fall. A story that crisscrosses political hot button issues from immigration, to domestic abuse, to gay marriage, *icarus burns* is a provocative, imaginative, and touching modern tale. If America is a melting pot, this is the story of how the modern dreams of its people are often the first to burn.

- **How do you identify yourself?**

    c. oscar peña: i would say i am a first generation honduran-american writer originally from california now living in new york. i would also identify as a queer writer. i am always all of those things, but i think different identities are highlighted at different times because of various reasons.

- **You use limited punctuation in your playwriting. How does this grammatical twist translate to the spoken word?**

    c. oscar peña: put simply, i believe that we are taught to write english in a very specific, grammatically correct way. but listen to the world, listen to your friends and family. no one actually speaks the way we are taught to write. everyone has their own rhythms and cadences and weird speech patterns. my goal is not to enslave an actor with my text, but instead to free them to use their own voice, using my words as a blueprint. so not using correct grammar or punctuation or capitalization, i think, helps that process.

- **Can you talk about the complex and cumulative factors that complicate James and Andres' relationship?**

    c. oscar peña: i think each of us, all of us, walk through the world in our own specific ways. this is the effect of our baggage, our past experiences, our histories. and though some of us share certain qualities, they don't always affect us the same way. in very simple ways, james and andres are both latino. they are also both gay. but these identities manifest in different ways for each of them, both because of how they express these identities, and how others perceive them. i would argue that james passes as white, but can't hide his gay-ness. andres can pass as straight, but can't hide his latino-ness. so even though they both share these identities, they go through life in different ways. it allows them to pass - regardless of peoples opinions of that idea. so do they pass? do they pass because they can? is passing a choice? and when it is, what do they choose and why? i think that they also resent the other for being ashamed of an identity and not of the other, not realizing that they are both ashamed of what the other can't hide. in many ways, they are both using their identities in similar ways, but think they're different. this idea of what we are, who we are, what we tell others, what they tell us is interesting to me.

- **James is highly influenced by the opinion of his brother Liam. How much is this opinion driving James' emotions in this scene?**

    c. oscar peña: i think james is afraid that his brother is right and thats a terrifying thing to consider. even though he would never consciously admit it, liams voice has crept into his head and is slowly gnawing at him, and causing him to spiral, chipping away at his ego and his sense of worth.

- **Where can we find the full text of the play?**

    c. oscar peña: you can contact my agents Olivier Sultan and Ally Shuster at CAA, or my manager Henry Huang at Heroes and Villains.

CHARACTERS

ANDRES: 31 (A person of color, of Spanish and Argentinian descent, immigrant, slight accent, and darker skin than James).

JAMES: 28 (A person of color, Latin American descent, Honduran, first generation American, light skinned, no distinguishable accent).

IN THIS SCENE

James and Andres' LA apartment. They just arrived home and are in the middle of a heated discussion.

ANDRES: Don't worry. I'll never cheat on you.
JAMES: I just can't believe the nerve he has

   Thinking our relationship isn't as good

ANDRES: I dont think-

   It didnt seem like thats how he felt

JAMES: yea well you wouldnt know any better now would you
ANDRES: Whas that supposed to mean?
JAMES: Nothing.
ANDRES: It's something. It's obviously something.
JAMES: There's no point.
ANDRES: Talk to me

   Will you communicate

JAMES: He thinks you dont value our relationship

   That its not important enough to you

   That if you did

You'd be out

And im not certain hes wrong

ANDRES: I thought you were okay with me not being out. I thought you understood.

JAMES: I put up with it. I deal with it because it's what you want. I never said I was okay with it or understood it.

ANDRES: What's the problem? I'm gay. I know I'm gay. You know I'm gay. I love you. We both know that. I don't follow.

JAMES: It's a character thing.

ANDRES: What? My character isn't good?

JAMES: It's weak. It's unknown.

ANDRES: Because I don't think that everyone needs to know who I fuck?

JAMES: Or who you love.

ANDRES: You know what I mean.

JAMES: It's human nature, basic human desire to want to be heard. To want to be understood. Everyone wants to know that they exist among the world. That they may be just one more atom in the universe, but they are at least that. Their own existent atom in the universe. But you-

ANDRES: Don't exist in the universe?

JAMES: Not the real you

When you were little, did you want to be a journalist? Did you always know that's what you wanted to be?

ANDRES: Always.

JAMES: Why?

ANDRES: I don't know.

JAMES: You must.

ANDRES: Did you always know you wanted to be a writer?

JAMES: Yes!

ANDRES: Why?

JAMES: Because I wanted to write the world the way I wanted it to be. The way it should be. Because it was the only world I knew how to exist within.

ANDRES: Oh.

JAMES: So?

ANDRES: What?

JAMES: So what about you?

ANDRES: My world was made up of Scandals. Lies. Gossip. The town I was from. They would say disparaging things about you to destroy you. They would find any reason to find political power over you. It was a vicious game of survival. I became a journalist so I could report the truth.

JAMES: Except your own.

ANDRES: I finally escaped all that. I don't need to give them one more reason to hold power over me.

JAMES: It's more than that. You refuse to be honest and therefore people don't really know you. In our own small world they know a superficial version of you, the surface. But in the bigger world, they have no idea that there's one more gay person out their living the life they want. Because you're not. How could you think you ever took the power back from them? And I. I got past that Andres. I left that behind. And now it's just one more thing Liam has over me.

ANDRES: This is about your brother and you're making it about our relationship.

JAMES: It's about what my brother has to destroy and I barely have to hold onto.

ANDRES: i need you to understand.

icarus burns

JAMES: I dont exist Andres

    Not in your world

    Not to your family

    Not at work

    The things you value in life-

    I dont exist in those places

    I'm not real there

    You show them what you want to

    You exist how you want to

    Youre something different there

    I dont exist

ANDRES: Youre who I go home to
JAMES: An unsayable secret
ANDRES: Youre important to me I love-
JAMES: I want to get married
ANDRES: What?
JAMES: You heard me

    I wanted you to ask me

    I had this stupid dream-

    This stupid idea that you would ask me one day

    But I dont know if you ever will or if you ever want to

    Liam thought Paris would be good for the honeymoon

And then I thought

He thought

We thought

If you came to Paris with me

Maybe you would finally ask me

Or i would finally have the guts to ask you even though its not the way I dreamed it

In my head

So i figured I would just ask

It sort of just happened

Silence
Silence
Silence
JAMES: Will you say something
ANDRES: I dont know if i can.

JAMES: Okay Oh god
ANDRES: I mean I'm not sure

Thats not a no

Its not a no

Its an I just dont know

JAMES: Definitely not the way i dreamed it happening
ANDRES: Im sorr-
JAMES: Dont.
ANDRES JAMES
JAMES: everything has a breaking point

It won't all melt away like a piece of ice the way you want it to

One day it's just going to break into a million little pieces

I think I'm going to go to Paris.

ANDRES: Is that what you want?

JAMES: Want is four letters that hardly ever seem to matter.

Swimming While Drowning

Emilio Rodriguez

Two teenage boys in an LGBT homeless shelter search for the home they've always wanted through anything they can hold on to including poetry, music, and root beer floats. As the story unfolds, we learn about the challenges of these two boys who are still looking for the love that their families took away from them. Culture, language, and discovery collide in a coming of age story that was deemed "heartbreakingly funny."

- **What inspired you to write *Swimming While Drowning*?**

  E. Rodriguez: I was inspired to write *Swimming While Drowning* when I first discovered that LGBT homeless shelters existed back in 2011. As I researched I learned more about the limited space and growing demand for shelter from LGBT youth kicked out of their homes or leaving their neighborhoods because of not feeling safe. As I got the opportunity to volunteer in these shelters I realized that there was a high percentage of Black and Latinx youth and most of them had families who were blatantly homophobic.

- **You incorporate spoken word and poetry in the play. How do you see it influencing the rhythm and speech of the characters?**

  E. Rodriguez: The poetry was something I originally included because I was a spoken word artist before I was a theatre artist. Poetry came naturally to me. I discovered a lot about the characters by writing their poems first. I think it seeped into their dialogue, which to me made the characters richer and increased the stakes of each scene so that even when they talk about root beer floats, you understand what a luxury a seemingly simple thing is in their world.

- **What suggestions would you offer to the actors?**

  E. Rodriguez: I would love it if the actors took the time to volunteer at an LGBT homeless shelter or a children's home. So, that they can understand these situations are real, they should honor their lives and bring a sense of truthfulness to their characters. The play has a lot of funny moments, but they only work if we are watching real people. Some people may believe that homophobia is dead because Ellen DeGeneres has a talk show or Neil Patrick Harris hosted the Tony's, but to young gay men of color, the intersections of racism, culture, homophobia, masculinity, and male intimacy are all very real experiences that shape their/our identities every day.

- **Where can we find the full text of the play?**

    E. Rodriguez: It can be found on the New Play Exchange.

CHARACTERS
ANGELO: 15, a gay Latino teen who knows that the only way to survive is to find someone to trust.
MILA: 15, a gay Black Latino teen who knows that survival depends on being very careful who you trust.

IN THIS SCENE
An LGBT homeless shelter a year earlier and a poetry lounge in the present.

ANGELO: ...Are you mad at me?
MILA: Just shut the hell up, alright.
(A long pause. Angelo decides to make it up to him.)
ANGELO: *(Beat)* If I tell you a secret, will you promise not to tell?
MILA: I told you mine, you should tell me yours.
ANGELO: You won't be mad at me anymore?
MILA: How am I posta promise that when I don't know what you 'bout to say?
ANGELO: I need you trust me.

MILA: ...Fine.

ANGELO: Not everything I said was true.

MILA: What's that mean?

ANGELO: I may have lied about something.

MILA: ...Your name's not really Angelo, is it? I bet you got a embarrassing name like Reginald or Preston or Cornelius. Yeah, your name's probably Cornelius.

ANGELO: My dad didn't beat me.

MILA: What...What the fuck?!

ANGELO: I made it up.

MILA: That's messed up, man. You got a kid kicked out.

ANGELO: You don't know that for sure.

MILA: He's not here no more, but you are. And Trey really needed this spot.

ANGELO: I didn't have anywhere else to go. All of the shelters were full.

MILA: There's kids out here praying for a bed that you already had.

ANGELO: If you could've seen the look in his eyes... It was worse than a beating. He looked at me like he wished I was never born.

MILA: But he never hit you?

ANGELO: You're not listening to me.

MILA: Did he hit you?

ANGELO: He didn't have to. He gave me that look for sixteen seconds; he sucked the air out of the room.

MILA: You out here begging for help cuz your pops stared at you the wrong way?

ANGELO: That was no stare. Staring is something humans do. This was something else. He was something else.

MILA: *(Beat)* You should give Trey his spot back.

ANGELO: You don't get it. It wasn't a choice. I did the right thing.

MILA: Poor you, your dad got mad at you.

ANGELO: I couldn't stay there.

MILA: Yes, you could.

ANGELO: He stopped saying he loved me. *(Beat)* You should know better than anyone how it feels to be hated for who you are.

MILA: I should know better?

ANGELO: Yes.

MILA: Why don't you tell me about the time you got fucked up by a gang cuz they found out you were a faggot... your own neighbors....same kids you used to walk to school with every day. And I bet you used to get the shit beat out of you for looking at some guy the wrong way, right? I bet you had yo ass knocked to the floor ...because your tía's boyfriend ...decided he liked you better than he liked your tía...No? Well, that's some people's story. That's some people's fucking poem, alright? ...That's some fucked up shit, right? That's some shit that none of that voodoo- Zero-bitch-ass shit gonna fix. Cuz, you know what, this—

(Mila rubs his forearm in a vigorous circle with his palm.)

This don't do shit out there. Out there you gonna go through some shit you got no control over. And there ain't no fucking superheroes to save you. Matter 'fact, why the fuck would I rub my arm to be invisible? ... I already am. *(Beat)* And that's how it feels to be hated for who you are. So don't ever try to come at me like we got the same life.

ANGELO: That's not what I meant.

MILA: Then you shouldn't have said it.

ANGELO: I'm sorry.

MILA: I don't give a shit.

ANGELO: No, Mila, listen. I'm truly sorry, okay? You're right. I don't know what that feels like. The shit you've been through, I wouldn't wish that on anyone...ever. I guess I just wanted to connect with someone so badly that I ...

MILA: Lied.

ANGELO: Yes...It was fucked up. I understand that. I just needed a safe place. You know I wouldn't have done it if I didn't have to.

MILA: ...You could've told me the truth.

ANGELO: I thought you wouldn't be my friend anymore. You didn't exactly welcome me with open arms.

MILA: So now I'm supposed to be your friend again? Cuz you're sorry?

ANGELO: From now on, I'm gonna be honest with you about everything.

MILA: I already trusted you once.

ANGELO: Mila, I'm never gonna lie to you again. I promise. Please. One last chance. If I lie to you or do anything bad to you I'll punish myself.

MILA: How?

ANGELO ...I'll hit myself.

MILA: Do it.

ANGELO: Right now?

MILA: Yeah. You lied. Hit yourself.

ANGELO: Okay...

Angelo smacks the back of his own head with his palm. A beat. Mila bursts out into laughter.

MILA: I can't believe you actually did it.

ANGELO: I want you trust me again.

MILA: *(Playful)* You still did it like a little bitch though.

ANGELO: So, you still mad at me?

MILA: Hell yeah I'm still mad at you. *(Beat)* But that don't mean I'm gonna be like your dad. Lying's fucked up, but you gotta do what you gotta do to make it out here.

EL PASO BLUE

Octavio Solis

Al has to take the rap for his pal Duane's botched robbery, but before he goes, he leaves his drunken ex-beauty queen wife Sylvie in the care of his father Jefe. In the year he is gone, Jefe and Sylvie fall in love, and when Al is granted early parole, he enlists Duane in a mad and murderous hunt for the fleeing lovers. In the course of their search, they meet China, a weird changeling who wields a water gun filled with ammonia and purports to know where his wife has been taken.

- **How do you identify yourself?**

    O. Solis: Mexican-American, Latino, dude.

- **The play is inspired by Oedipus Rex. Can you describe the fate vs. free will concept for both characters?**

    O. Solis: Well, it's not exactly consciously inspired by Oedipus Rex. I only noticed the connections and correlations afterwards. I was more concerned with the ways in which love can be so disastrously fickle, and then considered what a lover's most problematic rival would be if Love's arrow darted somewhere else. But for me, destiny and free will seem to be two distinctly different concepts. We all share the same destiny: we will meet the same end. We are predisposed to perish, one way or the other. That is our ultimate destiny. Free will is what we determine to do within the time frame between life and death. It's what we now call agency. Except that what I consider agency is often fueled by emotion, and emotion all too often causes our free will to crash directly into our destiny.

- **Duane has a metal plate in his head and can pick up radio signals. How does this manifest in the actor?**

    O. Solis: Duane's plate picks up all kinds of airborne signals, from late night call-in shows, to drive thru fast food joints, to ham radio transmissions and jet pilot communications. When he receives them through his plate, he undergoes something like an epileptic seizure and blanks out completely as those voices and their accompanying static crackle takes over his speech. They jockey for dominance in his head, causing a kind of word salad to spill fitfully from his mouth. When he is released from the seizure, he has no recollection of what has passed through him. He is a kind of accidental oracle for the lonely voices in the skies.

- **Why did you choose El Paso as the setting?**

    O. Solis: El Paso is where I was born and the strange aura of that town has stayed with me all these years. Since it is where the US meets Mexico in that culture-scarring border, it's the natural landscape for the endless border narratives that bounce around in my head. I grew up directly experiencing the weird, haunting, heartbreaking, violent consequences of America's relationship to its brown population.

- **Where can the full play be found?**

    O. Solis: The play can be obtained through Samuel French.

CHARACTERS
DUANE: Early 20's, Al's side-kick, took a bullet to save his friend and now has a metal plate in his head.
AL: Early 20's, Mexicano, a petty thief who feels he owes his life to Duane.

IN THIS SCENE
El Paso, the present. Duane and Al are brothers.
Duane has a big favor to ask of his brother, Al.
Duane enters with crying.

(Duane's frantic cries segueway to the year before. AL has long hair.)

DUANE: AL! AL! Jesus, you gotta do this for me! You gotta! Say yes!

AL: What's going on?

DUANE: Say yes!

AL: Fuck you. Can't you see I'm watching Hogan's Heroes?

DUANE: Al, no, this is important. This is real trouble! Where's Sylvie?

AL: Down at the liquor store. Now chill your ass out. CHILL!

DUANE: Okay, Al. I'm calm, I'm calm. Calm as a clam. You got any potato chips?

AL: All gone, buddy. Now, what's the problem?

DUANE: Okay, remember that Beauty Shop we said we were gonna do sometime?

AL: Which shop?

DUANE: LaShonda's Beauty Emporium, on Pershing. Remember that?

AL: Ah, shit, we talked about that a year ago.

DUANE: Yeah, well, it's been naggin' me, Al, every fuckin' night for the past year. It's been a real bear, man.

AL: Oh no. I know what you're gonna tell me.

DUANE: I did it.

AL: Asshole!

DUANE: I did it! I did it! I did it, Al! I broke in, man! I busted the place!

AL: How?

DUANE: From the video store next door. I got in a side door and then kicked in the sheet rock between them.

El Paso Blue

AL: You robbed the Video Store too?

DUANE: No, man. Those poor fucks are goin' outa business.

AL: So how much did you take?

DUANE: How much did I take?

AL: The loot. Let's see the loot.

(Duane opens his bag. It is filled with hair care products, rollers, bobby pins, etc.)

DUANE: It was dark and the alarm went off. Tension ruled.

AL: You are one big weenie, Duane.

DUANE: What could I do? My plate set the alarm off! The world was screaming for me! The cops, everyone!

AL: You really piss me off! If you'd asked me, I mighta gone and helped your ass around the deal. Unlike some buttholes, I can tell the difference between wads of bills and hair rollers!

DUANE: I know, Al.

AL: I shoulda been there!

DUANE: You kinda were, Al.

AL: What do you mean? What the fuck you talkin' about?

DUANE: The leather jacket you loaned me?

AL: Yeah?

DUANE: 'Cause I left mine in a bar?

AL: Yeah?

DUANE: You got your name on the inside pocket, right?

AL: That's right. Duane, where's my jacket?

DUANE: That's what I'm saying. Say yes. When they show up, say yes and I swear to you on my mother's fuckin' grave it'll be cool. The jacket don't mean nothin'! Sure it's evidence but a good lawyer'll reduce it to shit!

AL: I'm gonna reduce you to shit!

DUANE: *(picking up the police radio)* [Unit 21, reports indicate robbery suspect has been sighted heading south on Mimosa Street, over-cgcgccg--]

AL: OH MAN!

DUANE: Please, Al! I can't go to jail! I'm on probation already.

AL: Duane...

DUANE: If they nail me, man, I go do the big time. I'm way too young to spend my life in prison. I'll die in there!

AL: Well, if you think I'm gonna take the fall for you--

DUANE: They got your jacket, Al.

AL: No way, ese! I'm clean, I'm married now! Sylvie and me are squaring up our deal real fine. I'm not gonna lose her now.

DUANE: You won' t lose her, Al.

AL: No.

DUANE: What do you mean, no?

AL: No means no.

DUANE: Al, you owe me. We're camaradas, and as camaradas we do for each other, we sacrifice.

AL: Yo no te debo ni madre, cabron!

DUANE: You owe me! I took that bullet in the head for you. When my old lady aimed that shotgun, you were morgue meat. But who came out and took it point blank in the head and saved your fucking life?

AL: You did.

DUANE: I gotta metal plate right here instead of bone. I can't watch TV on account of it fucks up the reception. I can't even rob a goddamn beauty store without setting off the alarm. I'm a disabled man, Al.

AL: I guess you are.

DUANE: I'm askin'. Do this one thing for me and I promise

I will be your own personal dog, full-time, 24-7.

AL: Duane, I don't want you to be my dog. Best friends don't treat each other like dogs. Best friends trade ratchet sets.

DUANE: Fuckin' A.

AL: Best friends eat off the same plate.

DUANE: Best friends lie for each other.

AL: They do what it takes.

DUANE: Pals trust each other!

AL: Amen.

DUANE: Listen, pal, don't worry about Sylvie. I'll take good care of her.

AL: If it's all the same to you, Duane, I think I'll find someone else.

Scenes For Three Or More

MÁS

Milta Ortiz

A community struggles to hold onto their history, identity, and humanity as they fight to save Mexican American Studies (MAS) in the Tucson Unified School District (TUSD). Based on over 400 pages of interview transcripts, Más is a streamlined word for word recounting of the movement to save the Mexican American Studies program at TUSD. The play takes an intimate look at the people at the center of the movement, and how mounting pressure from the State affected their relationships.

- **How do you identify yourself?**

    M. Ortiz: I'm a playwright/performer/poet/deviser. I also identify as Chicana, but Salvi is perhaps a better term since I am Salvadoran American. I'm an Americanized Salvadoran immigrant, who almost forgot that I wasn't born here. Working with immigrant youth as a teaching artist at Mission High School in San Francisco reminded me where I came from.

- **You describe the play as a docudrama; what does that mean to you?**

    M. Ortiz: The people who shared their stories with me are the heart and soul of this play, without them this play would not exist. The play is written with the words of the people that were involved. All names, except for public figures, have been changed. Think of it as a redemptive remembrance; reflection of the events that make up this story. The players who take on this text have a hand in shaping/focusing these remembrances through the use of music, movement, tableau, and other theatricality.

    (For more about the banning, www.pbs.org/independentlens/films/precious-knowledge/).

- **What does *Más* stand for?**

    M. Ortiz: The title is *Más* like the word más in Spanish. MAS (in all caps) is the acronym for Mexican American Studies and is said M-A-S. The title is a play on words or acronym in this case. We need *más*. More programs like these, more gender equity, more women in leadership roles, more empathy, *más*.

- **The actors clearly break the fourth wall. Do you**

have any suggestions as how they should handle their relationship to the audience?

M. Ortiz: They are both present in the scene and observing/reflecting upon themselves. The play takes place in the collective unconscious and they are stating their case to the audience, who is in the sweat lodge with them, in community with them. And they are stating their case to each other and themselves. When an actor asked me in the early stages of rehearsal for the world premiere, I said you are stating your case as only you can.

- **Where can we find the full text of the play?**

  M. Ortiz: It's on The New Play Exchange.

CHARACTERS
MAESTRO: A composite MAS teacher. Hip. Mid thirties.
VICTOR: Co-founder and co-director of MAS. Very Chicano. Mid-late thirties.
RUDY: Co-director of MAS. Wears polo shirts, more conventional, late thirties
LIBERTAD: a composite Mexican American Studies (MAS) female student. Starts off unsure of herself. High school junior.
JEN: A MAS alumna and Chicana feminist. Determined. Twenty-two

IN THIS SCENE
We meet characters in their element. Jen aka Muxerista sets up the redemptive remembrance. We meet the two founders and Maestro. We see Maestro in his classroom with his students. Time in this space, the collective unconscious is fluid.

[This scene has been modified for publication.]

ALL: Seven years of battling does something to people.
(All exit, except Jen who speaks to the bookstones.)
JEN: We thought we could change the world together. The state is the enemy. That kind of state violence, the millions of dollars and resources focused on destroying a community for so many years... leads to in-fighting and deep divisions in what was once a unified community. It's fucked up when the system's working against you, and hurting you. But it's worse when it's your own brother or sister.
(exits)

ASI FUE: HOW IT CAME TO BE

(Rudy enters. Victor follows holding sage and a large Abalone shell. Victor stands near the bookshelf- altar and puts the sage and shell on it.)
RUDY: The Mexican American Studies department, MAS is created in 1997. Ray Chavez becomes director in 2001.
VICTOR: I'm first to join Ray Chavez in 2001.
RUDY: At the end of that school year, The Tucson Unified School District, TUSD comes to get me, when Ray leaves for Harvard. In 2002, I set up what we call Redemptive Remembrance-- comes from Paulo Freire, the belief in the circle not the structure of one. We have the capacity to continuously redeem our humanity through the reflection upon our actions and equally important is how we reflect upon those actions. How do we change our actions as a method of re-humanizing ourselves? We do good things and we make mistakes, so what are

the good things we've done? What are the mistakes we've made?

(pause)

I hate the term professional development. I facilitate the education of our teachers, the Redemptive Remembrance sessions from 2002 until 2009. Teachers say this is better than going to church. We start collecting data and see the impact we're having. Not just what the kids and parents are telling us, we see it quantified in terms of these kids are kicking ass! Holy cow! This is awesome! I don't mean to get overly spiritual-- I call it the good work and for me that's code for God's work.

(pause)

For our parent/student outreach forums, we tell the students, hey man you got to get your parents here if you want them to see what's going on. This way the forums are student directed. Low and behold almost without exception they're standing room only. You put the Chicano twist on it, and start adding food-MMM- se cago!

(pause)

Educators number one responsibility is to instill as much hope as possible. It gives us purpose. It motivates us. It gives us vision. It gives us direction. It's my responsibility to provide that to our teachers, and they become the facilitators of hope.

(pause)

I get chills thinking about it. It's fucking everything, todo madre!

VICTOR: I teach MAS at a charter school on the south side. We start MAS there and then move to TUSD. I'm the first teacher there to teach a MAS class in '98. It's a history course. Then Maestro and I teach together. He has literature and I have the history component. Juniors. Then it develops and develops into a huge K through 12 component. Rudy and I start working together. Leading it.

(pause)

We encourage our students to go out in the community. Take a certain unit, Vietnam or World War two, lot of WWII veteranos. The students go and interview them, ask them what was your experience as a Xicano/Mexicano during the war. Then the students present in class, or for their parents, or in a community setting. So beautiful. MAS is really community based.

(pause)

Our classes are about curriculum as colonizer, and why, and these are the historical examples. We discuss social issues, like current day oppression and how it relates to our 500 plus years of colonization. We carry the students through the American historical experience, and where Xicanos are within those American historical experiences. Cause history's important. Cause we were here before the American historical experiences, during, and here we are now.

(Maestro enters.)

MAESTRO: They bring us together. I don't know whose idea it is... I call them Vicudys-- get it Victor and Rudy-- Cause they hang out together so much. The two of them must have bounced it off each other. I can assume from the dynamics of the personalities how it comes about...I don't want to project ...I mean... Victor's calmado and Rudy, he's a lil more amped up, so I have a feeling he bounced the idea off of Victor and Victor went... simon.

(pause)

We don't have that deficit mind-set towards our students... What eventually makes the core curriculum is our default setting/

ALL: the belief in the power of our youth.

MAESTRO: That passion. For our students to have that calidad, that quality education right now, is intoxicating.

(Victor wafts copal into the space. Rudy distances himself.)

VICTOR: You want to go to the sweat?

(Maestro gestures yes. Rudy exits.)

MAESTRO: I don't know what to expect. I go in there and the stones come in. Man, they're glowing red and then all of a sudden water's poured on and shhhh shhh/

VICTOR & MAESTRO: Tsh shhh Tsh shhh Tsh Tsh shhh.

MAESTRO: We're introduced to things that were part of our culture for thousands of years. I feel I've done this before.

(pause)

There's this concept in the Mexican culture, its called Tezcatlipoca,

MAESTRO: which is our memory and our memory is in our DNA. It was being able to look in the mirror and really see yourself, not with your eyes, with your heart.

We can never get Rudy to go. He says, you go into a sweat and pray, but what about God? *(judging)* That element of Catholicism...

IN LAK' ECH

(Libertad enters.)

MAESTRO: In Lak' Ech is the embodiment of MAS. Our guiding principle as we engage in the beautiful struggle that is learning and teaching.

MAESTRO: It is a Mayan phrase that translates to/
MAESTRO & LIBERTAD: You are my other me.
MAESTRO: Each day as class starts, my students and I recite a verse from the poem In Lak´ ech by playwright Luís Valdez.
MAESTRO: Tú eres mi otro yo.
LIBERTAD: You are my other me.
MAESTRO: Si te hago daño a ti,
LIBERTAD: If I do harm to you,
MAESTRO: Me hago daño a mi mismo.
LIBERTAD: I do harm to myself.
MAESTRO: Si te amo y respeto,
LIBERTAD: If I love and respect you,
MAESTRO: Me amo y respeto yo.
LIBERTAD: I love and respect myself.

(Maestro moves to his wheeled desk chair.)

LIBERTAD :*(to audience)* You know, that poem's banned for being racist.

SO MANY STORIES

(A concha is heard in lieu of a period bell.)
(Maestro sits in the wheeled desk chair and lesson plans.)

MAESTRO: We're all developing Chicanos. I work with Rudy for years and say, man I can't call myself a Chicano. A Chicano is an activist, a person who's done, whose doing, whose acting. It's a political state of mind, a certain consciousness, right? I haven't done anything to merit that label.

(pause)

It wasn't until after a year or two of teaching in MAS that I say, you know what, soy Chicano.

CLOCK

Monica Palacios

For a lesbian couple, becoming parents is a big decision, especially when one partner wants to, the other one is freaking out and everybody has an opinion including Leti the Goddess of Fertility.

(Photo credit: Sunny Bak)

- **How do you identify yourself?**

  M. Palacios: Queer Chicana, Writer/Performer, International Hip Chick.

- **You are widely recognized as working at the forefront of Chicana/Latina, queer, lesbian, feminist performance. Where is *Clock* in that trajectory?**

  M. Palacios: *Clock* comes from receiving a commission from the Latino Theatre Initiative of the Center Theatre Group of Los Angeles. I could have written another one-person play but I wanted to challenge myself and write a multi-character play. At that time in my life, my friends were having babies and I was trying to figure out if I wanted to have a baby with my partner. *Clock* is a result of facts and fiction and many moments of familia.

- **You are also known as a stand-up comedian; do you have any suggestions on how the actors might approach the comedy of the scene?**

  M. Palacios: The comedy is fully present in the dialogue so go with the flow and have fun.

- **Where can we find the full text of the play?**

  M. Palacios: NewPlayExchange.org

CHARACTERS

ANGEL DEL MAR: Late 30s, Chicana. Loyal, loving. Can get a tad bit neurotic. Speaks perfect English and Spanish and does not have an accent. *(The name Angel is pronounced in English by everyone except Angel's mother.)*

MARIBEL GAITAN: Late 30s, Chicana, attractive, long dark hair, sensual. Angel's wife who is a no nonsense gal and the calm one in the relationship. Speaks perfect English and Spanish and does not have an accent.

TANIA DEL MAR: 45, Angel's sister, Chicana. She's goofy but smart, animated, and a single mother of a 15 year old boy. Not alcoholic despite her references to booze. Speaks perfect English and Spanish and does not have an accent.

NOTE: In the play notes, the playwright requests that Spanish names and words be pronounced correctly.

IN THIS SCENE

San Jose. The couple has come to the home of Angel's mother Graciela, to celebrate Mother's Day. The night before their Sunday brunch, Tania and Maribel are sitting on the guest bed acting silly, talking openly about sex. Receiving too much information, Graciela leaves the room and Angel, not wanting to upset her mother, runs after her assuring her the women are joking. Angel walks back into the room.

TANIA: You're so uptight. What's going on with you?
MARIBEL: I told her your mom doesn't care.
TANIA: *(jokingly)* Why mother is embracing of all lesbians.

ANGEL: I don't want us talking like that around my mom--OK?

TANIA: Oh, now it's my mom. She always says, "my mom, my dad, my this, my that!" You're so possessive.

Maribel shakes her head yes.

MARIBEL: Tell me about it.

ANGEL: I am not.

TANIA: You never say our mother, our dog, our...hostages--

ANGEL: Maribel, how can you agree with her when it's not true?

MARIBEL: Pretty girl, come here.

She extends her hand to Angel but Tania grabs it and pulls Maribel off the bed and twirls her around as if they were at a sock hop. Tania twirls her way towards Angel, but Miss Party Pooper just stands there while Maribel dances her way back onto the bed.

TANIA: You're a downer, man.

MARIBEL: Oh she's tripping because of our announcement tomorrow.

Angel shoots Maribel a hard look.

TANIA: What's the big secret? Those aren't your real boobs? You actually like Taco Bell? Your sex tape went viral? What? Tell me! Please!

Angel continues to stare at her mate as she answers Tania.

ANGEL: *(curtly)* It's nothing, Tania. You'll find out tomorrow at brunch with everybody else.

MARIBEL: Tell her, Angel.

ANGEL: I don't want to tell her!

TANIA: Oh, tell me, please. I love it when I get told a secret--

(enjoying sensation) It feels so nasty. *(continues enjoyment)*

ANGEL: God, Tania, get a room!

MARIBEL: Angel, stop being a butt and tell your sister we're going to get pregnant!

ANGEL: ARRRGH!!!

She plops herself at the foot of the bed and places her head in her hands. Maribel quickly rushes to her side.

TANIA: Wow--the both of you are going to get pregnant at the same time?! Ahhh mazing!

MARIBEL & ANGEL: Nooo!

MARIBEL: We're going to have a baby *(arms around Angel)* and I'm getting pregnant.

ANGEL: *(face in hands)* I wish you hadn't told her, Maribel!

TANIA: Pregnant--wow, you lesbians are sooo progressive. I'm ah...I'm, I'm surprised. I never thought you guys--I mean "ladies" wanted a child. I know you mentioned it from time to time. But I just didn't think—not that I believe you're incapable of producing children--because anybody can produce a kid. Hey, we're cloning sheep--so it's no big deal. But ah...congratulations? Yeah, yes, congratulations!

Tania attempts to hug them but Angel is not responding to her.

MARIBEL: Thanks, Tania, I knew you would understand.

TANIA: Sis, look at me.

ANGEL: I can't. I'm traumatized!

Maribel kisses Angel's ear.

MARIBEL: Angel, I'm sorry I blurted it out but it's a good thing she knows now. Less pressure for us, babe.

With her eyes, Maribel instructs Tania to be supportive.

TANIA: Yes, good thing. Of...course...a fantastic thing. Letting it out is...ah...glorious sensation, Angel. It's cleansing. It's pure. It's...it's....Joni Mitchell.

(pause) That's all I could think of.

Angel looks up at her sister.
ANGEL: Thanks--appreciate it.
TANIA: Look, I'm being supportive. *(jumps on bed)* Little mothers! Que cute! Do you want to borrow my turkey baster? It's never been used.
MARIBEL: Thanks, Tania, but we have selected our "alternative insemination process". But do keep the baster for us as our back up.
ANGEL: The turkey baster is a myth. It's insemination lore.
TANIA: Remember Cata who lived across the street from me?
The couple nod yes.
TANIA: Well the daddy of her first child was a turkey baster.
ANGEL: Tania, in our Lesbians Considering Parenting Workshop, the first thing they told us was to save our turkey baster for Thanksgiving. Maybe Cata said the guy was a "turkey bastard".
TANIA: Hmmm--maybe she did. *(pause)* So are you two going to have the guy shoot into a cup or a bucket?
MARIBEL: Tania, did you just drink a six-pack?
ANGEL: We didn't find some random guy in a porno shop. This is a very serious process.
MARIBEL: Yes, it took us a while to find this vegetarian Chicano who likes mariachi music and jazz.
TANIA: Sounds like a personal ad--can I meet him?
MARIBEL: No but our child can once she's reached 18. We paid extra to see his donor statement. You get to find out more about his life. You know, what his mother's like—does she eat waffles, does she wear pumps, etc.
TANIA: Does she? Or doesn't she?
MARIBEL: Only her hairdresser knows for sure.
ANGEL: I'm feeling violated and you two are acting like

school girls.

MARIBEL: Babe, we're just having a little fun. Isn't it great that Tania is not freaked out because of the news?

TANIA: I haven't puked. That's a good sign. Wait until Dolores hears about this--she might.

ANGEL: I told Maribel, Dolores and mom are not going to get it.

TANIA: Yeah, they're going to shake their heads a lot but so what. This is about you--not them.

MARIBEL: Thanks, Tania. That's what I keep telling Miss Thing here, but she isn't listening.

ANGEL: I am listening. You're not listening--telling them is going to be difficult!

TANIA: Then don't tell them! You two should disappear for a few years and have the baby. I'll tell them you guys were abducted by the student loan people.

ANGEL: Clever.

TANIA: *(annoyed)* And anyway, stop being mama's little girl!

ANGEL: Shut up--I am not!

La Gringa
Carmen Rivera

La Gringa* is about a young woman's search for her identity. Maria Elena Garcia goes to visit her family in Puerto Rico during the Christmas holidays and arrives with plans to connect with her homeland. Although this is her first trip to Puerto Rico, she has had an intense love for the island, and even majored in Puerto Rican Studies in college. Once Maria is in Puerto Rico, she realizes that Puerto Rico does not welcome her with open arms. The majority of the Puerto Ricans on the island consider her an American – a gringa – and Maria considers this a betrayal. If she's a Puerto Rican in the United States and an American in Puerto Rico, Maria concludes that she is nobody everywhere. Her uncle, Manolo, spiritually teaches her that identity isn't based on superficial and external definitions, but rather is an essence that she has had all along in her heart.

*(La Gringa is the longest running Spanish language play ever to run off-Broadway.)

- **How do you identify yourself?**

  C. Rivera: A New York Born Puerto Rican / New Yorker / American / Latinx Boricua. I feel I cannot select just one "box" to live in.

- **The play tackles the themes of identity and belonging. What makes the character of Maria relevant today?**

  C. Rivera: With the popularity of DNA kits and tv shows like "Finding Your Roots", the of idea "identity" and finding one's place is as popular as ever. People want a connection to the past, to place, to ancestors. *La Gringa* deals with that search. Throughout the years, I've met many people who have connected with Maria's search for her roots – people from all backgrounds and countries. But, given the increasing tension and political divisions in the United States and how the antagonism has focused specifically on Latinx immigration, I feel we are discussing more and more the idea of Latinx identity and citizenship. We -- as an American People -- are still dealing with becoming American; what does it mean to be American and who is truly American. Latina(o)s born and raised in this country face an added challenge – we're not considered American enough nor are we Hispanic enough. We (I include myself) are always being considered the other – we are living in a no man's land – a sort of Hispanic "Checkpoint Charlie" – "Checkpoint Carlos" if you will. In *La Gringa,* I posit that the individual person has every right to claim her/his identity, regardless of external definitions and categories…a life experience that cannot and should ever be defined by checking a box.

- **Can you illuminate the relationship between Manolo and Maria?**

    C. Rivera: I studied the archetypical Mentor / Nascent Hero relationship found in the wonderful book *The Cry for Myth* by Rollo May -- Manolo is the Mentor and Maria is the Nascent Hero (Shero). He teaches her, that what she was looking for, was in her all along.

- **Where can we find the full text of the play in both English and Spanish?**

    C. Rivera: Samuel French for both English and Spanish, or my website: www.carmenrivera-writer.com

CHARACTERS
MARIA: 22 year-old Puerto Rican woman born and raised in New York City.
IRIS: 24, her cousin.
NORMA: Maria's aunt, Iris' mother, Manolo's sister.
MANOLO: Uncle, has terminal cancer.

IN THIS SCENE
This scene takes place at the top of the second act. Maria, the protagonist, returns from a job interview, revealing that she wasn't hired because she isn't a Puerto Rican "National." Maria and her extended family then get into an argument about what defines a real Puerto Rican and what does that means for Puerto Ricans, living in the diaspora?

(Norma and Iris are waiting for Maria.)

IRIS: ... Do you think she'll get the job?

NORMA: She studied business.

IRIS: Y la gringa comes here and gets the job she wants. If this situation continues, I'm going to New York.

NORMA: And where are you going to stay? With Olga?! She'll throw you out as soon as you get there. She took Mami away from me, she's not going to get you. Olga just picked up and left to New York City, just as we were dealing with your grandfather's death.

IRIS: Mami, she left for economic reasons.

NORMA: It's true, we were poor, but we survived. She didn't have to go to New York.

IRIS: I am sure Tía didn't want to abandon her family to go to a strange country.

NORMA: As soon as she had the chance to leave Puerto Rico, she left. We needed her here, not in New York. But that's how Olga is. When your abuela died, Olga wanted to bury her in Rincón, where her family is from. I wanted to bury her near our house. Ah Dios mío, ¿para qúe fue eso? Olga called crying, she said mami wanted to be with her family in Rincón, not here. I told her to mind her business, since she lives over there in New York.

IRIS: Mami, maybe that's what Abuela wanted.

NORMA: So you think that Olga, who lives in another part of the world, knew what Abuela wanted better than me?

IRIS: I'm just saying that it's logical that she wanted to be buried with the rest of her family.

NORMA: I'm also her family.

IRIS: I'm not saying that. I understand Abuela's desire to be with her brothers and sisters.

NORMA: So I was wrong?

IRIS: No, mami, I . . .

NORMA: Your Tía Olga came for the funeral and with all of her money had her moved to Rincon. I'll never forgive her. I was so mad at her I didn't let her step foot in this house. And then she gets mad at me.

IRIS: I don't blame her. This is the family house.

NORMA: Olga doesn't think like that. She told me that this house is hers, she paid for it with the money she made working in New York and that if she wanted to she'd throw us out and then sell the house.

IRIS: She can't do that. Abuela put in her will that the house can't be sold, only passed down through the family.

NORMA: Olga doesn't understand family . . . She paid for the house, but I built it with my own sweat and blood. I told her to go to hell and that as soon as I can I will pay her back every single penny she sent to us! Olga thinks I'm stupid.

IRIS: Mami, Tía Olga is not that way.

NORMA: You don't know her the way I do. And now Maria...first, she wants to go to the cemetery to see Abuela, knowing that it will annoy me...and all these pictures she's taking of the house are not to show her friends how beautiful Puerto Rico is...they're for Olga, who wants to come back to Puerto Rico and live in the house . . . she's going to have a fight on her hands. I'm NOT leaving!!

(Maria enters crying.)

MARIA: Iris, thank you for the use of your dress, I'll give it back to you as soon as I clean it.

IRIS: Don't worry about it.

(Maria exits. Manolo enters.)

NORMA: Manolo, what happened?

MANOLO: Ay Dios mio! She's a mess.//
IRIS: What happened?!
MANOLO: The guy who interviewed her told her she can't work there because she's not a Puerto Rican national. Para que fue eso?! She left the office crying. Monchi and I took her to the beach to cheer her up. She wouldn't get out of the car.
IRIS: I told her it wasn't easy to get a job in Puerto Rico.
(Maria re-enters with her jacket with the Puerto Rican flag.)
MANOLO: Sh!
MARIA: Iris, I promise I'll clean your dress.
MANOLO: Maria don't let people tell you who you are!
MARIA: He said I wasn't a Puerto Rican.
IRIS: But you are American.
MARIA: *(to Manolo.)* You see?
MANOLO: She's Puerto Rican.
MARIA: Here's the flag of your country!! *(She throws her jacket on the floor.)*
IRIS: Tio Manolo, she's American!
MARIA: In New York City I was hired as the token Puerto Rican!
IRIS: You were born and raised in America, so you're American.
MARIA: You're born and raised in an American colony. Does that make you a gringa?!
IRIS: I was born here in Puerto Rico! And your first language is English, you are AMERICAN!
MANOLO: Speaking Spanish doesn't make you Puerto Rican.
MARIA: I'm not accepted in America . . . There is no place for me!! I am a foreigner in my place of birth. I am

La Gringa

exotic, I am from the island, I'm an immigrant who's taking American jobs away from the Americans, I am a welfare burden on America!!! A Spic!

IRIS: If your mother had moved to France, and if you were raised there speaking only French, you would be French.

MANOLO: If a cat gives birth in an oven, what is born, kitten or bread?

IRIS: That has nothing to do with what we're talking about!

MANOLO: Divide and conquer . . . united we stand, divided we fall . . .you're helping the powers that be keep us apart. If the Puerto Ricans all over the world united, our culture would never die.

IRIS: Then we should accept every gringo as a Puerto Rican?!

MARIA: Stop calling me a gringa . . . can't you get that through your head, jíbara?!

IRIS: Me, Jíbara?! Jíbaro is that plátano boyfriend of yours.

MARIA: I'm Puerto Rican enough to be dumped by Peter.

IRIS: Who?

MANOLO: The now-defunct boyfriend.

MARIA: Who dumped me because I am Puerto Rican, not a GRINGA. First, I'm rejected by Peter, then by my own people.

IRIS: I'm only saying the truth.

MANOLO: The truth is that she's Puerto Rican. She really wants to know about Puerto Rico, most people in Puerto Rico don't care about Puerto Rico.

IRIS: Just because somebody read a book on Puerto Rico doesn't mean that they're Puerto Rican . . . but she comes down here thinking that she can just stake her claim in Puerto Rico like all the rest of the Americans.

MANOLO: She does have a claim to a part of this island.

IRIS: Not on my island!

MARIA: I came down here to bond with my island, my people, my family . . . I never expected that they would stab me in the back.

IRIS: You can't expect to abandon Puerto Rico and then take it back when you want.

MARIA: I didn't abandon Puerto Rico.

IRIS: Your family left Puerto Rico.

MARIA: My parents left Puerto Rico to find work . . . believe me they didn't want to leave Puerto Rico.

IRIS: Well, when they left the island, they gave up the rights to the island.

MANOLO: If that were really true, there would be no Puerto Rico left! Puerto Ricans were taken all over the world to work, hasta Hawaii. Those people had kids, and they had kids who are still Puerto Rican.

IRIS: No they're not! They have no connection to Puerto Rico.

MARIA: God forbid those Puerto Rican-Hawaiians should want to connect with Puerto Rico . . . they'll be kicked right in their ass.

IRIS: OH, how beautiful you speak ...you live in New York, with a great job, why do you want to be here?

MARIA: Because this is a part of who I am.

MANOLO: Iris what are you protecting? You don't care about Puerto Rican culture. You only buy American things, clothes, food; you don't want to take her around, "I saw it before...it's boring..." According to you our culture is boring. She loves our culture, the history, the music . . . she looking for her roots, you can not say NO to her!

La Gringa

IRIS: Ah no, *(To Maria.)* NO!!

MARIA: Well, YES!.

MANOLO: Maria doesn't have to be born in Puerto Rico to be Puerto Rican. She will always be BORICUA. Discussion over.

IRIS: Well you're wrong!

MARIA: Fine! If I'm not Puerto Rican then we're not family and I'm the unwelcome guest in a stranger's house.

IRIS: You said it, I didn't.

MANOLO: You *(to Maria)* belong here, in your house. This house is for the whole family.

IRIS: Manolo, please, this has nothing with the house.

MANOLO: Of course it does, Maria has every right to be in this house, just like Olga.

NORMA: Olga will never step foot in my house!

MANOLO: Without Olga there's would be no house.

NORMA: We built it.

MANOLO: With her money.

NORMA: Our blood, our sweat built this house! Olga doesn't know anything about pain and suffering.

MARIA: The money that mami and papi sent back is full of their blood and sweat. You think they had it easy? They worked 12 hours a day, two jobs each. New York isn't for lazy people.

MANOLO: Mami left this house to the whole family, the whole family Norma!

NORMA: Don't raise you voice in MY house! Now go downstairs.

MANOLO: …Okay… I'll leave, not because you threw me out, but because I am pissed off!!
(Manolo exits. Lights fade.)

MISS QUINCE

Cynthia Santos-DeCure

An Americanized Puerto Rican woman walks into a quinceañera dress shop on her 45th birthday, demanding to have the rite of passage she never had as a teen. The women who work in the shop believe this woman must be crazy, but because the business is struggling financially, they agree to help her, even selling the dress meant for the shop owner's own fourteen-year old daughter. Throughout the course of the play, each of the women take center-stage and, standing on a dress pedestal, magically recall moments from their own quinceañeras, helping the shop women understand why Soledad needs to reconnect with her roots via this ritual. When the shop owner's teen returns to find that her dress was sold to this wealthy woman, Soledad is forced to reveal the real reason she now wants a quinceañera. This is a play about identity, transformation and forgiveness.

- **How do you identify yourself?**

    C. Santos-DeCure: Puerto Rican— raised on the island and now part of the Diaspora.

- **What drew you to the theme of quinceañeras?**

    C. Santos-DeCure: I was drawn to the ritual of the quinceañera because it is something that can be traced back to indigenous rituals. Rituals connect us to our culture. I did a lot of research writing the play, and was inspired by Gloria Anzaldúa and the concept of "nepantla," which she described as transformations that occur in "liminal spaces, between worlds."[1] I saw the quinceañera as a moment of transformation, and the character of Soledad as someone caught between worlds—desperate to reconnect with her roots. The quinceañera became the dramatic conduit for transformation, to reclaim and to affirm identity in the play.

- **Soledad is in crisis in this scene. Why have these identity issues come up now?**

    C. Santos-DeCure: Soledad is a mom who has put her own hopes and dreams on a shelf for the sake of her family. You can say she's having a "midlife crisis," but it's more: a crisis of her Latina identity, and the feeling she's denied the true essence of who she is as an artist, and as a Puertoriqueña. Soledad has put herself last in line, but now, at 45, she wants to reclaim all that. She wants to turn back the clock to that moment, at 15 years old, when she could have affirmed her Latina identity. What did she compromise for a better life?

---

[1] Gloria Anzaldúa - This Bridge We Call Home.

- **The women have three different Latinx heritages. What do they have in common?**

    C. Santos-DeCure: Latinidad. I wanted to bring these women from different Latinx heritages together to affirm our collective identity, our community—our Latinidad. Each of the women in the play is important because of how they uniquely cope with the many challenges facing Latinas today. The women ultimately understand the symbolic importance of the quinceañera for Soledad— at any age. They affirm that it's never too late to reclaim your identity and your dreams, and place yourself center stage.

- **Where can we find the full text of the play?**

    C. Santos-DeCure: The play can be found on the New Play Exchange.

CHARACTERS
SOLEDAD "SALLY": Puerto Rican, 45, an artist, wife and mom on the edge.
ELIZA: A sexy Salvadorean, late 20's's, judgmental, works in the shop.
BLANCA: A religious, older, Mexican (Aztec Nahuatl-speaking) indigenous woman, a healer, works in the shop.

IN THIS SCENE
In Carmen's Quinceañera and Bridal Party Shop. One spring day in a U.S. city. Soledad has chosen her quinceañera dress – and is waiting for it to be fitted. She is beginning to drink the champagne from her "deluxe package" quinceañera party. A pedestal sits center stage.

NOTE: Nahuatl words appear in Italics.

(Soledad is sitting in a chair. The dress is gone and all that's there is the center pedestal it was placed on. Eliza brings the champagne, pours and hands it to Soledad, who drinks it in one gulp.)

ELIZA: Are you sure you don't want something else? Maybe you need to eat something with that. The restaurant across the street – we order the food from them. The have the best frijoles...

SOLEDAD: No, thank you. I don't like beans.

ELIZA: You don't? Oh...kay.

SOLEDAD: I'm fine. The champagne will do.

(Soledad refills it and drinks more.)

ELIZA: Bueno, the cake will do.

SOLEDAD: Excuse me?

ELIZA: The samples of cake. I can get you samples. We order all our cakes from the bakery across the street. They are very good.

SOLEDAD: What's their best?

ELIZA: Well, I like the chocolate. But that's me.

SOLEDAD: I don't like it.

ELIZA: Their most popular is the vanilla with lemon filling. They say it's the best.

(Eliza points out the photos of cakes in the binder.)

SOLEDAD: Yes. *(pointing at one)* This one. I want the best.

(Soledad refills her glass and pours another and hands it to Eliza, who reluctantly takes it.)

ELIZA: *(toasting glasses)* Happy Birthday!

SOLEDAD: Thanks.

ELIZA: *(she sips)* Sally, right?

SOLEDAD: Soledad.

ELIZA: I like that name, Soledad.

SOLEDAD: I don't. I always thought it was filled with sadness.

ELIZA: Oh, no, it beautiful. And Soledad can be a good thing, trust me. Sometimes you discover a lot of things when you're in solitude-- especially about yourself.

SOLEDAD: Yes.

ELIZA: You don't have any children? You said earlier...

SOLEDAD: I have two boys.

ELIZA: Boys. Are you're gonna try for the girl?

SOLEDAD: *(a beat)* No, I did.

ELIZA: Oh. Sorry. I didn't mean... At least you have your boys.

SOLEDAD: Yes. They're big now, 16 and 17. They don't need me.

ELIZA: Boys always need their mother. *(Pause)* Anyway, you're still young.

SOLEDAD: I'm 45.

ELIZA: *(reacting)* Really? You don't look it. You look great.

SOLEDAD: Thank you. But I'm not 15.

ELIZA: Yes, we know... *(changing the subject)* But it doesn't mean you can't have a quinceañera dress, right?

SOLEDAD: You don't understand. I don't just want the dress. I want it all-- the ceremony, the favors, the music, all of it.

ELIZA: Today?

SOLEDAD: Yes, today.

ELIZA: At 45?

SOLEDAD: Yes, now. I waited a long time.

ELIZA: You didn't have one back when you were 15?

SOLEDAD: No. I didn't.

(The bottle of champagne is empty.)

ELIZA: A pues...

SOLEDAD: *(defensive)* It's not my fault.

(Blanca enters with measuring tape.)

BLANCA: I take your sizes. *(Pointing to pedestal)* You stand here.

(Lights change. Soledad crosses to the pedestal and Blanca helps her stand on it. She touches Soledad's shoulders. Soledad feels a chill. Soledad speaks directly to the audience. Coquí sounds can be heard in the background. Light floods the pedestal.)

SOLEDAD: *(feeling the champagne)* I was fourteen... I dreamed of it. A beautiful dress. A tiara. A blessing. The waltz with my father, the high-heeled shoes. But then everything changed. *(Remembering)* "Mami, why do we have to move away? I don't know anyone there... I don't want leave. What about Papi? A divorce?" *(Reacting to the coquí sounds)* Can you hear that?

ELIZA: What?

(Soledad steps off the pedestal and the sound stops. Lights change back to reality. Soledad looks around.)

SOLEDAD: That sound. Coquís. Thought I heard...never mind. They can only sing in Puerto Rico.

(Soledad gulps another glass of champagne.)

ELIZA: You're from Puerto Rico. I could tell when you walked in.

SOLEDAD: You could?

ELIZA: You said quinceañero. That's what you call it in Puerto Rico, right?

(Soledad nods and smiles. Eliza signals to Blanca.)

BLANCA: I need sizes for dress. I help you.

(Soledad stands beside the pedestal. As Blanca measures her, she is also examining her with her curandera powers.)

BLANCA: You lift your arms. *(She measures the bust)*

Trenta y cuatro. *(To Eliza)* Pues, esta es tan flaquita.
ELIZA: Y un poco tostada también.
BLANCA: Un corazon roto. *Yolokuakuatotl.* I do your waist. *(She measures)* Veinte y siete. (*Eliza writes*) Está vacía. *(to Soledad)* You skinny.
ELIZA: Yes, and you have two boys? You work out a lot, I bet.
(Blanca measures the length from the waist to the floor.)
SOLEDAD: They keep me busy. Sometimes I forget to eat.
ELIZA: Oh, I forget lots of things, but I never forget to eat.
BLANCA: You got to eat. *Tlakua.* Feed yourself.
(The cell phone rings again. Soledad ignores it. Blanca continues to measure the hips.)
BLANCA: Treinta y seis.
(Eliza writes.)
ELIZA: *(To Blanca)* No lo contesta. ¿De quien piensas se esta escondiendo?
BLANCA: Pos, quien sabe.
SOLEDAD: It's my husband.
ELIZA: *(startled)* Oh, I'm sorry. I didn't know you spoke Spanish. No sabía. You don't have an accent, I just assumed... I'm sorry, it's not my business...
SOLEDAD: He's calling because I left him.
ELIZA: Disculpe. Sorry, I didn't mean anything by that.
SOLEDAD: It's fine.
(beat)
ELIZA: What happened? *(no answer)* You know, I lived with this Venezolano and he couldn't get his... *(gestures).*
SOLEDAD: No, no, that's not why.
BLANCA: Pobrecita, you married a guerito, verdad? Pos, ya lo sabía!
(Soledad looks at Blanca.)

361

ELIZA: --Blanca!

BLANCA: I finish.

(Eliza hands her the notebook with the written measurements and Blanca smiles and exits.)

ELIZA: Blanca talks too much. She's an indigenous woman from Mexico. One day she just showed up, told Carmen that she had a dream about the shop and how much Carmen needed her so she came. She embroiders beautifully, so naturally Carmen took her in. Something about passing on the Aztec spirit. I think she's a bit of a *(whispering)*... bruja.

SOLEDAD: I like her. She sees things.

ELIZA: She sees things alright. She walks around talking to the dresses as if they were women. She prays for these dresses. Every single one of them. She's been doing that since she got here.

SOLEDAD: Really? How long ago was that?

ELIZA: Let me think... she got here right after Lucy was born. Lucy is Carmen's daughter. That's almost fifteen years ago. Blanca's always seeing things.

SOLEDAD: She guessed right. My husband, he's white.

ELIZA: Guero? Oh. *(beat)* What did he do? Did he cheat on you?

SOLEDAD: No, he just--

ELIZA: --My ex-husband was from Panamá, and he cheated on me, lots of times. Ese 'ijo e puta thought he was a Mormon, he had so many women!

SOLEDAD: He just forgot about me.

(Soledad is now feeling the liquor.)

ELIZA: That's it? I mean, he didn't beat you or cheat on you?

SOLEDAD: He might as well have. He's so selfish. All about him. His career, what he wants. His status. He did not want a daughter. He's "relieved."

ELIZA: Oh.

SOLEDAD: *(loud)* Why not? I gave up a lot for him. Do you know I even stopped speaking Spanish. I never taught my boys Spanish. All they ever heard me say was--- *(trying to spit out the word)* Coño!

ELIZA: Ohhh-kay.

SOLEDAD: Became this... "Sally Jenkins." I put my career on hold. You know, when I met him, I was called an "up and coming" artist, a painter.

(Soledad open another bottle of champagne and quickly pours another glass and gulps.)

ELIZA: You're an artist?

SOLEDAD: I thought I was.

(Soledad crosses to the chair and gets a newspaper article and a small painting out of her bag. It is the Virgen de la Providencia surrounded by the Virgen de Guadalupe illuminating rays. A mixture of the two.)

ELIZA: You did that? Wow, it's beautiful.

(Soledad reads from the newspaper article as Eliza examines the painting.)

SOLEDAD: "Ms. Jenkins pretends to understand the heart and essence of the Latina-Chicana experience. However, her paintings merely offer an outsider's view. They bear no authenticity." Ouch!

ELIZA: Critics? Don't listen to them. They don't know anything. This is good. You have talent. But... (looking at the painting) I can see why they said that.

SOLEDAD: What? You? How?

ELIZA: This painting is signed by Sally Jenkins. Sally Jenkins? You don't identify yourself as a Latina, and well... that's what we call a "vendida."

SOLEDAD: A vendida? Really? A sellout!?

ELIZA: A Latina, but one who doesn't claim it. *(looking at the painting again)* People looking at it... they probably think you're, what's it called... appropriating? They don't know--

SOLEDAD: ---You're right, critics don't know shit! No matter what I call myself. Most of them haven't painted anything themselves.

ELIZA: Sorry, I'm just saying what I see.

SOLEDAD: *(defensive)* Well, I paint what I see...

ELIZA: Maybe you should paint what's inside of you, that's real.

SOLEDAD: *(feeling the liquor even more)* Real? I spent years taking care of the house and the kids— everything for other people. I stopped dreaming for myself.

(Soledad tries to pour more champagne but spills a little.)

ELIZA: Cuidado.

SOLEDAD: ...then one day you look in the mirror and you don't recognize who you've become... I don't even know what's real. *(She stumbles and regains her balance)* I'm sorry, may I use your bathroom?

ELIZA: Through that door, at the end of the hall on the left.

(Soledad exits.)

ELIZA: Ay, ya se vomita esa loca.

Momma's Boyz

Cándido Tirado

A humorous, dark, but ultimately uplifting look at what happens when a young man turns back the hands of time to save the life of his friend from the violence of dealing drugs.

- **How do you identify yourself?**

    C. Tirado: First of all, as one who gazes at the stars, and who's trying to understand his short time here on earth. As it comes to geographical boundaries; I'm Puerto Rican, born in Puerto Rico. As for my secondary boundary, here in the United States, I consider myself Latino. Latinx. And whatever might come which will define my status best in the future.

- **This piece has been described as a triumph of the 'urban theatre' genre. What does that mean to you?**

    C. Tirado: I think because in this piece I show the humanity, complexity and innocence of the "urban youth," to a people who've only seen these characters as stereotypes in some TV show or movie.

- **What insights would you give the actors about Mimic, Thug and Shine's relationship?**

    C. Tirado: These are three good friends, who grew up together, but who have different ways of looking at the word. At this juncture in their lives they are beginning to drift apart. Their personal interests and philosophies are causing that separation. In this scene Mimic has taken Thug to watch a play, but more importantly he wants him to expand his horizons. Mimic has taken Thug out of his comfort zone - "the projects" - their neighborhood. Thug acted like an asshole with Mimic's "actor" friends. Mimic is disappointed and angry at Thug, who's trying to annoy Mimic by poking fun at his newly found world of theater. Shine, who at first is upset because he's had to wait for them, becomes the amused arbiter in this scene. Does he take Mimic's side or Thug's?

- **Where can we find the full text of the play?**

  C. Tirado: NoPassport Press: *Nuestras Voces – Latino Plays From Repertorio Español's MetLife Playwriting Competition.*

  CHARACTERS
  MIMIC: Age 19, smart, sharp, funny. Slim. He wants to be a movie star. He doesn't like selling drugs and isn't very committed to it. He does it just to be with his friends, Shine and Thug. Mimic represents the "heart" in the play.
  THUG: Age 19, aggressive, funny, acts dumb but he has common sense. Physically strong. He might lift weights. He dreams of becoming Tony Montana from Scarface. Thug represents the "body" in the play.
  SHINE: Age 19. Playful, smart, tough. He can't let things go – that may be his tragic flaw. He's a bit on the heavy side. He's the best businessman in the group. He has dreams of becoming a Rap tycoon like Jay-Z. He represents the "mind" in the play.

  IN THIS SCENE
  Shine, Mimic and Thug are best friends who decided to deal drugs to make extra cash. In this scene, Shine is waiting for Mimic and Thug to return from the theater so he can turn their drug corner over to them.

(Shine is on his cell phone. Mimic and Thug, who's eating potato chips from a bag and laughing at a furious Mimic, enter.)
SHINE: There they come. Finally!... I'll be leaving in a few. I have to give Mimic and Thug the lowdown... Fuck no, I ain't hanging up. Shit they made me wait. Now they have to wait for me.
(Mimic and Thug enter. They're in a middle of an argument.)
THUG: Don't ever ask me to go with you again.
MIMIC: You don't have to worry about that. Why did you have to act like my sister's two-year old?
THUG: I don't know what you're talking about.
MIMIC: I take you to see a play and you act like you've never been out of the projects. Thug, you know what you are? A project Hillbilly!
THUG: At least I knows my place.
MIMIC: What the fuck is that supposed to mean?
THUG: You from the projects and you go downtown to hang with actors and shit. Look around. You belong here.
MIMIC: Yo, I belong where I say I belong, dog. Nobody is cutting me down. Especially not you!
THUG: Mimic, get this through that big head of yours, those actors wannabee only let you hang with them because you got money and their broke ass don't. That's the only reason.
MIMIC: I can't wait when the day finally comes that you become a human being. Eating potato chips and peanuts in the theater. We weren't at a baseball game, dumb ass. You know how much noise cracking peanuts open make in a theater?

THUG: At least I didn't have to listen to that stupid play.
MIMIC: This is what I get for trying to open that little close mind of yours. There's a big world out there. This ain't all there is, ya feel me?
THUG: You worries 'bout you. I worries 'bout me.
(Thug throws potato chips bag on the ground.)
MIMIC: Pick that shit up. This is our block.
THUG: I don't work for no sanitation department.
(Shine hangs phone.)
SHINE: (to Mimic) Ya, mad late! Mimic, you knew I was waiting for you to get back. And you know that Jazmin is stressing me 'bout dealing. And ya make it worse by showing up late. And yo, it's been deadass dead out here as if all of a sudden, all the Crack Heads went on a crack holiday! The merchandise is right there in the garbage can. Almost the whole stash. So, what took ya so long?
THUG: Yo, we could've been here sooner. Way sooner if it was up to me. Blame your boy right here.
MIMIC: My bad, Shine. The cast wanted to go out to eat and they invited me. I couldn't say no. They're all in my acting class.
THUG: Dig this, Shine. They went to eat in this rat hole with no real food. I ask for a burger and when I bit into it I almost threw up. What kind of meat was that?
MIMIC: I've told you a hundred times it wasn't meat. It was tofu.
THUG: You hear that Shine? The motherfuckers eat toe-food. It tasted like toe jam.
MIMIC: How do you know how toe jam taste like? I bet he eats his toe jam.

(to Shine) It was a vegetarian restaurant. I'll take you

sometime. Good food.

THUG: Yo, what kind of animal is tofu? I never heard of it.

MIMIC: It's soybean, dumb ass.

THUG: Like I said - never heard of it!

MIMIC: Soybean! You never heard of soybean?

THUG: So, dig, Shine. I went to Mickey Dees and got me a triple quarter pounder with cheese and ate it in front of the faces of the toe food eating actors, right Mimic.

SHINE: Damn! That shit is ghetto, Thug!

THUG: That's how I dos. Yo, I just wanted them to know what they was missing. Yo, yo, I'm glad I'm back here at the projects where everything is normal.

MIMIC: Ignore him!

SHINE: So how was the play?

THUG: *(doesn't let Mimic answer)* That's another thing. I thought this motha was taking me to see The Lion King. That's the only reason I went, right.

MIMIC: I told you the name of the play was The Lion Is King. You should wash those ears sometime.

THUG: Yo, Shine, him and me are the only two idiots in the audience. And listen to this, in the play, there these people dressed in these cheap ass lion costumes with plastic rifles hunting people down and shit, right? What kind of retardeness is that? Oh yeah, and this is the best part, Shine. One of the wacked out actors pointed one of those cheap ass plastic rifles in my face. I snatched it from him and was 'bout to shove it up his ass but your boy here stopped me. That play was so dumb they should've killed the writer, I swear.

MIMIC: The play is too deep for you to understand.

THUG: Mimic, It's too bad for me to understand. It'll never become a movie, video, DVD or a Laser Disk. And it'll never stream in Netflix, Hulu or Amazon!

MIMIC: The play talks about how man is making lions extinct. And the writer is asking the question, how would man like it if the situation was reversed and man were the ones hunted down?

THUG: That's stupid 'cause that'll never happen. Have you ever seen a lion with a rifle? Ah? No, right? I rest my case.

SHINE: The boy thinks he's a lawyer now.

THUG: That's right. I watch my Law and Order!

MIMIC: But it does happen. We hunt ourselves down.

THUG: Are we going extinct? Are we going extinct? Ah? Ah? Ah? No! There are more people in the world today than ever. Rest my case again!

SHINE: Yo, Mimic, the play sounds mad cool.

MIMIC: I'll take you next week. I'd like to see it again.

SHINE: Cool!

THUG: You two are wack, I swear.

(Shine answers his phone.)

SHINE: Hey babe. I'm leaving right now. Wait for me in the stairway. Let me holler at you in a sec.

(Hangs up.)

SHINE: Yo, I'm out!

MIMIC: Yo, Shine, I'll make it up to you next time.

SHINE: No problem.

THUG: Shine, Shine, don't let him take you to see the Lion is King. You're going to regret it.

(Shine bumps fists with the Mimic and Thug and exits as he takes out his cell phone.)

THUG: Yo, if I EVAH see you acting in a bad play like that, I'll climb on the stage myself and beat your tofu eating ass like there's no tomorrow. The Lion Is King? I can't believe you took me to see that crap.

MIMIC: Are you going to keep talking about this?

THUG: I wanted to see Uncle Scar… Mufasa… Little Simba.

(sings.) "The circle – the circle of life!"

MIMIC: Shut up already!

The Editors

MICHA ESPINOSA is an Arizona-based artist, activist, teacher, and voice, speech, and dialect coach. She has performed, lectured, and taught voice and speech around the world. She is a proud 30-year member of SAG/AFTRA, and has performed in film, television, and regional theatre. As a performer she has been privileged to work with film and theatre directors including Oliver Stone, Peter Patzak, Tina Landau, Les Waters, and Aaron Landsman, among others. As a voice/dialect specialist she has worked with regional theatre companies such as The Old Globe, Oregon Shakespeare Festival, Southwest Shakespeare, Arizona Theatre Company, Mixed Blood, Phoenix Theatre, and the Coconut Grove Playhouse. She is a Master Teacher of Fitzmaurice Voicework, and Director of Diversity and Inclusion for the Fitzmaurice Institute. She is an Associate Professor at Arizona State University's Herberger Institute for Design and the Arts, in the School of Film, Dance, and Theatre, and affiliate faculty with the School of Transborder Studies. She received the Chicano Faculty Sangre de Arte Award commemorating her commitment to the Arts and mentorship of Latinx students. She was recently elected to the board of the Voice and Speech Trainers Association and won the Outstanding Service to the Profession Award. As an associate editor for the International Dialects of English Archive, Micha has contributed and analyzed samples from all over the globe. She has published several peer-reviewed articles in the Voice and Speech Review, the Journal for Intergroup Relations, and was a contributing author for *The Politics of Actor Training*. She is the editor of the award-winning book, *Monologues for Latino Actors: A Resource Guide to the Contemporary Latino/a Playwrights*.

CYNTHIA DECURE is an actress, voice, speech and dialects coach. She is an Assistant Professor of Theatre at California State University, Stanislaus. Cynthia is certified in both Knight-Thompson Speechwork® and as an Associate Teacher of Fitzmaurice Voicework®. She has taught at California Institute of the Arts, UC Santa Barbara, University of Southern California, and California State University, Los Angeles. A long-time member of Actors Equity and SAG/AFTRA, some acting credits include: *The Mambo Kings*, *CSI: Crime Scene Investigation*, *Days of Our Lives*, *The Bold & The Beautiful*, *General Hospital*, *All My Children*, among many commercials. Voice and dialect credits include *In The Heights* (Phoenix Theater and Chance Theater), *Shelter* (Center for New Performance, featured in American Theatre), South Coast Repertory's *The Long Road Today/Diálogos* (featured in American Theatre), Showtime's *The Affair*, as well as many actors for TV, film and theatre. A native of Puerto Rico, Cynthia is also a playwright. Her play *Miss Quince* premiered at the 2012 John Lion New Plays Festival and received a merit award from KC/ACTF, and was featured in NoPassport's 30/30 Festival with staged readings in Chicago, Dallas and New York. Cynthia serves on the Steering Committee of the Latinx Theater Commons. She is the Diversity chair for the Voice and Speech Trainers Association and has presented at conferences in Chicago, Washington D.C., London and Montreal on empowering underrepresented voices, speech, and accents of Spanish. Her published research and scholarship examine linguistic identity and representation in performance. She specializes in all accents of Spanish.